11 Maoz Zion, Kurdish moshav nr J-m.

# The
# Book
# of
# Jewish
# Women's
# Tales

# The
# Book
# of
# Jewish
# Women's
# Tales

Retold by Barbara Rush

JASON ARONSON INC.
Northvale, New Jersey
London

The author gratefully acknowledges permission to quote from *Daughters of Yemen* by Mishael Caspi. Copyright © 1985 The Regents of the University of California. Used by permission of the University of California Press.

This book was set in Korinna and Helios by Lind Graphics of Upper Saddle River, New Jersey, and printed by Haddon Craftsmen in Scranton, Pennsylvania.

**Library of Congress Cataloging-in-Publication Data**

Rush, Barbara.
     The book of Jewish women's tales / retold by Barbara Rush.
          p.   cm.
     Includes bibliographical references and index.
     ISBN 1-56821-087-6
     1. Jews—Folklore.   2. Jewish women—Folklore.   3. Tales—Israel.
     I. Title.
     GR98.R87   1994
     398.2'089924—dc20                                                     93-34959

Manufactured in the United States of America. Jason Aronson Inc. offers books and cassettes. For information and catalog write to Jason Aronson Inc., 230 Livingston Street, Northvale, New Jersey 07647.

This book is dedicated to my mother, Sarah Wishengrad Korn, of blessed memory, truly an *eishet hayil*, a woman of valor. Her values have been my guide; her work as a teacher, my inspiration; and her stories, of life and Jewish tradition, have led me to love the people and land of Israel.

# Contents

# Acknowledgments

To the following who made this volume possible, I am most grateful:

First, to the Israel Folktale Archives (IFA), a collection of almost 19,000 stories from ethnic groups all over Israel, housed in the University of Haifa, whose holdings served as the basis for my search for stories;

To Professor Dov Noy, my mentor and friend, founder of the IFA, whose library was always open to me, whose guidance was invaluable, and to whom I am especially appreciative for writing the foreword of this book;

To Professor Aliza Shenhar, academic head of the IFA, who made the archives available;

To Edna Hechal, the IFA coordinator, for her patience in answering my incessant queries, and for sharing with me her intuition and vast knowledge;

To Tsila Schwartz, a most talented calligrapher, for designing the cover;

To Yitzhak Greenfield, Peninnah Schram, and Howard Schwartz, for their support;

To Marc Bregman, Rabbi Micha Halpern, Eli Marcus, Ina Ruth Sarin, and Cynthia and Rabbi David Spritzer, for clarifying details in the text, comparative sources, and glossary;

To those who shared stories and personal remembrances: Joe David, Doron Elia, Tillie Farkash, Elizabeth Galiker, Haya Gavish, Ziporah Sibati Greenfield, Rafi Israeli, Hanan Rothem, Judith Zuckerman Kaufman, Naomi Sapir, Simha Shemesh, and Yael Weinberger. These moments of personal sharing were the warmest and most exciting of the entire project;

To Simha Shemesh, my dear friend, who did the bulk of the translation, and to the many others who helped with this work: Karen Dinur, Adi Elkayam, Jerry Fogel, Haya Gavish, Dov Gavish, Dalia Goren, Azariah Levy, Batya Marks, Atarah Salmon, Shlomo Sapir, and Sarah Spanier;

To Sarah Friedman, librarian at the Hebrew Union College library in Jerusalem, for her diligent assistance;

To Eve Kedem, for proofreading the manuscript;

To Cynthia Spritzer, for reading the manuscript;

To Arthur Kurzweil, my editor at Jason Aronson, for his encouragement at every step of this project, and to Janet Warner and Jean Pease, production editors;

And most of all, to my husband, Don, my partner in all my endeavors, who was always there when I needed him, attending to every clerical detail, acting as a springboard for ideas, and spurring me to continue collecting and retelling.

# *Foreword*

Folktales, the stories that have been handed down from generation to generation by word of mouth, are the voluntary expression of every culture. In our culture they are part of the heritage of each and every one of us, our having been familiar with many, even in early childhood. And the fact that the tales are told voluntarily is an indication of the strong identification that both the teller and listener have with them. This body of tales has long been recognized as the reflection of a people's soul.

What, then, are the messages, the secrets, that narrators (tellers) transmit to their listeners, and, in turn, that those listeners, as narrators, send to their listeners? Are there special messages that Jews send to other Jews? Are there messages, overt and covert, that women send to other women? Are there messages that Jewish women send to other Jewish women? The answer to these questions is "Yes."

In Jewish folk tradition the distinction can be made between the law (the *halachah*), which is binding, compulsory, and normative, and folk custom, which is local or even contemporary, and is performed by choice: songs sung, dress worn, and so on, at various times in Jewish life.

At Jewish weddings, for example, only the *ketubah* (marriage contract) is prescribed by Jewish law. The type of dress worn at the wedding, the food eaten, dances danced, songs sung, and customs performed (throwing rice, breaking of a glass by the groom, etc.) are the creations and choice of the individual Jewish ethnic group.

The same comparison holds true for literature, which is but one genre of creative expression, and is the concern of this book. The distinction can be made, for instance, between written, printed literature and oral literature, that of the folk. The reading of a biblical Hebrew text, read as a portion of the week on *Shabbat,* has a compulsory place (the synagogue), compulsory time (*Shabbat*), and fixed text, which cannot be changed. But on that same day and in that same place, Jews

may gather to tell a sermon that may include a parable or
legend, the exact wording of which is not fixed and not
important. This latter narrative, told voluntarily and without
prescription by law, is a folktale.

These tales, transmitted in the society from generation to
generation by oral tradition, reflect the wishful thinking of
that society and the need of the tale's creators, narrators and
listeners to escape from the "gray" of daily life, attaining in
the tales what they cannot attain in real life. These tales
contain the extraordinary, and sometimes supernatural, elements (the mythological elements) that testify to the creative
imagination of the society and to its craving for the unusual,
the remote, the unattainable. It is these elements that give the
tale its soul and that imbue it with the suspense and sense of
aliveness that enrapture the listener.

Through the careful and systematic study of the folktale, its
types and motifs, meanings and messages, scholars have
come to regard the folktale genre as belonging to the universal folk-literary heritage of many societies. The life-
histories of these tales prove that they have traveled great
distances from their place of origin to the places of their
present life. Using the historic-geographic method of folk-
narrative research, which makes extensive use of type motif-
indexing, parallel analysis, and comparison of as many versions of the same tale as are available in order to establish its
time and place of origin and the process of its geographic
diffusion, one can classify virtually all folktales into types,
motifs, and tale-families, forming a kind of creative morpho-
logical web that binds and connects the lives of mankind's
many societies.

Although many versions, narrated and collected all over the
world, clearly belong to the same tale type, specific folktales
are imbedded in the local context of a specific society. They
live and breathe in particular cultural environments, are narrated in and informed by different languages, and, in all
likelihood, carry highly characteristic messages. The problem
currently engaging researchers is: What are the factors that
shape the local version, the so-called oicotype, of the folktale?
Wherein (aside from language of transmission) lies the ethnic

uniqueness of the local version? Given the universal appeal of certain motifs, images, and metaphors, why (and how) are the travels of tale types almost never instances of wholesale transmission?

Every society questions, "What about this tale is unique to *our* culture?" However, to apply the above-mentioned questions to the enormous body of Jewish folk-narrative complicates the investigation further, for never did the Jews create or narrate in a hermetically sealed environment. There was always some form of culture interchange with non-Jewish neighbors, friends, and foes alike. The orally transmitted folktales and literary legends of the Jews contain many elements that are no less a part of the cultural heritage of Christian, Islamic, Byzantine, and a host of other traditions. What then is uniquely Jewish about the Jewish version of these tales?

During the decades of this century the predominant Jewish viewpoint of the East European Jewish community, from whence the founders of Jewish studies in the nineteenth century originated, was that of the *Haskalah* (Enlightenment) movement, spawned between the mid-eighteenth and mid-nineteenth centuries. It held that Jewish behavior and mentality are of a "realistic" nature and, therefore, that Jews have a natural aversion to the fantastic and mystical. This viewpoint, counteracted in the 1930s by the work of the Jewish folklorist Y. L. Cahan, was further repudiated by the progress, in the latter half of the century, of studies in the fields of anthropology and folklore, combined with the great influx of immigrants to the State of Israel, and the advent of objective field studies of Jewish folk traditions. Scholars of varied backgrounds and ideologies have proved that Jewish pluralism has strongly influenced Jewish folkways and attitudes, and the multidimensional creativity of the Jewish people as an integral cultural factor is now an accepted assumption in the realm of Jewish studies.

A milestone in the progress of Jewish folktale research was the opening in 1956 of the Israel Folktale Archives (IFA) and the initiation of the folklore collecting projects that continue to this day. The reliable, objective, and quantitative data assembled in the IFA, where almost 19,000 folktales collected from authentic sources are registered, bear witness to the commonality of motifs, images, and characters of Jewish and non-Jewish folklore. Stories borrowing heavily from the surrounding culture (in some instances retrieving material that originated in the indigenous Jewish culture, or else imported from other Jewish centers) have time and again been embellished and narrated by Jewish raconteurs in the East and West in various Jewish languages, and enthusiastically received and enjoyed by Jewish audiences.

Yet, in spite of this commonality, there do indeed exist differences, very often quite significant, between the Jewish and non-Jewish versions of the same tale. Instead of (as some have feared) vitiating the Jewishness of the traditional Jewish folktale, the universality of themes and content has given us the opportunity of looking beneath the universally shared fabric of the tale and discerning the unique ethnic component that makes the story a Jewish one.

The study of thousands of Jewish folktales preserved in the IFA and the comparison with similar stories of other cultures lead to one conclusion: The Jewish character of a Jewish folktale derives from the identity of the narrator and his or her audience and the setting in which the tale is told. It is the nuances, details, moods, and the emotional components inherent in the story-telling art—more than the specific plots, characters, and large-scale images—that define the identity of the story as a Jewish folktale. The allusion to biblical or Jewish characters and events is less critical to defining the Jewish character of a story than the fact that the story is being told (or imagined by the listener as being told) by a Jewish storyteller to a Jewish audience in a Jewish space at a meaningful time in the chronology of the Jewish year or life cycle for what can only be called a Jewish purpose, namely, to edify and convey a Jewish message.

To be more precise, a study of the wealth of the Jewish IFA folktales suggests what might be called a model of the Jewish folktale, revolving not so much around the content and punch line of the story, for as we have seen time and again, there is not a twist or detail of plot that is not found in many variations

throughout world folk literature, but rather around the storytelling event, that is, the context in which the story is told, be
it in reality or merely in the listeners' imagination. The model
consists of four main elements that characterize the uniquely
Jewish aspects of the Jewish folktale. They are:

1. *The Jewish time:* The time of the respective story is
closely related to the Jewish year cycle and/or to the Jewish
life cycle. Much, even most, of Jewish narrating was performed during the relevant "passages" within the realm of the
Jewish calendar: Sabbath and festivals during the year; family
celebrations occasioned by the "rites of passage" in an individual member's life: birth, coming of age, marriage, death.

2. *The Jewish place:* The locale for Jewish storytelling was
also identifiably Jewish, either because of the special events
and ceremonies that took place there—foremost being the
synagogue—or because of a special attitude in Jewish
thought toward that place—such as the home—guarded by
the *mezuzah* and considered a holy place, or the Land of Israel,
the very soil of which was considered imbued with holiness.

3. *The Jewish acting characters:* The hero of the Jewish
folktale is often a historical figure, usually postbiblical, but
sometimes of biblical origin. Many of the "ethnic" folktales
that derive from specific Jewish culture-areas (the hasidic
tale, the Yemenite tale, etc.) have as their protagonist a local
sage, usually widely known and venerated, upon whose grave
sacred miracles occur. The characters, even non-Jewish and
those adopted from other folk-traditions and "proselytized,"
as it were, behave as Jews and show many identifiable Jewish
qualities as understood by the particular Jewish society in
which the tale flourished.

4. *The Jewish message:* Probably the most characteristi-
cally Jewish element of the folktale is the introduction of a
"moral" or message. The universal folktale most often had as
its purpose the entertainment of the listener and the providing
of relief from the troubles of day-to-day living. The Jewish
folktale has as its clear and manifest *raison d'être* a lesson,
sometimes about life, but more often about man's duty to
God, to his people, and to his fellowman. The ubiquitous
instructional element of literally all Jewish folktales (even if,

at times, unstated and remote from the main thread of the story) distinguishes the Jewish storyteller from all others. Whereas the universal folktale appeals to the present psychological state of the listener, delighting him with a pat resolution in a formulistic happy ending, the Jewish folktale is future oriented, urging the listener to adopt an ideal or goal as yet unrealized, to improve his ways and change his attitudes.

The definition of the Jewish folktale is further complicated by the addition of gender. The question now becomes: What is female about the Jewish female folktale?

In order to answer this question, we may again follow the model used in defining the Jewish tale and add to it the feminine aspect: The Jewish female folktale is told by women to women, and enjoyed by them. It includes the same elements as the previous Jewish model but is also composed of specific female elements:

1. *The Jewish female time:* This refers to times in the life of a Jewish woman that follow the year or life cycle: the Sabbath; the festivals; rites of passage where women are obviously present: birth, weddings, aging, lamenting for the dead.

2. *The Jewish female space:* Many female folktales were told at home, which, as has already been pointed out, was considered to be holy. Often tales were told during times of female functions in the home, as "queen" or "princess" on the eve of *Shabbat,* while gathering to prepare holiday meals for the family, or while in the female portion of the synagogue, where women listened to stories in their vernacular Jewish languages.

3. *The Jewish female acting characters:* Again these are based on biblical or postbiblical characters, or on local heroines, women sages, and so forth.

4. *The Jewish female message:* For years many folklore scholars working largely in libraries and influenced by the teachings of Freud, often looked at the folktale from a general point of view and stressed the psychological approach. Such scholarship detached itself from oral performance, from the very society that acted as the tale's chain of transmission, and recognized no difference between the analysis of the written text and that of the oral tale.

However, during the last two decades the trend in folkloristics has changed. Emphasis is now placed on oral performance, on field work, on interviewing the teller, on determining the attitude of the audience to the tale, and the usage
of the tale. Questions are asked of the teller: Where is he or
she inclined to tell the tale? To listen to it? Of the audience:
What does this tale mean to him or her?

This shift is emphasized in general folkloristics, and the
fieldwork done by the staff of the Hebrew University and
others in the State of Israel, in particular, has brought to light
what it is that determines the female folktale: *by far the most
important determining factor in a female folktale is the female
message.* The fact that the tale takes place in a female setting
or in female time does not necessarily make it a female tale.
The fact that the main characters are female or that the
dominant person (often the very title of the story) has a female
name does not, in itself, make the tale a female one. It is,
rather, the female message, transmitted from the female
narrator to the female listener, that provides a lesson relating
to personal behavior of a woman, or about the woman's duty
toward God, the Jewish people, and other men and women in
the community that distinguishes the female tale. This instructional female message, given overtly or covertly, urges
the future generation (i.e., the female listener) to change or
improve her ways and attitudes and to adopt an ideal in
accordance with those adopted by Jewish women in the past.

These messages have come to light as a result of examining
data of fieldwork done on tales in the IFA, some of which were
narrated to me and to the author of this book. The material in
this collection, then, is not the written material produced
hundreds or thousands of years ago, for which we have no
evidence that it is still alive, but rather tales told within the last
thirty-five years, that we know to be extant and for which we
have evidence that the chain of oral transmission was from
female to female. Also, this is the first time that many of these
tales have been made available to the general public, particularly because in many Jewish ethnic groups, particularly
those from the Middle East, the tales were told in a single,
mono-sexual environment. These tales represent various

Jewish ethnic groups and span the time period from those first told in the early '50s to those told in 1991.

My research, based on studies of thousands of these tales, shows that in most Jewish folktales (in approximately 90 percent of such stories) the message is clearly anti-female, the root of this anti-female message lying in the interpretation of the passage in Genesis 2: "And from the rib which the lord God had taken from the man made He a woman, and brought her unto the man, and the man said, 'This is the bone of my bone and the flesh of my flesh.' "

If the first woman was created from the rib of the first man (i.e., man preceded her) and the society was dominated by men and by firstborn persons, then the message of male superiority is clear: man and wife should be one flesh and the body of the wife belongs to its legitimate owner, the body of man.

How different was the message in the story of creation in Genesis 1: "And God created man in His own image . . . male and female created He them." Here the message is one of a tendency toward sexual equality. However, it is not this passage upon which the male-dominated society chose to elaborate.

The *midrash* on Genesis 2 (according to Louis Ginzberg in *Legends of the Jews*) reads as follows:

> When God was on the point of making Eve, He said: "I will not make her from the head of man, lest she carry her head high in arrogant pride; not from the eye, lest she be wanton-eyed; not from the ear, lest she be an eavesdropper; not from the neck, lest she be insolent; not from the mouth, lest she be a tattler; not from the heart, lest she be inclined to envy; not from the hand, lest she be a meddler; not from the foot, lest she be a gadabout. I will form her from a chaste portion of the body." And to every limb and organ as He formed it, God said, "Be chaste!"

Ginzberg continues:

> Nevertheless, in spite of the great caution used, woman has all of the faults God tried to obviate. The daughters of Zion were

haughty and walked with stretched-forth necks and wanton
eyes; Sarah was an eavesdropper in her own tent, when the
angel spoke to Abraham; Miriam was a talebearer, accusing
Moses; Rachel was envious of her sister Leah; Eve put out her
hand to take the forbidden fruit; and Dina was a gadabout.
(*Bereishit Rabbah* 8:1, 17:6)

The fact that the male midrashic interpretation of Genesis 2
had an influence on later folktales throughout the Jewish
world is unmistakable. Let us look at the English translation
(from Arabic) of a Jewish Yemenite (folk) love song:

My darling, my beloved, what shall I do?
How shall I treat you?
If I carry you on my head, I fear the wind will scatter you,
If I put you on my eyes, I fear my eyelashes will blind you,
If you come to my bosom, I fear my breast will strike you.
If I put you on my belly, I fear my navel will engulf you,
If I girdle you around my waist, I fear Satan will lead you astray.

M. Caspi, *Daughters of Yemen*

The content may be different, but the structure is the same.

It is no wonder that male interpretation of the *midrash*
describing the very beginning of woman's existence in Genesis 2 gave rise to a confrontation between the two sexes, and
led to the creation of feminine antimale and antiestablish-
ment tales about Lilith, man's first and proud wife, who
insisted on enjoying equality with her husband. These are the
tales with which women could identify and into which they
inserted their female messages.

Sometimes we see how a folktale changes from a female
tale told by women to a male tale when told by men. In
*Moroccan Jewish Folktales,* story 1, called "The Young Man
Who Gave the King's Daughter the Power of Speech," tells of
a king who has a most beautiful daughter who cannot speak.
The king offers the hand of his daughter in marriage to the
young man who can make the princess speak. (In folkloristic
terms, making a young woman speak is the equivalent of
relieving her of her virginity.) Failure to make her speak will

be punished by death. Ninety-seven men try; all fail and are killed.

Now, in a certain family there are three sons who hear of the king's decree and want to try their luck. The first two sons try but fail and are also killed. The youngest brother goes as well. What does he do? He sits in the corner of the room, remains silent, and takes out a candlestick. (The English version uses the word "candlestick" which may, because of its shape, appear to be a male symbol; however, the Hebrew *ner* is clearly a female symbol, being a circular lamp used in ancient times; in fact, the Talmud refers to a woman who has two men as a *ner* with two wicks.) The young man sits by himself and begins to talk in most erotic terms to the lamp in front of him. The princess, incited by such talk, blurts out, "Are you mad? How can you talk this way?" Thus the silence of the princess is broken!

The king, however, does not really want to give his daughter away in marriage. What happens? In female versions the daughter sings and is joyous, and makes her father understand that her joy is due to the fact that news has come to her that the young man, with whom she has fallen in love, will soon return. Love conquers all and the tale ends in a happy wedding.

In the male version, that in the book of Moroccan tales, the wedding is replaced by the following:

The young man forces the king to consent to let him take the princess to his home in order to meet his parents. Once there, however, he cuts off her head and sends it to her father with the following message: "I do not wish to be the son-in-law of a murderous king. I do not wish to be the husband of a wife for whose sake my brothers died. Ninety-seven plus two have you slain. Here is the head of the hundredth!"

The fact that the princess loves the young man is of no help to her in this male version. The caring mother (found in women's tellings of the tale), who weeps and tries to dissuade her sons from going on the dangerous mission, is also absent from this male version. Obviously, the message in the two tellings is not the same.

The difference between male and female versions of these

tales, in terms of symbolism and ultimate message, is the concern of this book. The female message, transmitted from female to female, from Jewish female to Jewish female, is the subject of investigation of this book. Whether these tales are truly didactic or, rather, the representation of wishful thinking on the part of poor, frustrated, restricted women seeking to gain revenge against or to triumph over men—or whether they were told by women who knew no men at all—is uncertain in terms of folklore research on this subject at this time. Theories relating to this problem are discussed throughout this book.

The book represents an exploration of the role of women's tales from the point of view of the tellers, a focus of folklore research not previously explored in great depth. This contribution to the field of folklore research will be appreciated by the general public and by future researchers as well. The stories, told in the natural style of the storyteller, will be enjoyed by men and women, Jew and non-Jew alike.

Dov Noy
M. Grunwald Chair of Folklore
Director of the Folklore Research Center
The Hebrew University, Jerusalem

# Introduction

The love of stories that led to the writing of this book was instilled in me the moment I was born, for, as long as I can remember, my home was filled with books and stories, and I was an avid story listener years before I became an avid story reader.

My father, born in a small village in Poland, was, in his boyhood, a *talmid hacham,* an excellent student, who knew all of the Torah by heart, and this knowledge remained with him all of his life. I remember well how proud I was, as a little girl, when rabbis would come to ask him to recite portions of the Torah or Talmud. And so, my father's stories were, on the one hand, religious stories, and, on the other, tales of his *shtetl:* his father, the town miller, his days at *heder,* and even the demons with which the village was fraught. Other stories were about his life as a young *halutz,* a pioneer in Palestine, working the land. And these stories always had a message: hard work brings one closer to God. Daddy's love of Yiddish literature and Yiddish culture took him (and me) to the Lower East Side (of New York) on Sunday mornings to purchase books, my father buying Peretz or Shalom Aleichem, which he would then read aloud at home, and I receiving an English volume of classic nature: Jules Verne or Mark Twain, which I would read at night, by flashlight, when I was supposed to be asleep.

My mother's stories were of a different nature. Born in Palestine under the reign of the Turks, she told of life as the daughter of a pioneer, and, later, as a young housewife, living in an Arab village, of life under the British, and of her days as a student in the teachers' college in Jerusalem. Some stories were funny; others, tense and scary—and they always had a moral, a message about living together with other people.

Stories were, in my childhood, ways of meeting my Jewish family across the world—of learning Jewish history, greeting Jewish heroes. How else, except through story, can we learn of yesterday?

Although I knew that Mama had been schooled in Palestine, I never realized how well versed in Jewish sources she was until one day in New York, when I was already married and the mother of grown children, two missionaries came to our door. Mama rebutted every one of their out-of-context biblical arguments by quoting other passages and telling incidents from the Bible—and she ended by rebuking them with the statement, "Shame on you! Don't you even know the Bible?"

But it wasn't until years later that I got another insight into my mother's Judaic background, which she combined with her stories. Living in Israel, in a senior citizens' hotel, Mama would write faithfully every week, not only to me, but also to my children, one a soldier, one a college student, and we began to see clearly that her stories, often accompanied by talmudic or biblical quotations, had messages. One of our favorites was a letter sent to my son, who had just had a distressing incident in the army. The message of Mama's story was, "If you fall down in life, get up and keep walking." As Mama wrote, the Book of Proverbs tells us, "A righteous man falls down seven times and rises up." (Many years later, as my mother lay close to death, my son thanked her for that story—and that message—which served him well.)

And so I began to wonder, "When people tell stories, what messages are they imparting? When my mother, certainly steeped in Judaism, tells stories, what Jewish message is she sending? And as a beautiful Jewish woman, a wife, a mother, what female message does she want me to receive?"

We have long known that stories have traditionally been the vehicle through which Jewish values and ethics have been transmitted. The Talmud and the *Midrash,* stories told to represent different points-of-view, are certainly such examples. "But," I thought to myself, "those are ancient sources, written sources of long ago. Are people, are women, still telling stories, still sending messages today?"

Finding the answers to these queries, aided by my own experience, spanning twenty years, of collecting stories from Jewish women, and coinciding with the interest of the folklore department of the Hebrew University in this subject and of the work of the Israel Folktale Archives in Haifa, led to the compilation in this book. These stories are the evidence of my conviction that Jewish women *do* send messages, via their tales, of how to live as a Jewish woman—how to act toward other people, toward community, and toward God.

My major goal in presenting these stories is to share with you, the reader, stories that Jewish women are telling. These are stories from virtually every Jewish community, ranging from North America to Europe, to Ethiopia, to the hills of Kurdistan, or to Azerbaijan. Many are told by women whose lives, in many respects, are much different from our own. Many are stories that don't ordinarily reach Western ears. These are not stories that I have culled from written sources; rather, they are tales that were *told* during the last thirty-five years—and are still being told today. Some, miraculously, have been handed down through several generations of female telling! By reading these stories, you will have an opportunity to meet these Jewish women: to get a glimpse into their lives and into the where, when, and why these tales were told.

You will soon see that the tales are varied. Some tell of the Jewish year: religious tales about Sabbath and festivals, carrying their message of keeping *mitzvot*. Some are tales of the female life cycle, those times important in the lives of women: birth, marriage, motherhood, aging, death. Some are magic tales, full of supernatural beings and elements, akin to what one generally thinks of as fairy tales. Others are legends; still others are love stories, usually ending in a romantic and happy wedding. You will find tales of Jewish heroines, often based on biblical and postbiblical characters. You will find tales of conflict between women: a mother-in-law versus the new bride, or the wicked stepmother versus the innocent daughter. And, there are tales of male-female conflict: tales of incest or alleged adultery. And as you read and become familiar with storytelling settings, you will "feel" the goals these women had in telling their stories: some tales educate, others heal, and still others transmit values, tradition. What unites these stories is that they were told by Jewish women. My definition of a Jewish woman's tale, then, is: *a tale told by Jewish women to Jewish women.* And the tales all have messages. Some are overt, readily seen from the words of the

interviewing the teller or audience—or gaining an understanding of the role of women in that particular Jewish ethnic
group. In some tales, for instance, advice or reward may be
given by an older woman; the message here is that women
support each other. In other stories, a couple does not merely
live happily ever after; rather, they continue to do charitable
deeds or mete out mercy, as do their children after them. The
message here is that the Jewish ethic continues throughout
several generations.

More than reading these stories, *listen* to them—for these
stories are being told to you, as they were to the listeners who
first heard them and who passed them on. And, as you listen,
hear the messages these women are sending.

## Postscript

Whenever anyone hears a story and retells it, there is always a
change—in a word, a phrase, a beginning or ending. This is
because, by the very virtue of the fact that we are all human,
and, therefore, creators, we seek to re-create the story according to our own backgrounds and needs. And, with each
retelling and each change, there is always the danger that a
message, or other element vital to the story, may be destroyed. Thus, in order to best preserve individual style and
the message of each tale, I have, in my retelling, kept each tale
as close as possible to the original telling, and have kept the
title as close as possible to the one given by the teller. Titles
are messages too!

As an introduction to each story, I have presented whatever
background information I felt would give you a link to the
teller and to the story itself: the link with tradition, that is, the
name and ethnic group of the teller; in some cases, the tale
type, as classified in the Israel Folktale Archives according to
the Aarne Thompson Index, an index of universal tales, and
referred to herein as AT; the circumstances of the telling and
the importance of the story to the teller; and the Judaic
background of the tale, which gives you insight into the

connection between the oral telling and its traditional or written sources.

I have also attempted to point out the importance of each tale from the point of view of the woman teller. In the few cases where stories were told by men, I included those in order to add interest and to point out the differences between male and female telling of the same tale. This comparison has proven absolutely fascinating to me—as I hope it will to you.

Some of the stories I have chosen to share with you were told to me personally. This very process of collecting has added a sense of reality and excitement to the tales, and I hope that you feel this excitement, this reality, as I did!

But, by far the greatest number of tales in this collection represent a search of almost 19,000 stories in the Israel Folktale Archives, a treasure into which I have dipped many times. Even such a vast collection, which grows by approximately five hundred stories per year, is, nevertheless, limited. Thousands and thousands of stories, yet uncollected, have been, and are still being, told. There are stories in the families of every one of you reading this book—and on the tongues of your neighbors, your colleagues, your acquaintances. And, so, my first plea to you is to preserve these stories (listen to them, record them) and then pass them on, *tell them* to your friends or children!

My second plea is that this collection be but the catalyst for further research in the area of Jewish women's tales. For this reason I have included detailed comparative sources, to serve as a tool for those who wish to search further.

May you continue to find stories!

May you continue to tell them!

I

IN THE
BEGINNING

# Why Man Has an Adam's Apple

## INTRODUCTION

Where better to start a collection of Jewish women's tales than at the beginning, at the creation of the first woman? The story of Adam and Eve has, for centuries, piqued the imagination of men and women alike, causing them to create their own versions.

Numerous *midrashim* give evidence to the story's being a problematic one. Depending on the storyteller's point of view, the *midrash* may tell of Eve's having intercourse with the serpent or her tempting Adam to sin — or it may tell of Adam's tempting Eve or Adam's having sexual relations with animals. In addition, the *Alphabet of Ben Sira* gave this account of Adam's quarrel with his first wife, here called Lilith, and her subsequent departure:

> After the Holy One created the first human being, Adam, He said: "It is not good for Adam to be alone." He created a woman, also from the earth, and called her Lilith.
> They quarreled immediately. She said: "I will not lie below you." He said: "I will not lie below you, but above you. For you are fit to be below me and I above you."
> She responded: "We are both equal because we both come from the earth."
> Neither listened to the other. When Lilith realized what was happening, she pronounced the Ineffable Name of God and flew off into the air.
> Adam rose in prayer before the Creator, saying, "The woman you gave me has fled from me." Immediately the Holy One sent three angels after her.
> The Holy One said to Adam: "If she wants to return, all the better. If not, she will have to accept that one hundred of her children will die every day."
> The angels went after her, finally locating her in the sea, in the powerful waters in which the Egyptians were destined to perish. They told her what God had said, and she did not want to return. (*Alphabet of Ben Sira* 23 a-b.)

The following IFA oral tale from India is a reaction to both the *midrashim* and the passage from the *Alphabet of Ben Sira*. The account in Ben Sira, written by men, and this folktale, told by a woman, have many things in common: Adam's first wife leaves him; Adam complains to God; God punishes the wife. However, this oral tale, seemingly simple and naive, is a tale of protest. The female teller is saying, "All right, men, you got your way. God listened to Adam, and destroyed the first Eve, who was strong and assertive (like Lilith!). God created her anew, innocent, naive, the way Adam wanted — and look at what happened!"

Note also that in both stories there are consequences for the children of this first woman. In the male account, children are punished and killed (by God) every day. In the female tale, Eve seeks to protect her children by forewarning them of their future.

The tale parallels the biblical account of God's creation of the world in the Book of Genesis.

We have all heard stories about how the moon, sun, planets, or constellations got to the sky, or why various animals have their physical characteristics — or why another physical phenomenon came to be the way it is. Such a tale is called an etiological tale. This story is an example.

This tale was told to Haya Kornatski-Ben Avaraham by Avigail Nagukar, a member of the B'nei Israel from Bombay in India.

# 1

# *Why Man Has an Adam's Apple*

any, many years ago there was nothing in the world—only darkness and a great deal of water. God said, "Let us make order" and He created a beautiful world.

What did He do?

In the beginning, on the first day, He divided the world into four parts: one part, earth; three parts, water.

On the second day He created light and darkness, day and night.

On the third day He created animals, all the land creatures of the world.

On the fourth day He created flowers, trees, and plants.

On the fifth day He created fish and the creatures of the sea.

On the sixth day He created, from the earth, two images, and He called them "Adam" and "Eve"—and to each He gave a soul.

God said, "Adam and Eve, everything I created was created for you. Do as you wish, and eat from every tree. But do not eat of this tree that stands in the middle of the garden."

Adam and Eve had no clothing. Both were covered with a special skin that is found today only in the fingernails of men.

Now, Eve was a clever woman, and stronger than Adam. Therefore, Adam said to God, "Please God, I don't want this woman. Take her from me, and give me another in her place."

And God heard Adam's request and wanted to drown Eve in the sea. But she said, "Before you take me, I ask that you give me one right."

"And what right do you ask for?" asked God.

She answered, "At the time that I give birth I will come to my infant, on the fifth day of life, and tell him what future to expect." And so Eve continued to live for some time.

One hundred years passed, and, at last, God granted the request of Adam. He put him to sleep, and took a rib from his left side, and from it He created a new wife. She was beautiful, innocent, and quiet—and she, too, was called Eve. Thus Adam and Eve lived in the Garden of Eden.

One day a demon appeared in the form of a snake—long, smooth, and evil. He coiled himself around the tree of the forbidden fruit, and said to Eve, "Come here, Eve. Look at this beautiful tree, so high and strong. Do not be afraid. The fruit is sweet and good. Nothing will happen to you if you taste it."

Eve saw that this was true—and slowly, slowly she drew near to the tree. And the snake gave her one apple.

When she saw that the fruit tasted good, she said to the demon, "Give me another. I will take it to Adam, my husband."

So Eve took the apple and gave it to Adam. And he ate and

remarked, "Hmmm, this is good. Where did you get such tasty fruit?"

And Eve answered, "This is from the tree which God forbade us to eat of. Why did He say that? The fruit tastes so good."

When Adam heard those words, he was greatly alarmed, and because he was in the midst of swallowing the fruit, it got stuck in his throat, and he couldn't swallow.

From then on, all men have Adam's apples, as a reminder of part of the fruit that remained in the throat of the very first Adam.

II

THE LIFE
CYCLE

# Birth

The fascinating legend of Adam's first wife, Lilith, did not end with the story of creation. Instead, the legend grew and, eventually, came to have great influence on stories told by women, particularly on tales about birth, the time so special in a woman's life. Why and how did this come about? The development was a long and strange one.

As we have already seen, the Lilith legend was created and spread by men, as a commentary to the passage in Genesis 2. After she and Adam quarreled over their sexual positions, Lilith, refusing to acquiesce to Adam, asserted her independence by fleeing, and taking up residence on the shore of the Red Sea, thereafter becoming the lover of demons who lived there. As we have also seen, her refusal to return brought upon her the threat of one hundred of her children being killed every day. Lilith, until this point, had been concerned with issues of independence and sexuality; it is perhaps for this reason that her name has become a positive slogan adopted by modern Western women concerned with the same issues.

But here Lilith was infused (by men) with the characteristics of another demoness (possibly Ozibut, who was invoked by King Solomon in *The Testament of Solomon*, a first-century text). Lilith took on the characteristics of the less-known, life-destroying witch, and her activities took a twofold path, during both of which she attempted to divert the holy purpose of intercourse.

1. In one, she became the incarnation of lust, haunting men in their dreams. Whenever a man had a sexual fantasy, he was believed to be having intercourse with Lilith. Their offspring were believed to be half-human, half-demon—unacceptable to either population. And, so, many tales were created in which human and demon interact and even marry, living together in a demon (fantasy) world, or in which the man has orgies with the Queen Demoness herself. (According to my Yemenite sources, this male-attacking Lilith, called Sayat, was the evil heroine in stories told by men; she even went as

9

far as to drive men insane.) In such tales the man often escapes the clutches of the demoness, but she—and her offspring—continue to hold power over him. To men, then, Lilith represented fantasy, lust, and fear. No wonder that so many tales were told in which a stranger to a particular locality is queried with the fearful question, "Are you demon or humankind?" We will meet these tales in this book.

2. In the second case, Lilith became a child-destroyer, inflicting her evil in one of several ways: murdering newborn infants outright; exchanging a human infant for a demonic one; or, substituting a puppy or kitten for the human child. So widespread and horrific was this belief that customs arose throughout the Jewish women's world to protect the newborn child: keeping fires lit; keeping watch over the child day and night (particularly before the *brit milah*, during which time Lilith and her helpers were sure to lurk); using amulets (including the names of angels and the words "Out Lilith"); and the singing of lullabies (whose refrains of "Li-li-li" or "La-la-la" were meant to shoo away the demoness. Many tales, such as #3 in this book, reflect these customs.

To women, then, Lilith represented a child-destroying witch or spirit, *whom they feared and against whom they were willing to fight*. Stories, probably created in female circles, were told in which Lilith entered the room of birth, could change herself into a broom or any other shape, and could even become a single hair, slipping into the water pitcher of the new mother. In these stories the midwife would overcome the demoness by sealing the pitcher, causing the spirit not only to beg to be allowed to depart, but also to promise to bestow gifts upon the mother and child. *In these tales women overcame the demoness.* Such a story is number 4563 in the IFA.

These stories eventually gave rise to tales in which the midwife, *via her own virtue and goodness* (that is, via a Jewish ethic) overcomes the power of demons. These tales, as our evidence shows, were transmitted almost entirely by and to women. Such a story follows.

# The Midwife's Reward

## INTRODUCTION

This is one of my very favorite stories, one which I have told dozens of times. It is told in the first person, which makes it all the more believable. And I do believe the story. Whenever I tell it, I feel as if the story is mine and that Grandmother is my grandmother.

The tale was first related to the IFA over thirty years ago by a Kurdish woman from the town of Zakho in northern Iraq. And it was told to me personally about twelve years ago by another Zakho woman in her Israeli home in Maoz Zion, a Kurdish *moshav* near Jerusalem. I heard this story again from a Moroccan woman as we sat next to each other one long night on an El Al flight to Israel; her story was about her great-grandmother, the midwife. The story is known to Ashkenazi women as well.

I love this tale because it reflects the *mitzvah* of participating in the birth of a child, and what moment could be more intimate or rewarding to a woman! My own daughter, Avi, whose children were delivered by midwives, is herself a practicing midwife, having participated in many births. Midwifery is well established in Jewish tradition, based on the biblical Shifra and Pua, the midwives of the Hebrews in Exodus 1:15–21: "as a reward to righteous women the Israelites were redeemed from Egypt" (*Sotah* 11B). This, in itself, is a women's message.

I love this tale also because in it a Jewish woman who believes in the power of righteousness overcomes the power of evil. (As the Book of Proverbs tells us: "Good deeds deter even the most blood-thirsty of demons, the Angel of Death.") I love it also because it is a Jewish woman who transmits the ethic: the reward for a good deed is the deed itself (*Pirkei Avot* [Sayings of the Fathers] 4:2). This is a message my mother practiced and taught all her life.

But one of the special beauties of this tale is that it contains another message, a hidden one, that became known only after field-workers from the Hebrew University's folklore department questioned the teller of the tale. Let me share it with you: by telling this tale, the woman

11

narrator was instructing her young female listeners how
to act if a strange man approaches. In that Kurdish
community the message was: "Act as Grandmother did!
Don't panic or show fear! Remain silent! Think of what
to do!"

Recently I heard a story told by a woman in New York
City about her neighbor who had been raped. This woman
narrator inserted instructions for her female listeners:
"She (my neighbor) should have looked around to see
who was following her. She should have leaned against
the doorbell to call for help. She should have had her key
ready so that she could get in the house quickly." Yes,
we women are still telling the same kind of tale. Men who
told the same story about their neighbor or relative who
was raped did not include these instructions.

This story, about a brave woman, has traditionally been
told by women to women. At one point a version was told
about a *mohel* (male circumciser) as the hero, but it was
not transmitted from one generation to another, and the
version died.

# 2

# *The Midwife's Reward*

 y grandmother, may she rest in peace, was a
midwife. She was always ready for a knock on
the door that would call her to her work, to help
at the birth of a newborn child. Grandmother
worked for the love of it and never asked for any
reward. She was sure that her payment would be to go straight
to Heaven. Since there were neither doctors nor qualified
midwives in the town of Zakho at that time, my grandmother
had more work than she could handle.

One day she was sitting outside her house, embroidering.
She was very tired after a hard day's work. Suddenly she saw a
beautiful cat creeping quietly into the house, sniffing in all
the corners as if searching for food.

My grandmother took a liking to the cat and fed her. As she did so, she noticed that the cat was pregnant. "Ah, if only I could be this cat's midwife," Grandma said to herself.

Days passed, and one dark and stormy night my grandmother was awakened by the sounds of footsteps. There was a rap at the door. She rose quickly, dressed herself, and opened the door. There in the doorway stood a man, panting and sweating as if he had come in a great hurry. "Grandma, come with me," he said. "My wife is about to give birth, and there is no one to help her."

Grandmother listened quietly and rejoiced with delight. How lucky that such a request had come to her at this time! "Why, to bring a child into the world on such a stormy night and at such a late hour," she thought to herself, "would be like doing all the 613 commandments at once."

Now, Zakho is a small town, and Grandma strode up the main street behind the man. She could not understand why she did not hear the sound of his footsteps. Suddenly she noticed that they had gone beyond the last house in the town and were now walking in an open field.

Grandma trembled all over, knowing that no one lived there. She understood that the man leading her was none other than a *sheid*.

"Lord, have mercy on me," she muttered to herself, but she did not utter a sound. Soon they came to a bridge made of large stones and, thereafter, entered a huge cave. There Grandma heard a man's voice, "Grandmother, come in. You have reached the place."

Now Grandmother was really frightened. She glanced about; there inside the cave were *sheidim* and *sheidot*, prancing and dancing and meowing like cats.

"What dreadful company in which to find myself," Grandma thought to herself, but she did not say a word. The *sheid* with the longest horns took her aside. "If the newborn is a son," he said, "you will get everything you want, but, if it is a daughter, God forbid!"

Pale with fear, Grandma did not answer a word. She entered the room of the birth, and what did she see? The cat that had visited her a few days before was lying there.

"Dear, dear Grandmother," whispered the cat, "do not eat here or you too will be turned into a *sheid*."

My grandmother listened to the warning of the cat and did not eat anything in the cave during the whole night, even though she was offered the best and most delicious of foods and drinks. When the time for birth came, she rolled up her sleeves and set to work.

A male cat was born. What rejoicing broke out in the cave! Why, the cries of joy even reached the heavens! The chief of the *sheidim* called my grandmother to him and said, "Whatever you ask, even up to half my kingdom, I will give you."

"No, no, no!" said Grandmother, "I do not want anything. The reward for a good deed is the deed itself."

"That is impossible! You must take something! This is our custom!" warned the chief.

My grandmother was aware this was a serious matter. She looked around, and her eyes fell upon a bunch of garlic in the corner of the room. Grandma asked for a bit of the garlic, just to satisfy the chief of the *sheidim*, and before she knew it, the sleeves of her clothes were stuffed with garlic, and the *sheidim* quietly escorted her home.

Tired and discouraged, Grandma threw the garlic near her door and sank into bed.

The next morning her grandchild woke her up. "Grandma, Grandma," she called, "from where did you bring so much gold?"

Grandma looked at the door and saw that the garlic was, indeed, nothing else but pure gold. She divided the gold among her children, her grandchildren, and all of her family.

After many years Grandmother passed away. Her children and grandchildren are now scattered all over the world; my sister and I live in *Eretz Yisrael*, the Holy Land. And each of us keeps until this very day a small piece of golden garlic—to remind us of the reward of our grandmother, the midwife, and of her gift to us.

# A Yemenite Woman—Performer of Mitzvot
## and
## A Yemenite Midwife's Duty

## INTRODUCTION

These true-life happenings were told to me by Ziporah
Sibahi Greenfield, a beautiful Yemenite woman, steeped
in her tradition, and a dear friend, who lives in Ein Karem,
an outlying neighborhood of Jerusalem. In the 1950s,
after a large influx of immigrants to Israel from Yemen,
many settled in Ein Karem, and some still live there.
Ziporah heard the first story from Saidah Butel, a
Yemenite neighbor, to whom the incident occurred in
Yemen. The message of the story is: the duty of a
Yemenite woman is to be the doer of *mitzvot*. I share this
story with you as an introduction to the second tale, in
which a Yemenite woman performs two *mitzvot* concerning a birth.

The second story was told to Ziporah by her mother,
Nadrah, who, before she came to Israel, had been a
midwife in Yemen. To me this story has great beauty and
importance: first, because it takes me far away to Yemen,
and gives me insight into a Jewish woman's community
so different from my own.

Here we see the process of birth, an aspect of the life
cycle belonging only to women. Yet we also see the part
played by males; they too have a role in the birth. And
we see the *mitzvah* of the heroine, the midwife, without
whose help the male could not have performed his
Jewish duty.

Any change in the human life cycle is fraught with
psychological crises, leading to fear and anxiety. It was
at these times of crisis that evil forces, hostile to
mankind, such as devils and demons, were thought to
attack. And so, ceremonies and customs were developed
to ward off these evil spirits. The time of birth was a
particularly vulnerable time for both mother and child,
and, therefore, special prayers were needed and amulets
prepared for their protection. My own mother-in-law, of
Ashkenazi background, tells of metal objects and red
ribbons (both of which are believed to ward off demons)

being placed in the baby's crib, and similar beliefs spread throughout the Jewish world. In this second story these beliefs and customs are evident.

# 3 A

# *A Yemenite Woman—Performer of Mitzvot*

 aidah had been married for a whole year before she got her first menstrual period. She was thirteen years old, and the third wife of a man who was fifty-five. So she ran to tell her mother that her period had come.

In honor of this event her mother prepared a special meal: special *pita* and melted butter called *samneh*, on the verge of boiling.

She took a bowl, and broke the *pita* into small pieces in the middle of the bowl. Then she took her daughter's hand and put it in the bowl.

Saidah's mother then poured the butter, hot and melted like oil, on her daughter's elbow, so that it dripped down the girl's arm and onto her palm. As she did this, she repeated again and again, "Let this be a blessing in your hands. I wish your hand to be full of blessings. Don't be stingy. Do *mitzvot*."

And Saidah finished telling Ziporah the story by saying, "If I do *mitzvot*, my heart is quiet."

And Ziporah finished telling me the story by saying, "The Jewish woman is the one who paves the road to her family's protection by God."

# 3 B

# *A Yemenite Midwife's Duty*

n the middle of a Friday night *Dod* Yosef took sick with an illness called *subah*, from which one either recovers or dies; for seven days and seven nights there is a high fever. In the middle of the same night *Dodah* Sabrah, his wife, felt the pains of childbirth.

Now, at that time your father and I slept together in a big sleeping bag in our bedroom on the third floor. Sinyah, your father's sister, came in the middle of the night, shaking my leg, trying to awaken me, and so I accidentally kicked father with my foot. He nudged me. "What happened to you?"

"I don't know. Someone pulled my leg."

Sinyah laughed. She whispered, "Hurry! Sabrah is giving birth. Come quickly."

Father pulled off the strings of the sleeping bag, and I jumped out and ran. Father called me to come back and light the candles. One is not supposed to give birth in the dark, and it is permitted to light the candles on *Shabbat* to save a life.

Now Sabrah was giving birth on the ground floor, at the entrance to the house, right near the stairs. The corner for giving birth was nearby but Sabrah did not manage to get there; the baby was coming too quickly. I found her sitting on her knees, which was the position for giving birth, and I quickly embraced her, grasping my hands in front of her chest. With my knees I pressed on her back, exerting all my strength, and the child was born, the first child to be born to her. Then I cut the cord and held the child and took care of him as needed to be done. At that moment Sinyah, my sister-in-law, burst into "Hallelujah!" as an expression of happiness and also as an expression against the evil eye.

Suddenly *Dod* Yosef, still sick, came downstairs, dressed in a white robe and *tallit*. He was on his way to synagogue for, even though he was ill, he needed to offer prayers for his new son. But there on the threshold he was greeted with a puddle of blood and the afterbirth. Frozen with surprise, he didn't know where to go, what to do. He wanted only to get to the synagogue to fulfill the male's role of praying for his newborn son, but there he found himself in the territory of women, unable to pass. What could he do?

Quickly I summoned every bit of my strength and lifted *Dod* Yosef over the puddle of blood and outside the door. How I could have done that I still don't know for he was much heavier than I.

"Go, go, go to pray," I called.

"Watch over the boy and his mother," he shouted back.

Then I cleansed the baby, covered him with cloth and swaddled him. I covered the mother and tied her, as needs to be done after birth. Then I burst into "Hallelujah" to awaken the people in the house and to announce the birth.

We took Sabrah to the second floor and set her to rest on a high, soft mattress. She was so beautiful, especially at this time, that your father, upon returning from synagogue, rubbed two black stripes of *saberr* on her face in order to reduce her striking beauty, so that she would not attract the evil eye.

After prayers in the synagogue, everyone came to bless her, to wish her, "*Mazal Tov*." Her mother-in-law brought a special gift, an amulet prepared from skin, decorated with shells and beads, rolled and sewed in a beautiful way.

Surely with all the good wishes, the amulets, and especially the prayers of his father, made possible by the midwife's *mitzvah*, this eldest son of Sabrah would have a long and happy life.

# Marriage

Throughout the centuries, hearts of young girls all over the world have been weighted with the predominant questions, "Whom will I marry? Who will be my mate for life?" To answer these questions, people created stories that involved a variety of themes. One of these is "The Predestined Marriage" or the idea that fate cannot be changed. Another is the idea that even the poorest girl in the kingdom can eventually marry the prince himself.

Once the wedding takes place, the next concerns become, "What will my married life be like? How will my husband and my husband's family treat me?"

Many marriage stories contain conflicts between male and female: the father who wishes to have an incestuous relationship with his daughter, or the father who would rather see his daughter killed than allow her to marry (have sex with) another man. But these tales are full of female–female conflicts as well: on a familial level, the mother-in-law, sister-in-law, or stepmother becomes the girl's enemy. On a societal level, the rich, greedy, or lazy woman becomes the girl's foe. In these stories, piety, faith in God, and deserving behavior are rewarded. This is the Jewish women's message!

Above all, these stories show that Jewish women *do* have choices: whom to marry and how to behave as a married woman. True, the choice may not be an ideal one, according to Western, twentieth-century, "liberated" thinking. But, to women who in real life had little choice, the tales present an outlet for fulfilling subconscious dreams and wishes.

# *There Is No Escape from Fate*

## INTRODUCTION

Who doesn't love a love story, especially one in which a poor boy and a rich girl overcome all difficulties of social class, and are eventually bound together in marriage? Ah, the power of fateful love!

Such love stories (novellas) are based on *midrash*: forty days before the birth of the partners a match is irrevocably decreed in Heaven (*Midrash B. Sotah* 2b); this theme has made its way into many folktales, and has been the basis of some beautiful *hasidic* stories. Over one hundred versions of this tale (and its subtypes) are now in the IFA. The story has its parallel in *Midrash Tanhuma*, where King Solomon's daughter is locked away in a tower in order not to marry a predestined groom.

The story of the predestined marriage is basically a feminine one. On the surface the son may seem to be the active character but the women in the story are the ones who are truly active.

In some versions the father goes to elaborate lengths in order to dispose of the predestined groom—to no avail. In a Greek version, IFA 10084, the girl's father gives the infant boy to an elderly couple living in the woods, later retrieves the boy, has him butchered and left for dead.

In this version from Iraq the bride is rewarded by God, for her suffering and for her insistence on a Jewish marriage, by His sending Elijah to perform the wedding.

# 4

# *There Is No Escape from Fate*

nce, many, many years ago, there was a member of the *Sanhedrin* who had a grown daughter, not yet married. Every suitor who came to seek her hand was rejected, and her father was greatly saddened by her situation. At last the family went to seek the counsel of a fortune teller, known for her wisdom. "Your daughter will marry a poor beggar," they were told.

"What! My daughter, so beautiful, so learned, married to a beggar!" shrieked the father. And he went to seek the advice of King Solomon himself. Perhaps the king, who understood the language of every living thing on earth, who sat in judgment and issued wise decrees, would have a different answer. The king, indeed, listened to the problem. "Everything is in the hands of God," he announced.

Still the father could not accept the decree. And so he encouraged other suitors to appear before his daughter; perhaps one would find favor in her eyes. But none was worthy. This one was not wise enough; that one, not handsome; a third, not noble—and so it went.

The girl's mother was worried as well, and she too sought the advice of a fortune teller. "Your daughter's luck is to marry a poor beggar," came the counsel.

But the father could not accept this decree. "I will not allow my daughter to marry a beggar. It would be better to dig a cellar under the earth and there to hide my daughter, even if I should never see her again." So he thought, and so he did.

And so, far away in a deserted field, a cellar was dug. Each day a servant brought food and water to the daughter, and, thus, days and years passed, the young woman living in her solitary chamber.

But one day there was a loud knock on the door. "Who's there?" called the daughter in fright.

A man's voice answered, "I am a human being." His voice was harsh from the biting wind. "Even here my bad luck follows me. All day I have been begging and now I am lost. Please give me a place to rest."

And so the man continued to plead until, at last, out of pity, the young woman opened the door. "*Shalom*," she said.

"*Uvrachah.* I will stay only until morning."

But the two became acquainted and soon became friends, and the young woman told the story of how she came to be in that lonely place.

At last the two decided to marry, and the moment they declared their love for each other, a stranger, an old man, appeared before them. "I am Elijah the Prophet," he told them, "and I have brought you a *ketubah*, so that you may be married according to the laws of Moses and Israel." And so they were!

From then on the young girl asked the servant for double portions of food. A year passed, and a son was born. The woman asked the servant for another portion of food. And so, in the second year and again, in the third, a new child was born, and each time the servant was requested to bring to the cave additional quantities of food. At last the servant, wondering at the meaning of this, discovered the young woman's secret.

"You must write your father the truth," he told her.

And so, from her home deep in the earth, the woman wrote her father a letter. "Here in this lonely place I have married a beggar," she said. "Our wedding was performed by Elijah the Prophet, who brought the *ketubah* and made the *hupah*. Now we have three sons, who would like to see their grandparents, if they may."

The servant brought the letter to the girl's father, and stood trembling as the man began to read. Soon the father too began to shake. "There is no escape from fate," he mumbled. "There is no escape from fate."

As quickly as he could, the father went to find his daughter. There he embraced her and begged her forgiveness.

Then he built a beautiful house for his daughter and her family, and found work for his new son-in-law. And they and their children lived together in wealth and happiness all the days of their lives.

So may we all!

## The Match Made in Heaven

### INTRODUCTION

This is one of my most delightful finds in the IFA, told to Shalva Palestinsky by Sarah Beile, who heard the story from her great-grandmother!

Here we have an absolutely beautiful example of female transmission (four generations!), and a rare opportunity to see how the female storyteller inserts herself, as a heroine upon whose words the entire audience is dependent, into the plot of the story. Also, we can see how other female characters are brought to light as heroines: the rich man's wife, whose innocent suffering is rewarded; the baker lady, who, in death, intervenes in Heaven for the youth who aided her (in Jewish folklore, when someone dies, it is customary for the living to say, "May (s)he intervene in Heaven for me," as the dead have this power); and the daughter who keeps her faith in the promise of the baker lady (another woman!). And we see that the strong male character, Yosele, whose deeds are next to godliness, is aided and even overshadowed by women, and that the greedy rich man is thwarted by them.

I also found the "homey" language of the story to be most inviting, and could feel myself being one of the enraptured listeners as Sarah Beile told it. Sarah Beile swore that she heard every word with her own ears from her own great-grandmother, who, herself, was a righteous woman, a saint. That is to say, she would never tell a lie.

Enjoy the story as much as I did!

# 5

# *The Match Made in Heaven*

 n our *shtetl* there were two great people: one lived in great wealth; the other, in great poverty.

What do you think? If not for a match made in heaven, would these two have ever become *mehutanim*, in-laws? Never in this life!

Even if the rich man had an only daughter who had every good quality! Even if the poor man had an only son who had every good quality!

Yosele was his name. He was truly a *lamed vovnick*, I think an angel dressed in ordinary clothes. Why, the good deeds he did for people are plainly unbelievable!

There was an old, sick baker lady who could no longer work, and he would knead the dough for her. If his blessing went inside, even the king would have eaten the bread!

And there was an old Jewish water carrier, whose horse died exactly on a Thursday. If not for Yosele, who went to carry the water, the whole village would have been without water on *Shabbos*.

You hear, even if I'm only an old Jewish lady, as you see, I don't like to swear or curse. But just so you'll believe me, I'll swear for myself: may so much blood flow, the blood of Hitler and Stalin should run like water, Yosele didn't take money from the poor. From the rich he did take money, which he gave to the water carrier for *Shabbos*.

Now, whoever didn't see with what fright we jumped when Sarah Beile pronounced the name of Stalin never saw a fright! But Sarah Beile didn't fall down. She ended with an even voice, "Remember my words: Stalin's bones we'll live to throw out!"

At once there was an uproar amongst the crowd. People attacked each other and fell on Sarah Beile like wild animals, hiding her from sight.

But Sarah Beile couldn't remain silent, for time was short and wonders are great. So we who listened to Sarah Beile's stories, for whom her stories were like shots of morphine that quieted severe pain, made a contract with Sarah Beile: if she had a need to swear, she could do so only on Hitler's name, not on Stalin's. And so she continued her story about the heavenly match.

To the rich man, she said, there suddenly appeared in his dream the old, sick baker lady, who had since died. He didn't even know of her death. And she told him, "Soon your daughter will be married to Yosele."

The man, you should excuse me for saying, was a pig. "What *hutzpah*! What nerve of her!" he shouted. And so angry was he that he stuck out his powerful foot to strike the old lady in his dream, but instead he got his wife, lying beside him in bed. The poor woman, who was herself not guilty at all, suffered for a few days with severe pain in her lower back.

A few nights later, who's here? The baker lady appears again. Welcome!

And this time she said, "Because of your wife's suffering, because she suffers so innocently, you will be blessed with a wonderful groom, Yosele, for your daughter. *Mazel Tov!*"

The man, in a stew, hurried to another city to seek a bridegroom for his daughter. And, at last, to the father of the prospective groom he offered a large dowry. Conditions were agreed upon. A plate was broken, a date was set for the wedding, and the matter was sealed, according to tradition! The rich man spat on Yosele's name.

Meanwhile, the old baker lady, may her memory be blessed, went to visit the rich man's wife. "Because you endured your pains, you will have great *nachas* and a joyful heart. Your daughter and Yosele will soon be wed."

And to the daughter she said, "My daughter, I have intervened for you in Heaven. Yosele will soon be your husband, *in a guter sho*, may it come to good."

And from the daughter she went to Yosele. "Yosele, my son, I haven't forgotten the good things you did for me. I have come to tell you that on *Shabbos Bereishis* you and the rich man's daughter will be wed. When she stands under the *hupah*, be ready to come forward and marry her. *Mazel Tov!*"

And so, with these words, the baker lady returned to her grave, never to be seen again.

*Shabbos Bereishis* came. The bride stood under the *hupah*. The father of the groom wanted to finger his money in advance. The father of the bride said that he would pay afterward. Each one was angry at the other—so long and so wide that the bridegroom overturned the table, made a retreat, and disappeared—until today. And so, the bride stood alone under the *hupah*, waiting for the groom.

The whole village steamed. Tears—rivers of tears—fell from women's eyes. But the bride and her mother were at peace. After all, hadn't the baker lady told them that the girl and Yosele would be wed?

Her father announced, "Who is ready to take my daughter?"

Yosele came forward, and the bride greeted him with a smile. And so the two were married, and live happily and luckily to this very day.

## *Sarah and Shlomo*

### INTRODUCTION

This story about predestined marriage belongs to a particular subtype in which there is a proselyte: a foreign princess converts to Judaism because of her love for the youth. Female proselytes are well known in the sources: Ruth, Hagar, the wives of Solomon, Ziporah, Shifra, and Pua.

Interestingly, most of the fifteen versions in the IFA come from North Africa and Asia, where there is little conversion. Rather, the story's theme represents the desire of Jewish audiences, suffering religious persecution, to see Judaism triumph.

In the Moroccan version told here, the non-Jewish princess takes the name of a biblical heroine, as is customary. In other versions she is called Esther or Miriam.

The eagle, which plays a role in carrying the boy away from his parents — and towards his intended bride — is reminiscent of the eagle that brings the groom-to-be to the tower in which Solomon's daughter is imprisoned (*Midrash Tanhuma*). In so doing, the eagle is an emissary of God or fate. The eagle plays an important role in many Jewish folktales, such as "Lanjeh" and "The Widow and King Solomon," referred to in the notes to the story "The Judgment Against the Wind."

# 6

# *Sarah and Shlomo*

 nce there was a righteous woman who was barren, who couldn't bring children into the world. But she wanted a child so badly that she sought the advice of the rabbi. "Pray to God," he told her.

So the woman prayed, cried, begged, and at last God heard

her prayer. One night in a dream an angel appeared to the woman. "You will have a son, but when he is grown, he will be kidnapped. Do you accept the condition?"

The woman awoke and related the dream to her husband at once. "Let us consent to accept the child. Perhaps the prophecy won't come true," he said.

And so a son was born to them, a boy named Shlomo, who grew up to be handsome, studious, clever. And the dream was forgotten in the woman's heart.

One day, when the boy was eighteen years old, he went to the roof of his house, for there he would study Torah. Suddenly, a giant eagle swooped out of the sky, lifted the boy in its huge claws, and took him off to a faraway land. There it left him on the roof of a beautiful palace.

Now, the king of that country had a beautiful daughter, who, upon hearing the thud of the boy falling onto the roof, hurried with her servants to see what was the matter. There she found the handsome boy, unconscious, and set about nursing him back to health.

And when the boy regained consciousness, she asked, "Who are you? How did you get here?" So it was that Shlomo told his story. "I am a Jew, a student in a *yeshivah*, and one day, as I was studying on my roof. . . ."

The princess, who was not Jewish, had already fallen in love with this boy, and she agreed to become a Jewess. During the days and weeks that followed, Shlomo taught her the laws of the Torah and the customs of his people, the children of Israel. And each day the young boy and the princess fell more deeply in love.

But one day Shlomo said, "If we are truly to be a couple, if our marriage was truly ordained in Heaven, God will send us a sign." And, lo and behold! That very same day an angel dropped a *ketubah*, a wedding contract, in which the bride was given the name Sarah. And so the two were married, according to the laws of Moses and Israel. And during the years that followed two children were born to them.

Meanwhile Shlomo's parents waited and prayed for their son's return. But when months and years went by and he did not return, they remembered the prophecy, and mourned their son.

But one day, while Shlomo was out walking, the same giant eagle snatched the man, and brought him back to the roof of his former home. Just as quickly as he had vanished, so did he reappear.

The joy of his parents knew no limits. And although their son was unconscious, they were certain that he would soon be brought back to good health.

But Shlomo did not recover. The finest doctors were called. "Your son suffers from an illness of the heart," they said, "and this we cannot cure."

And so Shlomo grew more and more frail, until the day of his death arrived. But on that very day a strange woman appeared at the house. "My name is Sarah," she told Shlomo's parents, "and when my husband did not return, I set out on a ship to find him. For months I have traveled until I came to this place."

Without a moment to spare, Sarah entered the room of her husband. "Shlomo, Shlomo, I am here," she whispered. "Our children are here, and we will never leave you. You must get well."

At that moment Shlomo breathed and smiled at his wife. Soon, under her tender care, he regained his health, and the two lived happily ever afterward.

## *The Girl Swallowed Up by a Stone*

### INTRODUCTION

This story was told by Simha Shamaka, as she heard it in Libya from her mother, Idriya.

In the universal tale ("The maiden without hands") the plot is usually about a slandered or banished woman whose hands are restored at the end of the story. Here,

in this Jewish version, the story deals with the confrontation between a daughter and her father, who wants an
incestuous relationship.

In Jewish folk tradition the stone symbolizes fertility
and legitimate sex. This means sex intended for
compliance with the first commandment of the Torah: Be
fruitful and multiply. In the eyes of the unmarried female
narrator, any sexual act is illegitimate and is equivalent
to the abnormal sexual urge of the father wanting his
daughter. How does the woman narrator give us this
message? She excludes the father (and the other women
who are ready to marry her off) from any reunion. The
sexually endangered girl feels safe only with her small
(and sexually neutral) brother.

According to Jewish thinking, the story contains
several erotic symbols. The hair is an erotic symbol and
is probably related to the pubic hair. Women's covering
their heads with scarves or wigs in certain Jewish ethnic
groups is designed to eliminate the male's erotic desire,
for this would diminish his role of pleasure in performing
the *mitzvot* or commandments.

The opening of the door is also symbolic, The Hebrew
saying: *Beito zo ishto* means "His home is his wife." Just
as the home is the symbol of the wife, the door is the
symbol of the vaginal opening to her.

Several other IFA stories begin with the father's
finding a hair that ultimately proves to be his daughter's
and with his passion to marry her. In IFA 6861 she
disappears into the woods and takes refuge with several
lions (à la Snow White), one of whom she marries.
Neither this solution, nor the one of living inside a
stone, may appeal to the Western woman. But remember
that these tales were told in a male-dominated,
patriarchal society, where men could sell their own
daughters and where women had little say in their fate.
The fact that the girl's mother and sister went along
with the father's wish reflects "the way things were" in
that society. Yes, there are women in today's world who
live this way! Think, then, how strong the hidden
message of the story is: women *have* a choice. They can
determine their own lives. And, what could be a better
choice than to marry the strong king of beasts or to find
refuge within a heavy stone where *she* controls who may
or may not enter!

# 7

# *The Girl Swallowed Up by a Stone*

O nce there was a very rich man who had three daughters and three sons. And of all his children he loved his beautiful daughter, Fatma, most of all.

One day, as the man was walking through his fields, he chanced to look at the ground—and what did he see? Why, lying there beneath his foot was a long hair, the like of which he had never seen before. He picked it up and wound it, over and over, across his palm until the hair covered all of his hand. The man wondered at its great length and swore, "By God, I will marry the girl from whose head this hair has come, even if she be my favorite daughter Fatma."

And soon his servants went from house to house, measuring the hair of every girl in that home, be she rich or poor, tall or small, fat or thin. But the hair matched none!

At last the servants reached the house of the rich man himself, and when they measured the hair of his daughters, they found that it matched perfectly the hair of the beautiful Fatma.

Wedding preparations began at once. The cries of the family, their beseeching, the pleadings of Fatma that her father rescind his oath, were all in vain. The father was steadfast, and wedding preparations went on; the marriage was to take place in three days' time. Each day the mother cried and moaned to her daughter, "My dear daughter, will you be my husband's second wife?" And each day the daughter would answer in the words of the proverb: "My dear mother, by the time the meat cooks the savior will come." Thus the days went by and, indeed, on the evening of the third day the savior did come, as the words of the proverb said.

On that evening Fatma's little brother went to relieve himself in the yard, and he asked his sister to go with him. Fatma did so, but as she stood there waiting, her eyes fell on a large stone. "Stone, stone," she cried, "how good it would be if you would open and swallow me!" And suddenly, there in front of her brother's eyes, the stone opened and swallowed the girl.

The boy ran home and quickly told his family of the miracle he had seen. The family shouted, screamed, wailed, and the miserable mother ran to the stone.

"Oh, my dear Fatma," she begged, "open the stone so I may see you."

And the voice of Fatma answered, "Today you are my mother; tomorrow, my competitor. How can i open the door for you?"

So then her sister ran to the stone. "Oh, my dear Fatma," she called, "open the door and let me see you."

The voice of Fatma answered, "Today you are my sister; tomorrow, my daughter. How can I open the door for you?"

At last the father approached the stone. "Oh, my dear Fatma," he said, "open the door so I may see you."

And he too heard the voice of Fatma. "Today you are my father; tomorrow, my husband. How can I open the door for you?"

All the family stood near the stone, and all of their pleadings were in vain.

Finally, the little brother came to the stone, "Oh, my sister, my sister Fatma, let the door open for me."

And the voice of Fatma answered, "I shall open the door for you and only for you—for today you are my brother and tomorrow too."

Suddenly the stone opened, and the little boy was swallowed therein.

## King Solomon and Queen Kashira

### Introduction

This tale was told by Friha Susan, a sixty-year-old storyteller from Rabat, Morocco.

The story, a well-known novella or love story, is the second part of a folktale whose main subject (frame) is a discussion between King Solomon and an owl about the fidelity and devotion of women. The owl, who objects to the marriage of King Solomon and Queen Kashira, tries to impart to him "how much harm is done to men" by telling the king a story about a woman who mourns at her husband's fresh grave. When she meets the king's vizier, who is seeking a thief who has escaped from the gallows, the woman offers him her husband's corpse (AT 1510, known as "the Matron of Ephesus"). The owl's story, intended to show "how little trust you can put in a woman," is then countered by our story, told by King Solomon. The tragic ending of our story, illustrating the lack of man's sensitivity, is followed by the ending of the frame plot: "King Solomon concluded his tale, and then he took Queen Kashira for a wife." In other words, the pro-female argument won!

Most of the IFA versions of this tale type have been narrated by women. In those narrated by men the role of the woman is played down to some degree, and the rescue ascribed primarily to God's grace or favorable circumstances. However, the narrative plot and the fact that the wife was instrumental in rescuing her husband are not changed.

# 8

# *King Solomon and Queen Kashira*

King Solomon wished to marry a beautiful queen whose name was Kashira, but she agreed only on one condition—that the king first build her a palace made entirely of the bones of eagles.

And so the king, who knew the language of all living things and who had command over every beast on earth, ordered all the eagles of the world to commit suicide, so that he could build the palace. The wretched eagles came to the owl to ask its advice. "Come with us to the king," they pleaded, "and help us convince him to change his decree."

"No, I will go by myself to King Solomon," said the owl. "I will explain to him how much harm is done by women in this world and will ask him to explain why women are so honored and respected!"

And so the owl went to the king and told him the following story:

Once there was a woman who loved her husband very much, and indeed the couple lived very happily. The two agreed that if one of them died, the surviving partner would honor the memory of the other forever and never remarry.

Now, after some time the husband died, and, as was the custom in that place, the wife went to the grave to mourn her husband for three days.

And it just happened that, at that time, a blind man stole something from the royal treasury. The king handed the blind man over to his vizier with orders that the man be executed, but, on the way to the gallows, the thief escaped. In vain the police sought him. There was only one place which they had not searched and that was the cemetery. So the vizier himself went to see if he could find the blind man there. And, once there, he came upon the woman weeping over the grave of her husband. The vizier told the woman about the blind man who had fled, adding, "The king has threatened that if I do not catch him, I will pay with my own head."

So the woman said, "My husband died two days ago, and in the last days of his life he was blind. Let us take him out of the grave and hand him over to the king in place of the blind man who has run away."

"And so," concluded the owl, "that just shows you how much trust you can put in a woman."

"Now I too will tell a story," replied King Solomon to the owl. And he told this tale:

There was once a couple who loved each other very much, and they lacked for nothing. One day the husband received a parcel of excellent merchandise, and he knew that he could sell it in the neighboring town at a large profit. But the husband was reluctant to leave his wife alone, and so he did not go.

When the woman saw that her husband was sad, she asked, "What is the matter, my husband?" At first the husband denied that anything was wrong, but then she asked him again and again, and he told her the reason. The woman begged him to go and sell his goods. "You have no reason to be jealous," she assured him.

And so the husband took his goods and traveled to the neighboring town, but no sooner did he arrive when he was seized by the king and thrown in prison.

The woman waited and waited for her husband's return, and at last, after much inquiring, she learned that he had been arrested by the king. What did she do? She put on her finest clothes and presented herself before the king to ask for her husband's release.

But the king and the vizier decided that they would set the husband free only on one condition, that the woman invite them to her home. The woman listened and consented. She invited the king and his vizier, but what did she do? She laid her carpets outside in the courtyard, and smeared the threshold with glue. When the two men entered, they slipped on the floor and fell. Quickly the woman shut the door and said, "I will let you go only if you set all the prisoners free."

"I will set only your husband free," replied the king.

"No," said the woman. "You must free them all."

And so the king agreed.

The woman herself traveled to the prison to await her husband. She stood and watched as the freed prisoners passed through the gate. They numbered three thousand, and her husband was among the last to leave.

But the man did not recognize his wife waiting near him. "Indeed," he thought, "who is this wretched woman? What is she doing alone on the road?" And he walked past her without paying her any mind.

"And so," said the king to the owl, "here you see the loyalty, the devotion of a woman, contrasted to the forgetfulness, the neglect of her husband." Thus King Solomon concluded his tale, and then he took Queen Kashira for a wife.

# The Ten Serpents

## INTRODUCTION

If this tale seems like a classic fairy tale or a story that you heard before, the reason is that it is! It is told throughout the world: in Europe alone there are over 1,000 versions. The tale belongs to a universal type, which has as its main theme "the monster as animal bridegroom." This Jewish version, told by a woman from Bukhara, is one of the first IFA tales; ten other Jewish versions were later told to the IFA.

There are certain differences between the tale as told universally and the tale as told by Jewish women. In all versions the girl is married to a monster husband. He is a monster by day and a man by night. In Jewish versions the girl always sacrifices herself for her father and willingly goes to be the bride of the supernatural husband. In Jewish versions the monster always takes the form of a serpent. Adam and Eve's biblical encounter with the snake has given rise to the serpent being *the* monster in Jewish tales.

The monster always imposes a taboo on his new wife. In Jewish versions the taboo is always an oral one; she must not *tell* the secret. This may be based on the *midrash* about the lights being put out when Jacob entered the bridal room and was deceived by Laban into marrying Leah, the older sister, instead of Rachel, his intended bride.

The wife then becomes an active character. She comes to "love" her unusual mate (a euphemism to describe sex). She wants to be with him physically and to verbally share her sexual prowess with her sisters and mother. But this is forbidden by society. So, then, it is *her* sexual eagerness and *her* breaking the taboo that lead to her loss of her husband.

She then sets out to find him. The quest always involves overcoming difficulties: here she must descend into a subterranean cave. In many versions she is aided by an elderly or young female. "Women help each other" is the message! In this case the female child shows traits of cleverness and determination.

The story always ends happily and in true fairy tale fashion: The girl disenchants her husband, and they are married and live happily (and often, royally) ever after. In our Jewish version, the royal pair do more than live happily; they continue to give justice, charity, and mercy. The strong Jewish women's message is: Because of women's attributes and actions, her happy life continues *and the Jewish ethic continues as well.*

# 9

# *The Ten Serpents*

nce upon a time there was a poor orphan boy who was righteous and hard working. One night, in a dream, an old man appeared before him and put a diamond in his hand. "With this diamond you will become rich, build a house, and wed," he said. "You will have but one daughter, whom you must guard carefully, for you will have to return her in exchange for the diamond. If you do not heed this warning, you will become poor once again." Thus, the old man finished his words and disappeared.

In the morning the boy awoke and found a huge diamond in his hand. He sold it, bought goods, and began to wander from town to town as a merchant.

Years passed, and the youth became very rich. He had a pretty wife and a daughter who was so beautiful that she had no match in all the kingdom.

Now, one day, when the merchant was returning home, a serpent suddenly crept out of the forest. The merchant tried to make his escape, but it seemed as if his legs were stuck to the spot; he could not move. And the serpent crept nearer and nearer. Suddenly the merchant heard a voice from above, "Honorable sir! If you want to escape death, give me your daughter in marriage. If not, the serpent will kill you with its venomous bite."

Remembering his dream and the warning of the old man, the merchant agreed, whereupon the serpent vanished and the merchant found that he could move once again. Just then he heard the invisible voice. "Honorable merchant, if you cheat me, you will die."

Terrified, the merchant went home, and behold! His house, his garden, and even his servants had disappeared. In their place stood a run-down hut. The merchant's wife and daughter were poorly clad, and his own clothes, too, were in tatters. At once he regretted the promise he had made to the mysterious voice, and he told his family all that had happened; his sorrow was so great that he wished to die.

Now, when his beautiful daughter saw her father's distress, she cried, "Father, I will fulfill the promise for you. I am willing to live a life of anguish so that you may be spared."

Weeks passed, months went by, and the merchant's family grew used to their poverty. Then one night there was a knock at the door, and, upon opening it, the merchant beheld a huge and terrible serpent. It opened its mouth and spoke in a human voice, "I am the stranger to whom you promised your daughter."

The father turned to his daughter in anguish. "I would rather die than give you in marriage to this terrible monster."

"Oh no, Father," she cried, "I will gladly go in your place."

And so, in order to save her father's life, the daughter married the ugly serpent. The snake gave her a ring as a token of betrothal, and they went to the second room and shut the door. Suddenly the serpent shook himself and shed his skin, and behold! A handsome youth stood in front of the daughter. He said, "If you want to live happily with me, do not ask any questions and do not tell anyone, not even your parents, what you have seen. Every morning I will leave you, but at nightfall I will return."

You can well imagine that the daughter fell in love with this handsome young man and promised to carry out his bidding. As a gift she gave him her own handkerchief of fine lace.

In the morning the daughter awoke to find that the serpent was no longer there. In the meantime her parents, who had not slept a wink during the whole night, were full of fear for their daughter. They did not believe their eyes when they saw her leaving the room, safe and sound, in fact, joyous and happy. They showered her with questions. But, to their surprise, their daughter, who had always respected them, now refused to answer.

Thus a few nights passed, and the parents began to rebuke their daughter for hiding the truth from them. And so, at last, the daughter broke down and disclosed the secret. That evening the serpent appeared but did not shed his skin. "As you have broken your promise," he said sadly, "I must leave you. Do not search for me anywhere, for you will not find me."

The daughter did not even have time to speak; in the wink of an eye, the serpent vanished. The daughter, despondent at the loss of her husband, locked herself in her room, refusing to see anyone.

Now, nearby lived a poor family, who had one young daughter, and, during the short stay of the merchant's daughter, the two had become good friends. And it so happened that one day, as the daughter was playing in the street with her doll, a dog passed, seized the doll, and scampered off. The child followed. The dog ran beyond the streets of town, and still the child trailed behind him.

Suddenly, out of the bushes jumped a fox, which chased the dog. Becoming frightened, the dog dropped the doll and ran away. When the child reached the spot, she found the opening of a large hole, but the doll was not there. Then she realized that the doll had fallen down into the hole, and she crawled inside. Neither the darkness around her nor her many scratches made her turn back, and she crawled on until she reached a wide opening. Then, climbing through the opening, she saw there, before her eyes, a magnificent palace surrounded by a lovely garden. Just near the opening of the hole lay her doll. Being hungry from her long day's search, the child entered the palace in search of food, and there inside she found two large rooms; in the first was a table laden with ten dishes of food, and, in the second, ten beds made up for the night. When the child approached the table, she heard voices from outside, so she hid herself under one of the beds. Suddenly, into the room crawled ten huge serpents, terrible to behold.

The terrified child was on the point of screaming when the serpents shook themselves and shed their skins. And behold! They were no longer serpents but ten handsome young men, and they threw their skins out of the window. Then they knelt

down and prayed, a prayer no less strange than anything the
child had already seen. And these were the words of the prayer:

"We pray for a fair maiden to come hither, burn our skins,
and rescue us."

After praying, the young men ate their fill and went to bed.
As the child peeked out from her hiding place, she saw one of
the men take a handkerchief—a fine lace handkerchief—from
his pocket and kiss it. At once she recognized the handkerchief of her friend, but she was so tired that she fell asleep. In
the morning, when she awoke, the serpents had vanished. So
the girl left the palace and set off for town, looking carefully in
all directions so as to remember the way. She decided to run
straight to the merchant's daughter and to tell her of the
handkerchief and all that she had seen; and so she did. At
once the two made their way to the underground palace and
hid themselves under one of the beds.

Everything happened as on the previous evening. And,
when the serpents changed into men, the merchant's
daughter at once recognized her beloved husband. She waited
patiently till night fell, and when the young men were asleep,
she went outside and burned their skins.

Morning came and the youths arose and saw what had
happened. How they danced for joy! The merchant's daughter
embraced her husband, who then told her this tale: "We were
ten princes. Our mother died, and our father remarried and
had another son. Our stepmother bewitched us all to ensure
that her own son would succeed to the throne. But now that
our skins have been burned, the old woman is burned as well.
Her spell is broken."

That very night the merchant dreamed of the same old man
who had given him the diamond in a dream. But this time, in
the dream, the old man freed him from his vow.

A wonderful wedding was arranged that very day, and
guests came from near and far. When the old king died, the
young couple succeeded to the throne, and were beloved by
all. They lived modestly, gave charity freely, and dealt out
justice all the days of their lives.

# The Ugly Daughter

## Introduction

So beloved is the Cinderella story that there are more different versions of this tale, worldwide, than any other story. Hundreds of versions have come from Africa, China, Afghanistan, and virtually every corner of the globe. And, so, the story reached Jewish ears as well: the IFA has forty-two versions of the tale, AT 510 plus its subtypes. My random sampling of ten stories showed that all were told by women.

This story was told by Esther Daniel from Azerbaijan. Stories from this area of the world usually don't reach our Western eyes or ears, and that is why I chose it. This version follows the classic Cinderella pattern but has some differences:

1. There is woman-woman confrontation between the stepmother and stepdaughter. The stepmother, as usual, is treacherous, cruel, and evil.

2. The girl wishes to go to the ball and needs a fairy godmother to befriend her. This role is filled by the rooster, a male symbol. But the burial site of her true mother becomes the origin of life for her. This is a woman's message.

3. The girl goes to the ball where the prince falls in love with her. In this version, the taboo on her of remaining at the ball for too long is missing.

4. The stepmother cheats the prince by hiding the stepdaughter and substituting her own daughter. But the prince finds the right girl, who identifies herself by fitting into the shoe.

5. The prince and the beautiful girl are married.

In this story, the stepdaughter seeks advice from the old woman. This is a woman's message. The girl becomes the positive heroine, receiving the blessings of the old woman. This again is a woman's message. The evil daughter is cursed for her nasty behavior. So, here, we see a symbolic connection between the deed and its reward or punishment. This entire part of the story is AT

403, in which the kind girl receives the reward of jewels and treasures falling from her mouth; the evil girl is cursed with toads spewing from her mouth.

In this particular version, we see the cruel death punishment for the stepmother. There is no room in the teller's heart for peace or forgiveness. This may express an extreme attitude of women toward stepmothers or, rather, be a reflection of a woman's society where life is often harsh and where wickedness is punished severely. The cruel stepmother's punishment, too, is a woman's message.

In this version of Cinderella, as in most fairy tales, there are fewer overt Jewish elements than we find in religious tales or stories about the Jewish life cycle. But here, too, the teller will infuse the classic story with a Jewish value or ethic or a phrase from prayer or scripture. In this tale we see that the gift of the old woman is given in the form of a blessing, with the words: "May God give you beauty to which there is no second. May light shine in your face and may your eyes be like precious stones." This is akin to the traditional priestly blessing (or the blessing of the *Kohanim*), found in Numbers 6:22–26: "May the Lord bless you and keep you. May the Lord make His face to shine upon you and be gracious unto you. May He lift up His countenance upon you, and give you peace."

# 10

# *The Ugly Daughter*

nce upon a time there was a woman who had only one daughter. The woman took ill, and when she felt that her end was near, she called her daughter to her, "Take my dress and bury it under the tree." The girl did as she was bade.

Soon afterward her father remarried, but the stepmother, who had a daughter of her own, mistreated the girl. One day she brought a pile of wool and said to her, "Knit all this wool by nightfall or I will kill you." The girl, not knowing what to do, sought the advice of a wise old woman living nearby.

"First," said the woman, "I will bring you a comb, and you must remove the fleas." The girl willingly agreed.

Now, the old woman's house was full of wealth, but while she was gone finding the comb, the girl did not touch a single treasure.

"Next," said the old woman, "you must go to the stream to fill the bucket, so that you may wash the wool." Again the girl agreed. And as she looked into the stream, she saw that under the water, instead of stones, there lay a covering of silver, gold, and gems. Again the girl did not touch them.

When she returned to the house, the old woman blessed her, "May God give you beauty to which there is no second. May light shine in your face and may your eyes be like precious stones." Thereupon, the girl turned into the most beautiful maiden in all the country.

When the girl returned home, the stepmother, as you can imagine, was quite astonished, and very jealous! And so when she heard the story and learned the source of the girl's beauty, she sent her own daughter to the old woman.

But when this one was asked to remove fleas from the wool, she balked. And when she saw the wealth around her, she filled her pockets. Again, when she went to the stream, she grabbed handfuls of gems and stuffed them wherever they would fit into her already-crowded pockets. Upon returning to the house, she too received a blessing: "May you be the ugliest girl in all the land." And, indeed, when the daughter reached home, her mother took sight of her and fainted.

Some time afterward news came of a ball at the royal palace. The prince, it seemed, was seeking a wife.

The stepdaughter was left at home with a sack of rice, which she was ordered to sort. The daughter and the stepmother, nicely dressed, rode off to the king's court.

The stepdaughter, watching from the yard, cried bitterly. Suddenly, as she wept, a rooster appeared and began to speak. "Why are you crying, beautiful girl? Why are you sad? Under this tree there is a dress. Wear it. You too can go to the ball."

And so, with its beak, the rooster pecked at the ground until he unearthed a magnificent dress, silver shoes, and glistening jewels. Then the rooster crowed for a chariot to appear, and, at once, the vehicle set off, taking the girl to the ball at the king's court.

As she appeared, the dancing stopped, for everyone present stared with mouths agape, so dazzled were they by her beauty.

"You know, Mother, I think that is my stepsister," said the woman's daughter.

"Oh, you silly girl, you know your stepsister doesn't have such a dress."

The prince, setting his eyes on the beautiful girl, fell in love with her at once and danced with her into the night. But suddenly, knowing that she must get home before her stepmother and her stepsister, the girl ran out, dropping one of her shoes. Back to the house she ran, leaving her dress under the tree. And when, a short time later, her stepmother and stepsister did return, they found her, as always, in tattered clothes, next to the pile of rice, sorted for her by the rooster.

Sick at heart, the prince asked the wise old woman to disguise herself as a seller of needles and other notions and to find the girl who fit the shoe. Thus, the woman walked through the town, declaring her merchandise to one and all.

At each house where there was a young girl, she was asked to try on the special shoe, but on none of their feet did it fit.

When she reached the house of the stepmother, and the girl came out to buy threads and needles, the old woman knew her at once.

"Child, why are you so sad?" she asked.

"Oh, no reason," said the girl.

"Yet, my child, I feel a sadness upon you. Tell me your problem."

And so the girl told her secret, and, pulling the shoe from her pocket, she showed it to the old woman. At once, the old woman produced the second shoe and ordered her to try it on. Indeed, it fit perfectly! Without delay the woman went to tell the prince that the girl of his dreams had been found.

Messengers were sent to bring her to the palace. But when they arrived, the stepmother said, "Tell the prince to come by himself to ask for the hand of my daughter in marriage." And when they left, she tied the girl with ropes to the kitchen stove, her face close to the oven. Her own daughter was dressed in beautiful clothes and a veil placed on her face.

When the prince arrived, this was the girl he took to the palace to be his wife. But on the way, as he rode, the prince heard whispering voices, "The beautiful girl is in the oven. The ugly one is in your hands. The beautiful girl is in the oven. The ugly one is in your hands." The prince, not understanding the meaning of the voices, continued on until he reached the palace.

But there, when he saw the ugly face of his new bride, he grew angry at the deceit. Then it was that he understood the whisperings, and, following their message, he returned to the house, where he found the beautiful girl. There she donned her beautiful dress and returned with the prince to the palace, where she was greeted with great honor.

As for the mother and daughter, they received severe punishment. Tied to a galloping chariot, they were dragged in the road until they died.

No longer can they eat, drink, or know happiness.

But you, the listeners of this tale, may you feast and be happy.

# Seven Bags of Gold

## INTRODUCTION

In this tale told by Devora Fus of Lithuania, we see the conflict between women: one, good; the other, evil. Overtly, we see that the deserving girl is rewarded, and that jealousy and greed are punished. The importance of the family as the basic structure in Jewish life is seen here: the girl's reward is shared with her entire family. And so, although this story does not deal directly with the subject of marriage, I have included it here.

On the other hand, the family structure of the wicked woman is destroyed. Perhaps, in the eyes of this woman teller, not allowing another woman to perform the *mitzvah* of observing a festival is equal to being deserving of death. The tale has a religious woman's message. Note that only the wicked mother and the sons who help her are punished; the generous husband is not. He joins the family structure of his brother's family. This too is a message! His conclusion that one should not be envious is an important ethic in Jewish life.

Note also the strong active character of the old woman. She is the one who can mete out reward or punishment. In this tale she is not a neutral character, from the sexual point of view, as is Elijah. (See story No. 53.) Instead, she is a strong woman who has Elijah's powers.

The woman is similar to Frau Holle, the old woman in the Grimm tale, who, via a garden door, metes out golden rain to the industrious girl and black pitch to the lazy one. The source of this tale may be an ancient myth, typically told in the Mediterranean area, about the change from the rainy season to the dry one. In that myth the door of the garden symbolizes the entrance to the underworld; there, an old woman, Mother Earth, metes out good things and bad.

Several other elements in the story indicate that the source of the tale is in the Mediterranean. One of these is the death by snake and scorpion, not known in the north. It is believed that the tale traveled from the south to Lithuania.

# 11

# *Seven Bags of Gold*

nce there were two brothers: one, rich; the other, poor. The rich man loved his brother and provided for his family at every festival. But his wife and seven sons did not know of his deeds.

Now, the poor brother had seven daughters, each one very beautiful. Once, just before a festival, the rich brother went off on a trip to conduct his business, and forgot to provide for the needs of his brother. And so, what could the poor brother do? He had no choice but to send his eldest daughter to his sister-in-law for help. "Please wait here," the elder woman said, upon hearing the request. And she left the girl standing in the courtyard for a long time. She had no intention of giving money to this poor girl.

As she waited, the young daughter leaned against an iron door, which opened, revealing dazzling treasures within. Why, there inside the room were piles of jewels, gold, silver! The girl was frightened.

But, suddenly, there appeared before her an old woman. "Why are you so frightened, my child? Tell me everything."

And, so, the beautiful daughter told her story.

At once the woman handed the girl seven bags. "Here, give this to your father. This is a gift for all the daughters, may they have good health and good life. But say nothing of our meeting." And, with these words, the woman disappeared.

At home the bags were opened. Can you imagine the poor brother's joy and surprise when he found the bags full of pure gold! He was able to buy food, clothing, to repair his house, to see his family live a life of wealth and happiness.

Now, when the rich brother returned, he remembered his poor brother and went to help him. How astonished he was to see such sudden wealth! He wondered from whence it had come.

So, at last the eldest daughter was called, and her uncle entreated her to tell about the iron door.

The rich man hurried home to tell his wife. She, in turn, ran to the iron door, but, try as she might, could not open it. So then she called her seven sons to take the door down. And when they did, what did they find? An old woman stood before them. In her hand were seven bags. In her mouth were these words: "Go home, go home and open the bags."

The boys did as they were told and brought the bags to their waiting mother. She opened them and, before she knew what was happening, let their contents emerge into the room: scorpions, snakes, and mice, which attacked the woman and her seven greedy sons and ate their flesh down to the bones.

The wretched father realized what they had done. "One should not envy the wealth of another," he cried.

And so he went to live with his brother, whom he had helped for so many years. And the two lived together in much happiness and with much love.

### *The Garbage Girl Who Married the King*

This tale was told by Jewish women in Yemen. It is a novella or romantic tale, which always has a happy ending. This is one of the most popular kinds of stories because it fulfills the wishful thinking, the Cinderella dream, of every poor girl: how wonderful to be chosen to marry the king!

This is a tale of female-female confrontation. It is a woman's tale directed, not against men, but against society, and is a protest against rich women who exploit the poor. When I read it, I identify with the garbage girl both because she is a woman and because she is mistreated and poor.

I am drawn to this tale because it has a strong class message: The poor girl *can* achieve what the rich girl achieves. She *can* elevate her socio-economic status. Here her actions and faith in God play an important role. The girl's recurring faith in God echoes the biblical passage: "He lifted the needy out of the dunghill" (Psalms 113:7), and is indicative of the strong religious convictions of the Jewish Yemenite woman.

# 12

# *The Garbage Girl Who Married the King*

 n a faraway country lived a wealthy king named Elhaj Munis, whose large and beautiful palace stood in the capital city. In the same country lived an orphan girl who, in the morning, asked for charity in the streets of the capital, and, in the evening, slept in a cave at the edge of town. And could she exist on the handouts of others? No! What she did not receive from charity she earned by gathering garbage.

The women of the city, passing her cave on their way to the well to draw water, would laugh at the garbage girl and call mockingly, "Oh, garbage girl, we'll marry you to the king." And she would answer, "The hand of God will not be short; for Him nothing is impossible."

Now, one day the king, Elhaj Munis, became engaged to his niece, but that one betrayed him and went to sleep with another. And so, on the night of the scheduled wedding to the king, the bride was about to give birth.

What could her poor mother do? Remembering the garbage collector, she called the orphan to her, cleansed her, dressed her in the garb of a bride, and said, "Tonight you shall play the role of the king's niece and you shall wed the king. After three days come to the orchard outside the city, and there you shall receive your payment."

And, so, the garbage girl, in her disguise, and the king were married. And, on the night of the wedding, the new husband gave his bride a beautiful bracelet and a belt, as a token of his love.

Three days later, still playing the role of the king's niece, the garbage girl begged permission to visit her mother outside the city, but when she got to the orchard, as planned, the old woman disrobed her and left her alone with no reward. On the same day the king's niece moved into the palace and assumed the role of wife of the unsuspecting king. The garbage girl, poorly clad, returned to her cave, with only her bracelet and belt as reminder of her wedding.

Some time later she gave birth to twin boys, who grew up not knowing, of course, that they were the sons of the king. Their mother continued to gather garbage, while the town women, passing by, continued to mock, "Oh, garbage girl, we will marry you to the king." And she continued to answer, "The hand of God will not be short; nothing is impossible for Him."

At times some of the women would wonder, "Who is the father of these bastard twins?" Others, taking pity on the poor mother, would care for her from time to time and bring her food.

Now, when the boys were nine years old, the king made a large feast to which all of the people of the city were invited. The two sons begged, "Mother, let us too go to the feast."

"No, you are too young. How will you behave in the royal palace?"

But the boys insisted, "We too are invited to the king's feast. Please Mother, let us go." And so at last their mother consented. She dressed her sons as best she could. Then to one she gave the bracelet, and, to the other, the belt. And as they left, she ordered, "Stand at the palace gate. If you see someone enter, push him. If you see someone leave, push him as well. And if anyone yells at you, answer, 'This is our house. This is the feast of our father.' " And, so saying, she kissed her sons and sent them forth.

The children did as they were told, and it was not long before the king himself received word of two boys pushing at the gate, claiming the house as theirs and the feast as the feast of their father.

"Bring the boys to me!" ordered the king. And when the two boys were brought before him, one carrying a bracelet, the other holding a belt, the king was shocked.

"Who—who gave you this bracelet and this belt?" he stammered.

"Our mother," answered the children.

"And who is she? Where does she live?" demanded the king.

"Our mother gathers garbage and makes her home in a nearby cave."

At once the king summoned his messengers to bring the woman forth. But when the servants arrived at the cave and stated their mission, the woman protested, "How can I face the king? I am hardly dressed."

The messengers left and soon returned with beautiful clothing, and when the woman was bathed and dressed, she went to the palace and stood before the king.

"Whose children are these?" asked the king.

"They are mine, your majesty," she said, without lifting her eyes.

At this the king begged, "Please, be at ease. Tell me the truth. Hide nothing."

And then the garbage girl lifted her eyes and told the king all that had happened. She closed her story with these words, "And from our wedding night these sons were born."

The king listened but said nothing. At once he wrote a *get*, a divorce, but told no one.

On the following day he called his wife. "I have heard," he said, "that your father is ill. Take horses and messengers and go to stay with him. And when you arrive, give him this letter."

The wife left and arrived soon afterwards at her father's home. There her father read the letter from the king and, indeed, began to look ill.

Three days passed, and his daughter announced, "Father, it is time for me to return to the palace, to my husband."

"That is impossible." answered the father, "for you are divorced."

"What? What are you saying, Father?"

"You are divorced," shrieked her father, "for you and your mother are both cheaters."

And then the woman knew what had happened. "But," she cried, "what was done could not be undone."

Meanwhile, at the palace the wealthy king Elhaj Munis took the garbage girl for his wife.

The hand of God is not short.

Nothing is impossible for Him.

# The Baker's Daughter and the King's Son

## INTRODUCTION

The Song of Songs (4:12–13) tells of a beloved maiden compared to beautiful spices and trees. Among these is henna, a plant whose roots and leaves give off a distinctive red dye. Before the wedding, in order to ward off evil spirits that might be lurking about the bride, henna is smeared on the body of the girl. This custom is common among the Jews of Yemen, Tunisia, Morocco, and other oriental communities. The bride and groom, dressed in the elaborate wedding garb of the particular ethnic group, march in a procession, accompanied by women carrying lit candles and incense burners, or playing drums, shaking bells, and singing, in order to ward off these spirits. The custom of the henna night is described in this tale, told by Jenny and Shoshana Elmaleh, from Tunisia.

This is another in the group of tales which fulfills the Cinderella dream of marrying the prince or a rich man. Here this is achieved via the wit and cleverness of the girl. This particular tale is most popular in the Orient.

One of the conditions in the story is that the lights be put out in the bridal suite. This may refer to *Bereishit Rabbah*, in which the lights were put out when Jacob was fooled into marrying Leah instead of his intended Rachel.

# 13

# *The Baker's Daughter and the King's Son*

nce upon a time there was a baker whose only and beautiful daughter helped him in the bakery, which was very close to the royal palace. One day a fortune-teller passed, and the daughter called, "Come, read my hand and tell me my future."

At that same moment, at the palace, a pet dove flew away from the prince. So the prince went up to the roof to find the bird, and what did he hear? The baker's daughter calling to the fortune-teller. The prince laughed, "Let's hear what the woman tells her." And, as he listened, he heard these words: "You will marry a prince."

Now, the baker's daughter had no money, so she paid the fortune-teller with oil and bread, and the woman went on her way. The prince laughed again, "Can it be that the baker's daughter will be my wife? I mean to marry my cousin."

So the prince went and asked his uncle for his cousin's hand. Now, that girl was very ugly, so her father told him, "Only on one condition, that you don't put on the lights in the bridal suite."

The boy agreed.

Before the wedding, the prince passed the window of the bakery. "Good morning," he said.

"Good morning to you, morning of light, happiness and health," the girl answered.

The prince asked, "Do you remember what the fortune-teller told you? Well, I'm going to marry my cousin."

"Congratulations!"

"What a waste of bread and oil you gave her," said the prince.

The girl said nothing.

In honor of the betrothal night, the ugly bride had been bought fine clothes, but her mother was greatly worried, for in her heart she feared, what if someone asked the prince, "How can you marry such an ugly girl?" What would happen if he listened to them?

So the mother of the bride decided that for just one night she would exchange her daughter for a pretty girl. Then everyone would say: "How pretty is the prince's wife!" And, since she knew the beautiful baker's daughter, she immediately thought of her. She offered the girl five hundred pounds, and the baker's daughter agreed to take the bride's place. She told her father: "Tomorrow I must go to the king's palace to clean the rooms. I will receive a lot of money." If not for this explanation, her father would not have agreed to let her go.

So it was that the baker's daughter took the bride's place at the engagement party. Everyone who saw her said: "A pretty bride! A lovely bride! A fine bride!"

The girl received her money from the bride's mother and returned home.

The next day the prince again came to the bakery. "Yesterday I became engaged to a pretty girl," he said. For he never imagined that the baker's daughter had taken his bride's place.

"Congratulations!" said the baker's daughter.

"What a waste of bread and oil you gave the fortune-teller!" he laughed. This time too she did not reply.

The wedding night came, and again the baker's daughter was dressed in fine raiment, and when the prince sat in the coffee house, everyone said to him, "What a pretty bride you have! What a pretty bride!"

The prince was so curious that he took a sheet, wrapped himself in it, and mingled with the women to see his bride. And when he reached her, he kissed her and placed his ring on her finger. The baker's daughter knew very well who he was, but he did not suspect her at all.

Later the groom was told, "The bride must enter in the dark." And he thought: "No matter! I've already seen her!"

But at night the baker's daughter changed places with the real bride. When the husband felt the real bride's hands, he found them to be very skinny. Her whole body was skinny and, in addition, she had a grating voice. "We'll turn the lights on and see who it is," he thought. And when the prince saw the bride, he was very angry. "They showed me a pretty girl, a beauty, and gave me an ugly one!" he cried. And he picked the bride up and hung her on the chandelier.

The next day, when the mother appeared, she heard her daughter calling, "Mother, help me! I'm strangling on the chandelier!" Finally the woman broke down the door, lowered her daughter, and took her home.

Then the angry groom went, as was his way, to the bakery. "Did you know that I was married last night?" he asked the baker's daughter.

"Congratulations!"

"Why did you give the fortune-teller oil and bread?"

"And why did you give me a kiss and a ring for no reason?"

Then the prince understood what had happened and returned home, angry, overexcited, and ill. For days he could neither eat, drink, nor sleep. His mother, the queen, immediately sent for a doctor, who examined the prince and said, "He lacks nothing; he is only lovesick."

So the prince was offered girls and women, but he insisted, "I want only the baker's daughter!"

Then his mother took a sum of money and, with another woman, went to the bakery. There they offered the baker money for his daughter to be married to the prince.

"I'm prepared to give her even as a maid, for we are very poor."

Wedding preparations began at once, but the baker's daughter had one demand: "Let the groom come to me in the dark."

The condition was agreed to.

Soon afterward the bride approached the pastry chef. "I will give you anything you want and even double your wages," she told him. "Look at me and study my features well, and make a cake shaped like a doll who looks exactly like me. Fill her with honey and put a cord at her neck, so that when the cord is pulled, the doll will nod her head, as if she is speaking."

At night the bride put the doll in her place and she herself hid, holding in her hand the end of the cord attached to the doll's neck.

"So in the end you succeeded in getting me!" cried the groom.

The bride pulled the cord and the doll nodded her head, as if she were saying, "Yes." Then she raised her head.

"Now, too, you pick up your head?" The prince grew angry, pulled out his sword, and, at once, slashed off the head of the doll. The honey started to pour out toward the groom's mouth, and he began to feel remorse. "What a sweetheart! What a pity that I killed her! Oh, dear, oh, dear! What have I done? Now I'll be accused of murder!" The prince was bewildered and was about to kill himself.

"It's just a doll's head. And I am alive and well," laughed the baker's daughter, coming out of her hiding place.

The prince rejoiced and the couple were married. They lived their life happily and in joy, and, from that moment on, all their deeds were blessed.

## *The Mountain of* Sheidim

### INTRODUCTION

The story of the Jerusalemite is the only Hebrew folktale with a scholarly background dating back hundreds of years. The story is told by both men and women, possibly for different reasons, and the elements, the plot, *and the ending* are always the same. This particular version, a male version, told by Jefet Shwili, is from Yemen. A female version is IFA 1048 from Morocco.

In this story the man has a negative side; he does not keep his promise, either to the old man, to the king, or to his bride (to three generations). Therefore, the faults are his. When men tell the tale, it is probably for its religious message: since the man is ethically at fault, he must be punished. When women tell the tale, it has an additional message: when a woman has been wronged in this way, when she tries to get justice via legal means (in some versions she goes before a *beit din*, a religious court), but to no avail, she gains the power of life or death. The female viewpoint requires a happy ending, which it has. The honor of the abandoned woman is rectified.

The theme of the kiss of death stems from the Jewish legend of Moses going to his death; according to the *Aggadah*, he is kissed on the forehead by the *Shechinah*. In the oral tales the kisses become erotic; by taking away the husband's breath, she brings him an erotic kind of death. Since the crime is an oral one, the punishment too is given by mouth; the manner of punishment fits the manner of the crime.

The question asked by the watchman, "Are you human or demon?" is one that is found in many folktales. Its basis is in "The Weasel and the Well," a tale alluded to in Talmudic Tractate *Taanit* 8.

# 14

# *The Mountain of* Sheidim

nce upon a time there lived a king who had two daughters and one son. Of all his children he loved his son most of all. When the prince grew up, he loved to hunt, and his father would say, "My dear and only son, perhaps you should not hunt so often. I fear for you, for, God forbid, while you are away at the hunt, the *sheidim*, the demons, may harm you."

"Do not fear, Father," replied the lad, "for as long as I have strength and good sense, the *sheidim* will have no power over me."

"May God be with you," said his father.

Now, one day when he was away on a hunt, the lad came to a mountain that was two hundred meters high. And behold! Smoke was rising from within its inner depths.

'What can that be?' thought the prince. 'I will go and see!'

So the young prince approached the mountain and, when he was almost there, who should appear before him but an old man. "Where are you going?" asked the old one.

"Oh, I am on my way to the mountain," replied the lad. "I want to find out how it is that smoke is rising from within."

"Turn back! Do not go to that mountain," said the old one.

"But I must," replied the prince. "I must know the secret of the smoke."

"Very well then," said the old one. "If you must go, then go with caution, and remember this advice: Never break a vow which you have made."

The prince gave his word, and, just as quickly as he had come, the old man disappeared.

And so the son climbed the mountain and found therein a huge hole, big enough for him to climb into. And when he had done so, he descended into an enormous cave, where three hundred tables stood, one near the other, laid out with the finest foods he had ever seen. The lad, amazed at what he saw before him and hungry from his day's journey, tasted from every table. Then, hearing the heavy sounds of footsteps, he crouched in a corner and hid.

Into the cave strode the *sheidim*, led by their king, for this was their home.

"What is this? Our food is gone!" they cried, as they ran from one table to another.

The cooks were called forth. "What has happened? Where is our food?" demanded the king.

"We know nothing," replied the cooks. "We put the platters on the tables as usual. Nothing was missing."

"In that case, some stranger must be here," declared the demon king. And they started to search but found no one. And so the *sheidim* ate their fill and went to bed.

The next day, while his hosts were away, the prince crept out of his hiding place. Again he ate from every table—a bite here, a taste there—until he was full, and crept back to his corner. When the *sheidim* returned and found their plates disturbed, they once again searched the cave, but found no one. The king was puzzled.

"Let us leave a watchman in hiding," he declared, "to see who is stealing our food!"

And so, the very next day, when all the *sheidim* seemed to have left, the prince again approached the tables. But this time, as he began to eat, the watchman caught him.

"Who are you? Demon or humankind?"

"I am of humankind," answered the prince.

"Then what are you searching for? Who bids you welcome here? Do you not know the dangers of this place?"

"B- b- but—I saw the smoke coming from the mountain and I only wanted to know where it was coming from—so I climbed inside," the prince protested.

"No matter," answered the watchman, "for now you shall remain here with us."

And before he knew it, the young prince was standing in front of the demon king.

"So you are the one leading us by the nose!" declared the king. "Why did you steal from us? Why did you hide? We wouldn't have harmed you—but now you are our prisoner."

And within moments the prince was led to a cell inside a

small prison. From there he could look out through a small window and see the open sky and the world outside.

Now, one day as the prince looked out, he saw a lovely girl, the demon princess, Ufrut, bathing in a nearby pond. At once he was struck by her beauty, and whistled to gain her attention.

The princess turned quickly. "Who is that whistling? Why, from the time I was a child I have been bathing here, and no one has ever whistled." So she dressed quickly and ran to her father.

And when the king heard her question, he sent his guards to search. They looked everywhere, and after searching near the pond and finding no one, they knew that the whistler could be none other than the young man in prison. Once again the lad was brought before the demon king.

"Why did you whistle?" the king asked.

"Only because I saw a beautiful girl bathing in the pond and fell in love with her at once."

"That beautiful girl is none other than my daughter, Ufrut," said the king, "and if you truly love her, you may have her hand in marriage. But you must swear never to break your marriage oath—for you are human and we are *sheidim*."

"I swear and will do as you wish," answered the young lad. "If I marry your daughter, she will be my wife forever, even though she be a demon."

And so the two were married, with Heaven and Earth as their witness, and remained in their home within the mountain.

Meanwhile, the lad's father, the king, was greatly worried, for his son had been gone for many weeks. Every able person in the kingdom was called forth to help him search. At last they came to a high mountain, two hundred meters high, but, search as they might, found no trace of the missing prince. Suddenly, smoke began to rise out of the mountain, and the astonished king went closer to find its source. And, just as suddenly, there in front of them sat an old man.

"Who are you? Demon or humankind?"

"We are humans," answered the king, "and I have come to find my lost son who came to hunt in this region."

"I too am human," answered the old one, "and it is my job to look after these mountains. Some time ago I saw your son descend into the mountain, but he never came out."

The king thanked the old man, and at once set off with his followers to climb the mountain, but when they tried to do so, each and every one of them slipped and fell! The king wanted to turn to the old man for help, but he noticed that the old man had disappeared. Tired and discouraged, the group at last turned back for the palace, where the king and his wife cried for seven days over the loss of their son, who, they felt, was surely dead.

Many years passed. The demon princess gave birth to a son, whose name was Badrus, and by the time the boy reached the age of eighteen, he was a fine horseman. His father's horse was the only horse in the demon kingdom, and the king grew afraid for his grandson. Perhaps the horse would hurt him. To his son-in-law he said, "Why do you let your son ride? The sport is dangerous! Kill the horse!" To this the boy's father replied, "That I will never do—for the horse reminds me of my home and my dear parents whom I long to see."

And so the prince's longing grew stronger and stronger, until one day he decided to run away and find the palace of his earthly parents. But the demon king's guards were too clever for him, and soon he found himself standing once again before the king.

"Why did you run away?" the monarch asked, to which the prince replied, "For eighteen years I have not seen my parents. My longing grows greater each day."

"Very well," said the demon king. "I will make an agreement with you. Go and visit your parents for four years, but after that time you must return."

The prince, thankful to the demon king, readily promised to keep this agreement, and soon he took Badrus, his son, and climbed out of the mountain. There he met the old man, who asked, "What brings you here? Have you broken your oath?"

"No, I have an agreement to take leave for four years."

"Then go in God's name."

The prince soon came to the home of his parents, who, of course, did not know him. "Have you a son?" asked the prince.

"We had a son," said the king, "but he died long ago."

"Father, Mother, it is I, your son," screamed the prince, and he gave some signs of recognition that only his parents would remember. The joy of the couple was unbounded. And so, for four years, the prince remained with his parents, and they lived together in happiness.

But when the four years were over, the prince did not return to the demon kingdom. The demon princess begged her father to let her go and seek her husband, "He took me as his wife before Heaven and Earth as witness, and so I must go."

At last, despite the danger, the demon king let her go forth, and she arrived as her husband sat in the house of prayer, his aging parents near him.

"Is this how you behave?" she asked. "You made an agreement with my father for four years, but you did not return! Don't you know me? Am I not your wife? At least give me my son!"

"Under no circumstances," answered her husband. "The boy and I remain here."

The people around were astonished.

"To whom are you speaking?" they asked, for they saw no one.

"For heaven's sake, to my wife!"

"Wife? What wife? Where is she?"

And then the prince told his parents of his marriage to the demon princess. "Yes, I have no way out," he declared. "I married her before the eyes of Heaven and Earth, and so I must return."

And so the prince took leave of his parents and went back with his son to his cavernous home.

But his longing for his parents arose again, and leaving his son Badrus behind, he soon escaped and returned again to the home of his parents.

"What are you doing here?" cried his father in surprise. "My dear son, you married your wife before Heaven and Earth as witness, so we cannot accept you. Come to visit us from time to time but always return to the wife you chose."

"No, never!" shrieked the son, "I will never return to the kingdom of *sheidim*." And so he remained in his parents' home.

This time the demoness took her son and went forth to earth, and came before her husband in human form.

"Come back and live with us," she begged.

"No, I don't wish to do so," he said.

"Then take your son and give me a *get*, a divorce, so that I may be free."

"No, I do not wish to do that either."

The demon princess then turned to her husband's father. "Talk to him," she pleaded.

But the old king answered, "I can do nothing. He is in your hands. Do as you wish."

"Very well," said the demon princess, "let me give him a farewell kiss, and I shall depart."

And so the prince approached his wife. She came toward him and kissed him—and took his soul.

## The Giving of Charity Is Repaid

### INTRODUCTION

This story belongs to a universal tale type called "the maiden without hands," popularly developed in the Middle Ages. It is also known in the tradition of *The Thousand and One Nights*. The universal tale usually begins with the girl refusing to marry her father or with the girl being slandered by her sister-in-law. It is a tale of magic in which the persecuted girl eventually gets a royal husband.

In the Jewish oicotype, of which this version from Tunisia is typical, the story does not begin with a sexual overtone. Instead, the girl refuses to stop giving charity. This ethic of giving charity, an important one in Jewish life, has its foundation in talmudic-midrashic literature: "Every man should give charity, even a beggar who lives on charity" (*Gittin* 7, 72). "Charity is equal to all the precepts put together" (*Baba Batra* 9, 72). The conflict in the story, then, is based on the father's attitude toward his daughter's giving charity and her refusal to obey, or, sometimes, on the attitude of the cruel step-mother, who usurps the virtuous, deceased mother. In these versions the father is the one who severs the daughter's hands.

Other versions involve a confrontation between sisters-in-law. In such cases, it is the brother who believes his wife's slander and cuts off the hands of his sister. In one such version, IFA 6895, from Lebanon, the maimed girl, upon drinking water in the forest, is bestowed with golden hands. In both versions, the girl, who has not sinned, is completely innocent and shows no sign of weakness.

In these Jewish versions, the punishment is one of "measure for measure" (*Nedarim* 32, 71); the hands that gave charity (and, thereby, disobeyed the father) are cut off. There is a direct connection between the girl's act and her punishment.

Some Jewish versions involve an admission, at the end, of the girl's innocence, and contrition and penitence on the part of the male. Sometimes, as in the Lebanese version, the brother divorces his wife and goes to live with his sister. This act of contrition, plus the appearance of Elijah as restorer of the severed hands, changes a universal tale of magic into a Jewish religious tale.

This tale involves a great deal of cruelty; a Bukharan Jewish woman's version tells of the girl's arms being severed, after which she is buried in a hole, with only her face in the open air. In the same version the jealous sister-in-law kills her *own* child, in order to blame the other woman and cause her to be punished. This cruelty, as unpleasant as it may be, arouses sympathy and pity for the victim, and fear for all mankind. The listeners, who enjoy the cruelty, to a point, wonder to themselves: "How can such a thing happen?" However, the cruelty comes to a climax, and the audience's sense of fair play gives suggestion to the teller to finally rescue the heroine.

Some versions end with the cruel punishment or death of the man. When women are treated cruelly, they would like to respond in kind; by telling this tale, they have the chance to do so. The end of the story, then, often gives a "measure for measure" punishment, as was previously given the girl; in the folktale presented here, the father becomes a magician who must use his hands to gain his livelihood. In other versions he becomes a beggar, holding out his hands for alms, or his hands fall off or wither away. Justice is served!

The storyteller, wishing to leave the audience with a

positive feeling, often ends the story by alluding to a biblical verse, such as, "Woe unto the wicked! It shall be ill with him for the reward of his hands shall be given him." (Isaiah 3:11)

This Judaized version of a universal tale is so full of Jewish characters, events in Jewish time, and other Jewish elements that they need no explanation.

The theme that charity saves from death is treated in greater depth in stories 33 to 36.

# 15

# *The Giving of Charity Is Repaid*

here was a man who had an only daughter who loved to give charity. Her mother supported her actions, but her father demanded that she be less generous. When the father saw that the girl continued to aid the poor, he said to her, "Bring me such and such a thing from the cellar."

And when the young girl went down into the cellar to fulfill her father's request, he closed the door behind her, and there she was trapped. The young girl began to weep and to cry, "My father, my father, is this how you behave toward your only daughter? Have you no pity?"

But the father remained insensitive to the beseeching of his daughter.

At midnight heavenly angels descended into the cave. "What would you like to eat, my child?" they asked.

"Whatever you give me I will eat."

So the angels brought the most delicious food, and drink such as comes from a flask of perfume. And on her forehead they inscribed the words, "Charity saves from death."

And thus for three weeks the two angels appeared daily to feed the girl.

In the meantime the father was seized by remorse, and one

day he decided to go down into the cellar. When he opened the door, he was astonished to see his daughter in good health. "What happened?" he asked.

And she replied, "You see, Father, that charity saves from death. It is because I gave charity that I am still alive. Thanks to heavenly help I have lacked for nothing while I was imprisoned."

To this the father answered, "I will release you from this terrible place, and from today onward you may give as much charity as you wish." So the young girl left the prison, continued to help the poor, and gave even more charity than she had before.

Now, one day the girl's mother died, and her father remarried. But the second wife complained to him that his daughter gave too much of their money to the poor.

So one day the man said to his daughter, "Come with me. We will take a long trip to visit the garden of my father." At midnight the two began their journey, and, at last, arrived at the forest. The father then lifted the girl from the carriage, cut off her hands and feet, and, thus, abandoned her. The girl began to weep and cry, "My father, my father, what have you done to me? Why do you punish me like this?"

At nightfall the Prophet Elijah, may his memory be blessed, appeared to her and asked, "What happened to you, my daughter?"

And when the young girl told her story, the Prophet said, "Do not worry, my child. I will return your hands and your feet."

The Prophet did as he promised, and soon the young girl was whole again. Then the Prophet asked that, in return, he be the *sandek*, the godfather, when she would one day bring a son into the world. And the girl willingly and readily agreed to fulfill the request.

She remained in the forest, and one day a poor man passed by, and, seeing the young girl alone and abandoned, spoke to her. "This is a strange place for a young girl. What are you doing here?"

Then she told him all of her story. The poor man responded by taking her back to his home, where he treated her with great respect; all that he earned he gave to her. After some time the two married, and within nine months a son was brought into the world. And on the day of the *brit milah*, the circumcision, Elijah the Prophet, may his memory be blessed, did indeed serve as godfather. The young wife asked him to bless her, to which he replied, "This will be my blessing: When your husband says grace after the meal, he will find five hundred coins under the mat."

And so it happened! Every time the couple said grace over their food, five hundred coins appeared. Soon they were quite wealthy, lived happily, and had great joy in watching their son grow.

Meanwhile, the girl's cruel father had lost his wealth and had become a magician, traveling from town to town to perform in the markets. One day his daughter spotted him at his work and asked her husband to invite this magician to their home.

Of course, the father did not recognize his daughter, but he said, "You know, once I had a daughter who looked like you."

"Father, I am your daughter," she replied. "You left me for dead in the forest, but, see, as I always told you, charity saves from death."

The father was astonished—but even more so when, after saying grace, his son-in-law lifted the mat to reveal five hundred coins. And what did the cruel father do? He ran to the king to tell what he had seen.

At once the king summoned the husband to the palace and commanded him to bring the magic object which brought forth money. And, so, the frightened man brought the mat, protesting, in vain, that it was the words of the blessing, not the mat, that produced the coins.

That night Elijah the Prophet appeared to the man to console him. "Do not be frightened, for no misfortune will befall you. In fact, the king will give you even more money than before."

Soon afterward the king, overjoyed with his new magic object, called his ministers and servants to show them how it worked. He placed the mat on the table, and pronounced, "I want five hundred coins." Then he lifted the mat, and there, behold! An army of scorpions surged forth, attacking everyone in the palace. Nothing the king could do could ward off the creatures!

At last the king called for the owner of the mat. "Please, please," he begged, "just get rid of these nasty scorpions and I will give you any sum you wish!"

So the husband said grace and lifted the mat, and behold! The scorpions disappeared. In their place lay five hundred coins.

The king kept his word and gave the man a large sum of money. "And, as for your wicked father-in-law," he said, "I will have him hanged from a high tree." And so the deed was done!

And then the young couple returned to their home, where they lived happily all the days of their lives.

# Great Are the Deeds of God

## INTRODUCTION

This tale was told by Fahima Shaharabni, a Jewess from Iraq. The biblical title (Psalm 111:2) and closing refrain (2 Samuel 2:6) are evidence of the teller's faith in God; He punishes the stingy and rewards the generous.

The heroine bears the name of the biblical Dina, daughter of Jacob and Leah, who was sought and defiled by a Shechemite prince, which thus incited the wrath of her brothers (Genesis 34). In pre-Solomonic narratives this was truly a sad incident involving women. But here, in our story, Dina becomes a strong character, independent and clear about her deeds as a Jewish woman. She is a turnabout from the passive and violated Dina of the Bible. To a woman teller, living in a society where she is passive, and sometimes violated, the wish fulfillment of this story is: "I too can be a strong, independent woman, just like this Dina."

# 16

# *Great Are the Deeds of God*

**M**any years ago there lived a rich, educated, God-fearing man who had a beautiful daughter named Dina. She herself was wise and intelligent and, above everything else, loved to help the poor. Indeed, every beggar who came to the door was welcomed at a fine table, and then given money to help him on his way.

Now, among Dina's many suitors was a certain wealthy man, owner of flocks and herds. And so Dina agreed to marry him, and the wedding feast lasted for seven days, according to custom.

What Dina didn't know was that her new husband was stingy, miserly, selfish. He had never given as much as a crumb of bread to the poor.

One day a ragged beggar appeared at the door. He was quite weary, not having eaten for two entire days. Dina received the beggar warmly, as was her way. "Welcome to our home. Come and eat with us."

But her husband was adamant. "Beggars are not allowed in this place! Leave the house at once." And so the husband continued to shout.

Now Dina understood the character of her husband. She left him and returned to her father's house.

In the days that followed many a suitor came to seek her hand. But each one, upon hearing of her generous nature, refused to marry her. "Just think of how much money she will spend. Think of beggars eating with us at our table! No, no, no." And each returned to his own home.

But at last a wealthy man appeared who was most pleased with Dina's character. "What could be better than a woman with a good heart!" And so the two were wed.

One evening, as the two were dining, there was a knock at the door, and when it was opened, there stood a poor man, weak and tired from walking on the road. Dina rose to welcome him, and then, upon facing the man, collapsed as in a faint. The beggar was none other than her first husband, who had lost his wealth.

Then it was that her new husband revealed himself. "And I am the beggar of long ago, whom you threw from your home."

Indeed, great are the deeds of the Lord.

He enriches and impoverishes.

He lifts up, and humiliates.

Great are the deeds of the Lord.

# The Deceived Girl and the Stone of Suffering

## INTRODUCTION

This tale is one of the first collected by the IFA in the 1950s. It was recorded by Sara Bashari, a Yemenite-born high-school student, as told by Leah Nakhshon, from southeastern Yemen.

The tale belongs to a type called "The Ghoulish Schoolmaster and the Stone of Pity." In most versions the stone bursts as it loses its patience.

Here we see the suffering that a woman must endure; life, indeed, can be cruel. Once again we see female-female conflict between the deceived girl and the wicked one, with the deceived and virtuous one eventually marrying the wealthy man. We also see the devotion of the mother, who remains with her daughter throughout her travails, and the support of the parents, who go into poverty in order to supply the girl with her need for food. These are strong messages.

The pattern of the seven years of hunger, thirst, and servitude may be based on the dream interpretation given by Joseph in Genesis 41, or the seven plus seven years in which Jacob toiled for Rachel and then for Leah (in Genesis 29).

The tale is well-known in southern Europe, the Middle East, and central Asia (India, Persia, Uzbekhistan). There are seven Jewish versions in the IFA.

# 17

# *The Deceived Girl and the Stone of Suffering*

rich and respected family had an only daughter, whom they looked upon as the apple of their eye. One night the girl dreamed a fearful dream. An old man with a long white beard fell to his knees before her and proclaimed: "For seven years you will be hungry, and no matter how much you eat, you will still be hungry. Seven years of thirst will follow, and no matter what you drink, you will still remain thirsty. Then you will spend seven more years tending a dead man in a locked-up house. Only after twenty-one years of suffering will happiness come your way and be with you until the end of your days." The frightened girl related her dream to her parents, who became terrified.

After a few days she began to feel famished. Her parents spent all their money on food and kept selling their property until they were impoverished. Still they could not satisfy their daughter's hunger. The fond mother wandered with her daughter from town to town, from village to village, asking for food.

Seven long years of hunger, misery, and exhaustion passed, while the mother continued to wander with her daughter. Then began the years of thirst. The daughter was always thirty. Her thirst became greater and greater and could not be quenched, not even by rivers and streams. So the two wandered from town to village, from village to town, from mountain to valley, and from valley to mountain. Everywhere the daughter drank water, yet her thirst was not quenched.

Seven years of thirst, hardship, and suffering passed, and one day the mother and daughter reached an isolated place in the desert. They saw a huge house that looked like a king's palace. The house was open, and the girl asked her mother to wait while she went inside. As she entered the house, the doors were bolted behind her, and she found herself in a room where a dead man lay upon a bed.

Thus, she realized that she had ended the seven years of thirst and come to the years of exhausting care of the dead man. She knelt down and bathed him. Then she washed and cleaned his clothes and aired the room. Day after day she carried on the burden of this work. All the time the corpselike body did not stir from its place.

The mother, knowing of her daughter's fate, came to live in the nearest town so as to follow her doings.

The years of suffering had nearly come to an end. The girl, exhausted from hard work, was on the point of a breakdown. Then one day she saw a pretty young girl on the road in front of the house, so she called out to her, threw a rope down below, and pulled her inside. From that time on, the young girl started to help with the work.

One day, when the daughter was in the adjacent room, she heard voices. The young girl was speaking to the sick man, who had recovered from his deathlike sleep. "Was it you who cared for me all this long time?" the man asked.

"Yes!" came the positive answer.

The man continued: "You have suffered enough for me. From now on your burden will be lifted. You will be the queen of this house, my beloved companion."

"For days and nights I did not close my eyes," lied the girl. "How good that the long and exhausting torture will come to an end!"

"Did you bear all this anguish alone?" asked the man.

"Indeed, I had a helper," answered the young girl's voice, "but she was wicked."

The daughter understood that, after bearing her miserable fate for twenty-one years, she had been cheated by the pretty young girl.

The wedding day drew near. All the time the poor daughter worked hard, at the orders of the young girl. One day the man decided to go to the nearby town to make purchases for the household and for the wedding. So he asked the daughter, too, what she would like him to bring her.

The daughter asked, "Bring me, my master, the stone of suffering."

Now, the master had never heard about this precious stone, but he promised to bring it, and, after much searching, at last succeeded in procuring it. He was told by the merchant that he who reveals all the sufferings of his past to this stone brings it to life, whereupon it swallows up the storyteller.

The man was quite surprised that the girl had asked for such a gift, so after he had given it to her, he hid behind the door and heard her entire story: "Alas! Stone of suffering, years of hunger passed over me, then years of thirst grieved me, then years of care . . ."

The story was a long one, and all the time the stone grew bigger and bigger. Suddenly the door opened, and the man just managed to catch the stone before it turned to life. In a trembling voice the man asked, "Why didn't you tell me that you were the one who suffered? How good that the truth has been revealed to me at last! To you and only you belong all the joys of happiness and delight."

At the magnificent wedding that took place the mother and many guests were present. And what of the wicked young girl? She disappeared, and the couple never saw her again all the days of their happy life.

## The Enchanted Princess Who Became a Bouquet

### Introduction

The opening words of the tale, "Nothing can happen unless decreed by God," changes this universal tale into one with a Jewish message. The ethic of keeping one's word, so important in Jewish life, is seen in this story as well.

This version, told by Sarah Gad from Afghanistan, has many women's messages. In this story we see the polarity of Eve and Lilith, complete opposites of good and evil, in the totally good and totally evil women characters. The Jewish message of the story may be that good, temporarily destroyed, is victorious. From a woman's point of view, love, temporarily separated, is reestablished. And, the support of the baker lady is yet another message of female help and solidarity.

The theme of the woman's talking to the doll is found in "The Deceived Girl and the Stone of Suffering" and "The Clever Wife" (nos. 17 and 65) in this book. In this tale the style of the girl's lament to the doll is similar to the songs of lament and other songs sung by women in Sephardic communities.

# 18

# *The Enchanted Princess Who Became a Bouquet*

othing can happen unless decreed by God!

Once there was a king who had an only daughter. His wife died and the king remarried, for a king must not be without a wife. At first the stepmother treated the girl fairly. But when she became pregnant and had a daughter of her own, she began to hate the stepdaughter. Day after day she harassed her, starved her, and beat her. The king knew nothing of this, for he was occupied with matters of state.

The princess suffered until she could bear it no longer. And so, preferring death to her stepmother's beatings, she ran far away until she reached a strange city. There she came to a beautiful park, in the middle of which was a large pool, surrounded by tall trees, where the people of the city would come to drink. The girl climbed a tree and sat in its branches. And so, when night fell, that tree became her bed.

In the morning the prince of that city was riding on his fine horse. Reaching the pool, the prince stopped his horse so that it might drink. But the horse, seeing the girl's reflection, jumped back and refused to move. The prince wondered at this and tried again to water the horse. But, once again, the horse retreated. So the prince dismounted and pulled his horse toward the pool until he himself saw the reflection of the girl. He looked up into the tree and stood still with his mouth agape. The girl was a beauty: her hair was long and silky; her eyes, radiant and sparkling. In an instant the prince fell in love with all of his heart.

Then it was that the princess told the prince how she had been harassed by her envious stepmother. To this he replied that his own parents would take care of her, if only she would marry him. The princess, whose heart had gone out to the handsome prince, consented at once. The prince then removed from his neck a golden ornament, gave it to the princess as a token of his love, asked her to wait for him, and rode off to the palace to tell his parents the good news.

Meanwhile, a maid of that city was sent to the pool to fetch water. She was an ugly girl, with thinning hair, eyes that went each in a different direction, face pocked with holes, and legs that were crooked. The girl came to the pool, looked down, and saw the reflection. "Oh, my," she said aloud, "if I am so beautiful, why do I need to serve others?" And so she threw down the jar, breaking it to pieces.

When she returned home, her employers asked, "And why did you come back without water?"

"The jar fell and broke," she said.

So they gave her a leather pouch. Again she returned to the pool, and, again, she saw the reflection. "If I am so beautiful," she thought aloud, "why do I need to serve others?" And she tore the leather pouch and threw away the pieces. At home, her employers asked, "And now why did you come back without water?"

"A dog attacked me and tore away the pouch."

So they gave her a vessel of copper, and the girl returned to the pool. Once more she saw the reflection in the water. "If I am so beautiful, why do I need to serve others?" she said aloud, and she kicked away the metal vessel.

Now the princess, looking down upon this, was growing impatient. "Why are you breaking the vessels?" she called out. "This is not your reflection. It is mine."

The maid looked up and was astonished to see a beautiful girl sitting in the tree. Asking permission to join her, the maid climbed the tree and saw the beautiful dress, the jewels, and the golden ornament, given by the prince. When asked what the beautiful girl was doing in the tree, the princess replied that she was waiting for the king's son to take her to the palace.

"And while you are waiting, may I try on your dress for just a moment," asked the maid, "for never have I had such a dress?" The princess, being kindhearted, agreed. In this manner, the maid borrowed the jewels, shoes, and even the golden ornament, until she, herself, was dressed as a princess. And, asking the princess to move a bit, then a bit more, and then even a bit farther along the branch, the maid pushed the girl into the pool.

At once the princess was changed into a bouquet of beautiful and delicate flowers that floated on top of the water—for it seemed that the moment she touched the waters, they became enchanted. Meanwhile, the maid, now appearing as the princess, waited for the prince's return.

At the palace the prince excitedly told his parents about the beautiful princess he had met and who had agreed to marry him. The king and queen, excited as well, invited entertainers, dignitaries, and important people of the court, and they went to fetch the princess, while the prince rode at the head of the procession.

But his heart darkened when he saw the ugly girl instead of his beloved. "Why are you so ugly? What has happened to your silky hair?" he asked.

"I waited for you for so long," said the maid, "that the ravens plucked my hair, one by one."

"And why is your face full of holes?" he asked.

"Because the branches pinched my face," she said.

"And why are your eyes crossed?"

"Because I looked into the sunlight to see if you were coming."

"And why are your legs crooked?"

"Because I ran after you and couldn't reach you."

The prince, disheartened, had no choice but to take the

maid to the palace, for he had been taught to keep his word. After all, wasn't the girl wearing the golden ornament he himself had given her? As they left, the prince noticed the beautiful bouquet floating on the water. Never had he seen such fragile flowers. So these he took to the palace as well, where they were placed in a vase and watered by the prince every day. How he loved to smell their fragrance and enjoy their beauty! And, wonder of all wonders, the flowers never withered.

A year passed. And the maid, to whom her husband paid little attention at all, was jealous of the bouquet, and plucked its petals one by one, scattering them about. At once they were turned to logs, which were then fashioned for a cradle, for the maid, in the meantime, had given birth. But so much pleasure did the cradle give the child as it rocked back and forth that the maid broke the cradle to pieces and ordered the logs to be used for the fire in which their bread was baked. But, when the baker lady appeared and saw those logs, she thought, "Such fine logs! I will take them home and use them for a door for my house."

Now the baker lady was an elderly woman who lived alone. In the morning she would leave her house, unswept, untidy, dirty dishes strewn about, and in the evening after her day's work, she would return. But, from the moment that her new door was put into place, a strange thing happened. Every night when the woman came home, she would find her house shiny, her clothes laundered, her dishes washed. "Who has done all this?" she wondered. Little did she know that, during the day, the princess would come out of the door, do all the cleaning, and return to her place at the end of her work.

At first the baker thought that the door had been left open and that a stranger had come in to do the work. So she locked the door. But again the house was cleaned in her absence. The bewildered woman ran to a magician for advice. "You must make a doll of china," he said. "Put it in bed in place of yourself, and hide to see what is happening. Cut your finger and rub salt into the wound so as not to fall asleep." And so the woman did. Next to the doll she placed a big mirror, and hid.

The next morning, as usual, the girl emerged from the door. And what should she see but a beautiful girl staring back at her from the mirror. And, as she looked at her own reflection, her heart opened and she began to pour out her troubles to the china doll:

"Daughter of my fate who has come out of the door, goddess of china, my heart is bursting or your heart will: I had a nice and dear mother who loved me. My mother died and my father remarried. . . ."

Thus, the whole sad story poured out, including the part where she fell in love with the prince and the maid pushed her into the pool and she was turned into a bouquet of flowers by the envious maid and turned to wood to be saved by the baker lady. Each part of her story was told in rhyme and ended with the same refrain, "Daughter of my fate who has come out of the door, goddess of china, my heart is bursting or your heart will." As the girl finished telling the story, the doll burst into many pieces, and broke.

The baker lady calmed the princess and caressed her. Then she went to the prince and told him the story. And so it was that the prince and princess were reunited.

As for the jealous wife, she received her punishment. Tied to a horse's tail she was dragged through the streets of the city, and torn to pieces.

The prince married his beautiful princess, who was loved and beloved by all, all the days of their lives. And, for as long as they lived, the prince continued to bestow golden ornaments on his enchanted princess.

## The Pomegranate Girl

### INTRODUCTION

This story has very special meaning to me. It was told by Flora Cohen, originally from Egypt, to her daughter, Elana, who collected over eighty of her mother's tales and contributed this rich collection to the IFA. Flora was a captivating storyteller who made a wonderful contribution to storytelling in Israel, and it was my pleasure to listen to her on many occasions and my privilege to appear with her in storytelling programs. I can still see and hear her telling these stories, as she closed each one with her own stylistic ending, a play on words of her name, Flora: "I have three flowers: one for the teller of this story, one for Flora Cohen, and one for me."

The tale is obviously a variant of Grimm's "Snow White." In Hebrew versions her name is often "Shalgiah" or "Snow from God." There are no overt Jewish characters as, for instance, in religious or festival tales, but there are some Jewish elements and symbols.

One is the name of the heroine herself, for the name Romana is Arabic for "*rimon*," Hebrew for pomegranate. This fruit, prized and cultivated in Palestine, was used to decorate the robes of the high priest (Exodus 28:33), the pillars of Solomon's temple, and the silver shekel of Jerusalem, circulated about 140 B.C. Today it is still used as a ceremonial object, adorning the Torah, and, in Jewish folklore, signifies fertility, as was its function in this story. For the same reason it is customary to eat the pomegranate on Rosh Hashanah.

The pomegranate is also found in many Jewish stories. Legend has it that Rabbi Hiyya Bar Ashi, a famous interpreter of *Mishnah* in the time when the Talmud was being written, was tempted by his wife, disguised as a prostitute. She requested a pomegranate from the top of a tree. This he brought to her, and then took his pleasure of her. Later, after he had confessed, she revealed herself, proving her identity by showing him the pomegranate. (Note that legend is not necessarily historically accurate!)

Another folk motif, AT 852*A, of which there are four versions in the IFA, tells of a hero who finds a pomegranate and eats it. He later regrets his act, and seeks the owner in order to pay for the pomegranate. Instead of asking for money, the owner demands that the hero marry his crippled daughter. She turns out to be a beauty.

The second element is the Jewish wedding, lasting for seven days and seven nights. Wedding customs, so important to a Jewish bride, are often inserted into a basically universal tale.

This story deals with female/female conflict (the wicked stepmother vs. the innocent stepdaughter). The strong woman's message is: the virtuous, the innocent woman is rewarded, and the wicked is punished.

Note the sexual overtones in the story when the thief who finds Romana asks, "Are you a woman [sexually experienced] or a girl [virgin]?" When she answers that she is a daughter, the thieves treat her as a sister and do not violate her sexually. According to Professor Noy, tales told by women have three times the number of sexual themes as tales told by men. The structure of the thief's question to the girl is a paraphrasing of the question often asked in folktales, "Are you human or demon?"

# 19

# *The Pomegranate Girl*

nce upon a time there lived a king and queen who had no children. One day the king an-nounced, "You know, my dear, we have been married for many, many years and still don't have a child." These words hurt the queen very much, and she sat and wept, afraid that the king would marry another in order to bring forth an heir.

As the queen sat thus, crying hysterically, behold! An old woman appeared and asked, "Beautiful queen, why are you crying?" And so the queen told her story, to which the old woman replied, "Don't cry. I will give you a pomegranate. Eat half and give the other half to the king. Soon you will give birth to a daughter, and, when you do, name her Romana." So saying, the old woman disappeared.

Exactly nine months later the queen gave birth to a baby girl, who was so full of joy that she cast light in every place she went. The girl was as beautiful as she was joyous, and her mother named her Romana, as the old woman had instructed.

A few years later the queen died, and the king took a second wife, a woman who was quite pretty but whose beauty could not compare with that of Romana. Because of this, the new queen envied her stepdaughter. Now, the king and queen had a daughter of their own, who was not very pretty at all, and this made the queen even more jealous than before.

Now, the queen had a friend who was a wizard, a man who could perform all sorts of magic—and evil magic at that! One day she invited him to come to live at the palace. And one day, as the two were talking, she asked him, "Tell me, who is more beautiful than I?" The wizard answered:

I am handsome,
You are fairer still. But no!
The girl Romana's beauty
is a thousand times more so.

The queen glared in envy. "And how can I get rid of Romana?" she asked.

"Take a dirty piece of cotton, call Romana to the cellar, and there bid her knit the cotton into stockings."

So the stepmother did as the wizard advised. And soon the girl sat in the cellar, crying miserably.

But, behold! There appeared before her an old woman, the very same as had appeared before her mother years ago. "And what happened to you, my dear? Why are you crying?" the old one asked, to which Romana told of her sad plight.

"Don't worry. Listen and do as I say," said the old woman. "A stream of red water will pass near you. Ignore it. A stream of black water will appear near you. Do not go near it. Then a stream of white water will flow near you. Into this water dip your cotton and with it wash your face and hands."

So saying, the old woman disappeared.

Romana did as she was told, and when she dipped the cotton into the white water, the cotton at once was trans- formed into knit stockings. And when the girl washed her hands and face with it, why, she became even more beautiful than before.

Now, when the stepmother saw what had happened, she was quite astonished, and forced Romana to tell her about the appearance of the old woman. And what did she do out of jealousy? The queen took the cotton to the cellar, where she brought her own ugly daughter, and bade her wait for the old woman to appear. And just as the woman had come to Romana, she appeared before this girl as well. But the daughter was not as well-mannered as Romana, and shouted harshly at the old woman. So the old woman instructed her: "A stream of red water will appear before you. Ignore it. A stream of black water will appear near you. Into this water dip your cotton and with it wash your hands and face."

So the girl did as she was told, but no sooner did she wipe her face with the cotton than, behold! She was even uglier than before. Meanwhile the king had gone abroad, and the queen, not knowing what to do to gain revenge against Romana, asked the wizard's advice. "Send the king a letter telling him that his daughter is going out with young men and coming home way into the late hours of the night," he instructed.

This the stepmother did, and when the king read the letter, he became so enraged that he sent his vizier at once to have his daughter slaughtered and to bring him her blood.

So it was that Romana soon found herself in the midst of the forest, understanding full well that she was to be killed. "Oh please," she begged, "have mercy on me and leave me here. Slaughter a dog and give its blood to the king in place of mine." And so, because the vizier was fond of the beautiful girl, he had mercy on her and did as she asked, sending her off into the forest by herself.

The girl wandered until she saw a flickering light in the distance. And as she approached a small hut and entered, she sensed at once that it belonged to thieves.

There on the table she found fresh vegetables, which she washed and cooked and later ate. And when she heard the thieves coming, she hid herself in a corner.

Now, the thieves felt the presence of someone in their house but did nothing. The next day, however, when they left for their daily work, one stayed behind and hid. And when Romana, thinking all the inhabitants had gone, came out of her corner, the thief pounced upon her. "Are you a woman or a girl?"

"I am a girl," she answered.

"Then you will be a sister as well." And so Romana remained with the thieves, forty in all, preparing their food, tidying the house, and receiving a new gift from her "brothers" every day.

Now, one day at the palace the queen happened to ask the wizard, "Tell me, who is more beautiful than I?" to which the wizard answered:

I am handsome,
You are fairer still. But no!
The girl Romana's beauty
is a thousand times more so.

"Romana?" shrieked the wicked queen. "But she is dead!"

"No," answered the wizard, "she lives in the forest at the home of the forty thieves. If you want to be rid of her, go to her and pretend to be a seller of jewelry. Place this ring on her finger, and she will die."

The queen quickly did as she was told, and the girl fell into a deep sleep. Then the queen returned to the palace, happy to be rid of Romana at last.

When the thieves returned and saw their "sister" dead, they grieved, for they had come to love her very much. Tenderly they placed her in a glass coffin in the forest, so that they could gaze upon her beauty every day.

Now, one day a king's son went hunting, and shot a bird, which fell out of the sky right onto the coffin of the sleeping princess. And so it was that the prince cast his eyes upon Romana and fell in love with her at once. He asked permission of the thieves to move the coffin to his home, where she could be properly buried.

Soon people were called to cleanse the body and bury the girl, and, when they began to work, they removed the ring. Then and there the girl came back to life.

The prince, astonished beyond words, confessed his love to the beautiful girl, and asked her to marry him. She agreed at once, upon the condition that the forty thieves, whom she loved like brothers, be invited to the wedding. And so, for seven days and seven nights there was feasting and rejoicing as the couple were wed.

Sometime later the queen found herself again in the company of the wizard. "Tell me, who is more beautiful than I?" she asked. The wizard said:

I am handsome,
You are fairer still. But no!
The girl Romana's beauty
is a thousand times more so.

"But Romana is dead!" cried the queen.

"No, she is not dead. She has married the prince."

"And what can I do to be rid of her?" asked the queen, her eyes glaring.

"Go to the palace and say that you are the mother of the new princess and you wish to see her. When you are admitted to Romana's room, stick this pin into her head. At once she will become a dove and fly away. Then send your daughter to take Romana's place. Say that she is ill and that you wish to stay and nurse her."

So the stepmother did as she was told. And the moment the pin was stuck into Romana's head, the girl became a dove and flew off into the forest. She flew at once to a favorite orange tree that had grown in the spot where she herself had thrown the pits. Day after day the dove ate the fruit of the tree, for only from this tree did she gain her nourishment. Day after day she would fly near the head of the gardener, chirping, "Water the orange tree! Water the orange tree!"

But one day the gardener fell asleep and did not give the tree its water. For several days the tree was not watered, until at last its roots dried up, and the dove too began to wither.

The prince, meanwhile, walking in the forest, found the dove, spread his net over the trees, and caught her. When he saw how weak she was, his heart went out to her. "Oh, you poor dove," he cried. "I will take you home to the palace and nurse you back to health." And so he did.

The next day the queen, visiting her friend, the wizard, asked idly, "Tell me, who is more beautiful than I?" The wizard answered:

I am handsome,
You are fairer still. But no!
The girl Romana's beauty
is a thousand times more so.

"How can that be?" shouted the stepmother. "She became a dove."

"Yes, but the prince caught her and nurses her, more than he cares for your own daughter."

"And what can be done?"

"Go to the prince and tell him you dreamed that he caught a white dove and that if he slaughters it and spreads its blood on his sick wife, she will recover."

Once again the queen did as she was told. And so the prince believed her story, went to the dove and lifted it to be slaughtered, but, as he did so, the pin became loose, and, at once, the dove was transformed into his beautiful princess.

Then the prince understood what had happened and thought of a plan to punish the wicked queen. He stuck the pin back into the head of the girl, after which she turned back into a dove. Then he invited the woman—and the king and all the ministers—and the wizard too, to witness the curing of his sick wife. And so, when all were present, he held the dove in one hand and lifted the knife, as if to slaughter it, in the other. Instead, he quickly pulled the pin, and there in front of everyone stood the beautiful young princess, looking radiant, as always. The queen and wizard had no choice but to tell the truth.

Then everyone present took a twig or branch in hand. "Let all who love the king come and add oil," cried the prince. And before long a bonfire blazed high, into which the queen and the scheming wizard were thrown.

After that the king, the prince, and the princess Romana lived together in happiness and health.

☙❧

# The Girl with the Cow's Face, Redeemed by Elijah the Prophet

## INTRODUCTION

This tale, first set down in written form by Farhi and later by Bin Gorion, has crept into oral tradition; eleven versions are found in the IFA, coming from Morocco, Syria, Yemen, Iraq, Persia, and Poland; this one was told by a Jewess from Persia. And, because it contains specific elements not found in the universal tale type, but unique only to Jewish society, the tale has been given its own number as a Jewish oicotype, 873*A.

These elements include: The girl is the daughter of a rabbi or scholar; the groom is a scholar; the two are married according to the laws of Moses and Israel; the Jewish family is the framework in which events take place; the husband leaves his wife a prayer book and his *tallit* or *tzitzit*; Elijah the Prophet brings about the miracle of curing the deformity; the husband is found at prayer in the synagogue; etc.

At the onset of the tale, the girl is born with some sort of monstrosity (the horns of a bull, the face of a donkey, one-half of her face discolored). Extreme deformity is known in talmudic-midrashic literature: two-headed men (*Menahot* 37a), and many hybrids are to be found in the *Aggadah*. Such deformities sparked great interest in the folk imagination.

Biblical and postbiblical sources play another role in the tale as well: The emphasis in all versions on the shock of the groom, upon seeing the bride, is based on the biblical association with the story of Jacob and Leah (Genesis 29). The woman's covering her face is based on Rebecca's veiling her face when she saw Isaac (Genesis 24:65). Precedent for this tale is found as well in the story of Judah and Tamar (Genesis 38:18). Only in the Polish IFA version does the groom see the bride before the wedding. "It is forbidden for a man to wed a woman until he sees her" (*Kiddushin* 41a), but in that version the groom marries the monstrous bride anyway in order to fulfill the vow he made to her father.

The quality which draws the groom to the girl is her wisdom. Throughout the generations there has been precedent in several outstanding women sages: Rabbanit

Osnat of Kurdistan and Hannah Rodel Werbermacher of the Ukraine are but a few. Inclusion of the wise heroine provided the fulfillment of wishful thinking for the women tellers of the tale, usually uneducated themselves.

However, in all versions of the tale, it is not the woman's wisdom which reunites her with her husband but, rather, the love and perseverance of her son. This story begins as a novella, a love story between a man and a woman, and it does end in a happy reunion, as should the typical love story. But the foremost love here is the love of the son; this is evidenced in the title of a Moroccan version, IFA 4510: "The Good Son Who Made Peace Between His Parents," which ends with the following statement: "He (the father) was very happy because of his beautiful wife and his wise son, who was so anxious for the happiness of his parents' home."

The later appearance of Elijah the Prophet changes the story from a novella to a sacred legend, with elements of the fairy tale thrown in.

I can see why this tale appeals to women and is transmitted by them, for it gives expression to every bride's suppressed desire to be appreciated for her inner virtues. As *Pirkei Avot* 4:20 tells us, "Pay attention to the contents, not the container." The story alleviates the unexpressed fear, "Maybe I won't be good enough for my groom!", a fear felt by every bride.

My examination of all versions in the IFA showed the tale to be told by both men and women, with slightly more women tellers. There was little difference in the tale itself (some women's versions were slightly more expanded, beginning with the midwife's delivering the child), but the major (and fascinating!) difference is to be found in the titles. Men's titles, such as "The Genius-Protegé (Husband) of Skardish," IFA 1338, point out the virtues of males; women's titles ("The Clever Daughter ..." or "The Rabbi's Daughter with Horns") stress the deformed girl and *her* wisdom.

# 20

# *The Girl with the Cow's Face, Redeemed by Elijah the Prophet*

nce there was a girl, the daughter of a rabbi, who had been born with the face of a cow. In order to hide her deformity, to keep her from being laughed at, her parents kept her hidden in a room at their home.

Now, the girl's father was a great teacher of Torah, and young men would come from distant cities to be his pupils. The daughter, who was very curious, would listen, from her place behind the wall, to her father's teaching until she became even more clever than her own father.

One day the father asked his students a particularly difficult question. No one could answer it. But suddenly, from behind the wall, a girl's voice gave the answer.

One young student was caught in wonder. Where was the voice coming from? "I must marry the girl who has given such a wise answer."

"But she is ugly," cried the father. "You must not marry her." Still, despite the rabbi's protests, the young man insisted.

And so the two were married. But that night, after the wedding vows had been recited and the bride and groom had consummated their marriage in their chamber, the husband saw his wife's face.

At once he regretted what he had done, and, in the morning, told his wife that he was leaving to visit his parents in a faraway city.

"And what shall I do if I am pregnant?" cried the wife. "What sign shall I have for my child that he has a father?"

And so the husband took off his ring and gave it to his wife. Then he handed her his *tzitzit* and prayer book, and set out.

Nine months later the woman gave birth to a fine and handsome son. He was beloved by his mother and his grandparents, and grew into a fine boy. And all that time the father did not return.

But when the boy was old enough to go to school, the children mocked him. "You have no father!" they cried. "You have no father!" And the boy was ashamed.

At home he kept asking, "Who is my father? Where is he?" But no false answer of his mother or grandparents could satisfy him. Years passed in this way, until they had no choice but to tell him the truth.

"I must find my father! I must find him!" the boy repeated, and so, seeing that her son was so determined, the mother told the boy the name of the place where his grandparents lived. "Perhaps you will find your father there," she said. And so, taking the ring, the *tzitzit*, and the prayer book that his mother gave him, the boy set out in search of his father.

Weeks passed, and at last the boy came to the town and entered the synagogue. There he saw a kindly man, engrossed in prayer, who was none other than his own father.

"Who are you? Where do you come from?" asked the man, when prayers were over. And the boy, not knowing who this man was, told of his long journey and of his father who had deserted his mother many years before. Then he took out the ring, the book, and the *tzitzit*. Upon seeing these, the man grew pale.

"I—I am your father," he stammered, as he recognized the objects as his own.

Then the boy embraced his father. "Please, please come home," he begged. "Mother has missed you so much. I have missed you. I want us to live as a family." And so his father promised to wind up his affairs and follow after him in a few days.

Meanwhile, the boy started on his own journey home, and one night, on the way, he fell asleep under a majestic tree. In his dream Elijah the Prophet came to him. "Here is a flask of special oil. When you reach home, rub it on your mother's face," he said. And when the boy awoke, behold! There was a flask of oil beside him, just like the one in the dream.

Remembering the Prophet's words, the boy reached home and did as he was bade: he rubbed the oil on his mother's face, and, behold! The hideous deformity began to vanish. The boy repeated this for several days until, at last, the cow's face was completely gone—and his mother had become a radiant beauty.

And so, when the boy's father returned, as he had promised, the three lived together in great happiness, and they continued to follow the ways of God.

# He Who Has Found a Wife Has Found Good

## INTRODUCTION

Riddles have long played an important part in folktales; they are fun for the listener to answer, and help alleviate tension in the story. This particular type (AT 875) is found in Grimm and is widely known throughout the world.

But riddles have had a special place of significance in Jewish lore. In biblical times storytelling and the art of asking riddles was a highly esteemed practice. The riddles of Samson (Judges 14:12) and Sheba (1 Kings 10:1) are well known.

Riddles were often told at Jewish weddings, where they helped ease the tension between the bride and groom, who often had never before seen each other. Separate riddles were told to the bride and to the groom. In addition to biblical riddles there were many others, and these often were full of sexual symbols.

There arose also a body of folktales in which the main plot revolved around the hero or heroine's telling or solving riddles as a condition to marriage.

It is no wonder, then, that this story found its way into written versions (Gaster, Cahan, Bin Gorion) and to the mouths and hearts of so many Jewish tellers; over ninety versions are found in the IFA, from virtually every part of the Jewish world. Here I have combined two women's versions, one told by Mazal Yakobi of Persia, and another told to Ilana Cohen Zohar by her mother, Flora Cohen, from Egypt.

The last part of the story refers to a *midrash* (Talmud

*Pesikta*), where a husband seeks a divorce after ten years of childless marriage. The wife is allowed to take her dearest possession; she chooses her husband. The two are then blessed with a child.

In this folktale told by women, a clever woman sends the man to another clever woman; she, in turn, solves three sets of riddles, thus proving that she is truly wise. Men's versions of this tale are not as full. They sometimes eliminate the part where the wife chooses her dearest possession, and they contain no more than two sets of riddles. Also, a clever woman does not refer the man to another wise woman. In other words, the wife is not depicted as being as clever in tellings by men as she is in tellings by women.

The title of the story comes from Proverbs 18:22.

# 21

# *He Who Has Found a Wife Has Found Good*

 certain king wished to marry a wise girl, but he would be wed only to a bride who could be given one *lira*, one coin, and from it bring him raw meat to eat, a mirror, and a map, and then return to him the one *lira* she had been given. And so he ordered his minister to find such a girl, threatening him with death if he failed.

The minister was frightened. Where could he seek to fulfill the king's request?

Now, his own daughter noticed his sadness. "Father, what is bothering you?" she asked. But when the minister told her of the king's demand, she began to laugh. "You need not be sad, Father. Go to a certain field and find the shepherd who feeds his flock in that place. Ask him if he will let you speak to his daughter, who is very wise and will surely give you your answer."

And so the minister found the shepherd in the field. The two agreed to walk together to the shepherd's house, where the minister could seek the counsel of his daughter. But not even a quarter of an hour had gone by when the minister asked, "Shall I carry you or will you carry me?"

At these words the shepherd was bewildered. "I have worked hard, walking all day with my flock. Does this man expect me to carry him?" But he said nothing.

As the two walked along, they saw a farmer, planting his seeds. Said the minister, "Are the ears of corn already eaten?" Again the shepherd was bewildered. "Is the man crazy?" he thought. "How could the corn be eaten if the farmer is just planting the seeds?" But again he said nothing.

And as the two came nearer to the shepherd's house, they came upon a funeral procession on the way to the burial. "Is the man dead or alive?" asked the minister. Now the shepherd was even more bewildered. "Is the man dumb? How could a corpse be alive?" he wondered. Again he did not answer.

But when they arrived at their destination, the shepherd could hardly contain himself, and quickly sought out his daughter. "Daughter, you are known for your wisdom. Please, can you explain the strange questions our guest asked me on the way?" And he told his daughter the three riddles.

"Of course, Father," laughed the girl. "The first question meant: 'Who will tell a story on the way?' You know, Father, that whoever tells a story carries his listener, for he shortens the way.

The second question meant: 'Is the harvest already sold?,' for, you know, Father, that if the corn is sold, it is as if the ears are already eaten.

The third question meant: 'Does the dead man have sons?' You know, Father, that if a man has sons who bear his name, it is as if he is still alive."

The shepherd was pleased with his daughter's wisdom. He told her of the minister's request and asked for her help. She replied that first the family have their evening meal, after which she would give the answer.

So the family sat down to eat, and the minister, being the guest, was asked to serve the chicken, set before them on a fine platter. At once he took his knife, cut the fowl, and divided it as follows: the head to the father, the feet to his wife, the wings to the daughter and, since there was no one else to serve, the remainder went to himself. The shepherd watched in amazement. "Why did he give me only the head and keep so much for himself?" he cried. "Why did he give me only the head?"

"Oh, do not be troubled, Father," replied the daughter. "The meaning is quite clear: You received the head of the fowl because you are the head of the family. Mother received the feet because she is the one who stands on her feet and cooks for us. I was given the wings for I will someday marry and fly away. Could anything be clearer?"

Upon hearing these words, the minister was most impressed. "I see that you are quite clever," he said "and are able to decipher riddles. Can you solve this for me? The king has sent you one *lira*. From it you must bring him raw meat to eat, a mirror, and a map, and then return the *lira* to the king."

The girl's eyes sparkled as she thought quickly. "Give me three days and I will appear before the king."

So the daughter took the one *lira*, and, with the money, bought a lamb. This she sheared and, from its wool wove a map in which she embroidered the figure of the king, bending in prayer. Then, just before appearing at the palace, she had the sheep slaughtered, sold its meat for a *lira*, which she then returned to the king. Thus, she brought him: raw meat to eat (the sheep's heart), the map (she had sewn), the mirror, that is, the picture of the king himself (which, after all, is what he would have seen in a mirror, isn't that so?).

Upon seeing these objects, the king was struck by the great wisdom of the shepherd's daughter. "I will take you for my bride," he told her, "but only on one condition. You are not to interfere in matters of court, for, the moment you do, I will divorce you."

"I agree to be your wife," replied the girl, "but I too have one condition. If I do anything to displease you and cause you to divorce me, I must be allowed to take from the palace the one thing that I find most precious."

To this condition the king agreed, and a lavish wedding was planned at once.

Now, one day, at the palace, while the king was holding court, two men came before him to be judged. The first presented his case. "My dear king, this man and I share a barn. There I keep my horse and he keeps his donkey. Yesterday, my horse gave birth. His donkey gave birth to a stillborn donkey. Then he switched his dead donkey for my horse."

But the second protested. "My dear king, this story is not true. My ass gave birth to a live horse."

The king judged in favor of the second man, and, with a wave of the king's hand, the two were dismissed.

But when the shepherd's daughter, who had secretly been listening to the matters of the court, heard this judgment, she became angry. She ordered the first man, the owner of the horse, to appear before the king the very next day, and instructed him on what words to say.

"Your honor, I ask for judgment. I planted cucumbers, and this other man's fish ate them."

Said the king, "Stupid man, do you expect me to believe that fish eat cucumbers?"

"May God watch over you and give you long life, your honor the king. Certainly fish do not eat cucumbers. And could this man's donkey give birth to a horse?"

At once the king realized his foolish mistake and granted the horse owner his new foal. The man left in a happy mood.

But then the king turned angrily to his wife. "I know that this was your wise advice," he declared. "You have disobeyed my instruction never to meddle in affairs of the court. And so, according to our agreement, we are now divorced."

"I accept your verdict, my husband," answered the shepherd's daughter, "but remember that I have the right to take with me one precious thing. I will decide by morning."

And so, that evening at their dinner meal, the queen mixed a sleeping potion into her husband's food. Then she ordered a long box to be upholstered with fine velour. And when her husband had fallen into a deep sleep, she laid him in the box, and ordered him transported to her father's house.

In the morning the bewildered king awoke. "How—how did I get here?" he stammered.

"My dear respected and honored king, my beloved husband," said the queen, "according to our agreement, I took from the palace my most precious possession, you—for I have nothing more precious in all the world."

Upon hearing these words, the king realized the true wisdom of his wife. "If you love me so much," he said, "please come back to the palace. There you will sit at my right hand and, from this moment on, will help me to judge in righteousness and wisdom."

And so the two returned to the palace, where they shared great love, had many sons and daughters, and lived a long life.

## *The Bough of Amber, the Mountain of Gold*

### INTRODUCTION

This story was told to me by Simha Shemesh, one of my dearest friends, who heard it from her mother, Dina Elbar. The family came to Israel from Fez, Morocco.

The story seems to contain a combination of many fairy tale themes: the father asks each daughter to name a gift; the father orders his daughter to the forest to be killed; some sort of blood or animal part is to be shown him as proof of the deed; etc.

The story, being a combination of many, deals with many conflicts: female-female (the innocent daughter vs. the jealous sisters), male-female (the king vs. his daughter). Some of the minor characters (the protective mother and the wise old woman), via their actions, give strong female messages.

The title of the story is structurally similar to the "mountain of gold and palace of pearls" found in "The Lost Princess," a well-known tale of Rabbi Nahman of Bratslav. In that allegorical story, the mountain of gold represents the holy city of Jerusalem.

Another Jewish element of the story lies in the girl's selection of her husband as the most precious gift; this is based on a similar happening in *Midrash Pesikta*.

# 22

# *The Bough of Amber, the Mountain of Gold*

n a faraway country, across seven seas, seven rivers, and seven mountains, there lived a king who had seven daughters. All were beautiful, gentle, and clever, but the youngest, a girl of twelve, was the most beautiful, the most clever, and the gentlest of all. And so, of all his daughters, the king loved her the most.

Now, one day the king was about to leave on a journey to visit the seven lands that surrounded his kingdom, and he asked each of his seven daughters what gift she would like upon his return.

"Oh, Father," said the first, "I would like a dazzling crown, unlike any crown any princess has ever worn."

"Oh, Father," cried the second, "I would like a dress of sparkling cloth, unlike any dress any princess has ever worn."

"Oh, Father," stated the third, "I would like a sash of the softest wool, unlike any sash any princess has ever worn."

And so the fourth daughter, the fifth, the sixth asked for a special gift. But when it came the turn of the youngest, she answered simply, "Oh, Father, your safe return will be my most precious gift."

"Still, daughter, if you think of anything you would like, anything at all, do not hesitate to tell me."

Upon hearing these words, the other sisters grew angry. "What! Will Father think our youngest sister loves him more than we?" And they went at once to an old woman named

Mother La Guz, which means "mother old one," known for her clever ways. They asked her to think of a plan to rid themselves of their youngest sister.

And what did the old woman do? Why, she disguised herself as a very old woman and, appearing outside the palace window, called, "Oh, where is the youngest princess? It is my one wish to see her before I die."

And when the princess did, indeed, appear at the window, the woman said, "Oh, you are so beautiful. Please, put on your most beautiful gown and your most precious jewels. It is my wish to see you so dressed before I die."

And when the princess dressed herself and appeared in all her finery, the woman sighed, "Ah, you are truly beautiful. But there is one thing you lack. Yes, if only you had that one thing, you would be the most beautiful woman in all the world."

"And what is that?" asked the princess in wonder.

"What you are missing is the Bough of Amber, the Mountain of Gold."

Upon hearing these words, the youngest daughter ran to her father, the king, who was just about to leave on his journey, and asked him to find her the Bough of Amber, the Mountain of Gold.

"What a strange request!" thought the king. And, in order not to forget, he wrote down his daughter's request and put the paper in the pocket of his robe, assuring his beloved daughter that he would fulfill her wish.

And so, as the king journeyed through the first six lands surrounding his kingdom, he easily found each gift his first six daughters had asked for. But search as he might, nowhere did anyone know where to find the Bough of Amber, the Mountain of Gold. And yet the king was certain of his daughter's request, for, after all, had he not written it down!

At last, he came to the shore of the seventh land, and just as he was about to despair at not finding the gift for his beloved daughter, he came upon a small hut. And, after knocking on the door, he saw that his hostess was an old woman, mending a fisherman's net.

"Please, may I come in?"

"Yes, my king."

"And how did you know that I am a king?"

"Oh, I know many things," the woman replied.

"Then, perhaps, you can answer this question. Where can I find the Bough of Amber, the Mountain of Gold, for my youngest daughter?"

The woman was greatly surprised. "And how old is she?" she asked.

"Why, what is the problem?" asked the king.

"In truth," answered the woman, "the Bough of Amber, the Mountain of Gold, is none other than the powerful king who rules this kingdom."

"What!? My young daughter wishes to have a husband. Why, I am so angry that I would have her killed."

The king did not forget his anger, and when he returned to his kingdom, he ordered his vizier to take the girl into the forest, kill her, and bring back her heart. When the vizier protested, the king threatened him with death if he failed to obey.

And so the man and the young girl set out for the forest. "Have pity on me! What have I done?" she cried.

Now, the truth is that the girl was so sweet, so kind, so beautiful that the vizier spared her life and brought back to the king the heart of a sheep. That night the vizier told the queen what had happened. And she, rushing at once to the forest, brought her daughter back to the palace, where the girl was hidden in the cellar and there fed every night. So she remained in her dark home for five years! At last, on her seventeenth birthday, the girl was so unhappy that she cried to her mother, "I would rather die than remain here. I must find out why Father was so angry. I must find the Bough of Amber, the Mountain of Gold."

At first, of course, the mother was fearful, but at last the girl persuaded the queen to give her horses, provisions, and a servant for her journey. She too crossed the six lands as had her father before her, and, she, too, came to the shore of the seventh land and sought refuge in the tiny hut where the wise woman dwelled.

"May I come in?"

"Of course, my princess."

"And how did you know I am a princess?"

"Oh, I know many things," replied the old woman.

"Then perhaps you can answer this question. Where can I find the Bough of Amber, the Mountain of Gold?"

This time the old woman was not surprised. She said, "As I told your father, the Bough of Amber, the Mountain of Gold is none other than the powerful king who rules this land."

"Is that what I asked for? Then that is what I shall have. And where can I find the king?"

"Oh, but you do not understand," said the old woman. "You must not go, for the king is very cruel. Each night he takes a new young maiden to his chambers, and, in the morning, he has her killed."

"Do not worry. I will be safe." And, so saying, the princess donned her most beautiful dress, her most precious jewels. And, when she stood before the king at the palace, he was, at once, struck by her beauty.

Then the king, as was his custom, took the girl to his chambers. But, he was so overcome by her gentleness, her beauty, that he could not bear to have her killed. Instead, he banished her to her own kingdom, on the condition that she never return.

"Very well, my king," answered the girl, "but allow me to take one sign that I have been here, so that my father will know that I speak the truth. Allow me to take the thing I like best."

The king agreed. "Very well, very well, you may take one gift, only one."

That night at dinner the princess gave the king much wine to drink. And when he fell into a deep sleep, she had him moved to the old woman's hut.

At last he awoke. "How—how did I get here?"

"Oh, my king, you agreed I could take the one thing I liked best, the one thing that was most precious to me. And so I took you."

"What! Are you making fun of me?" cried the king in anger. "Go back to your own land, and never return!"

And so it was that the princess returned to her kingdom, to her place in the cellar of the royal palace.

But, in the days that followed, the Bough of Amber, the

Mountain of Gold missed the princess very much and realized how much he loved her. And, so, he gathered five hundred soldiers and rode forth to her kingdom.

When the king, the girl's father, learned of the strange army that was approaching, he was quite puzzled. Quickly he gathered gifts and rode forward to meet the neighboring king.

"Welcome to my kingdom. I bring you gifts in welcome. But what is it that you wish?"

"I am the Bough of Amber, the Mountain of Gold, and I wish to marry your youngest daughter."

"My youngest daughter? But she is dead."

Then it was that the vizier confessed what he had done, and the king was happily reunited with his daughter, for he had long since regretted ordering her to be killed.

The princess and her beloved king knew that each had found, in each other, what was truly the most precious. A royal wedding followed thereafter, and the two lived happily ever after.

# A Yemenite Woman's Protest

## INTRODUCTION

The Yemenite girl was married as soon as she got her first menstrual period, usually about the age of twelve. But to circumvent the law of Islam which said that orphans were to be converted to that faith, an orphaned girl would be married at any age, sometimes as early as six or seven. She would live in the house of her mother-in-law, and then, after her first menstruation, would live with her husband. In some cases he would be twenty, thirty, or forty years older than she.

In the 1950s, when many Jews came to Israel from Yemen, one girl, a neighbor of my friend, Ziporah Greenfield in Jerusalem, wanted to go to school. Her husband shouted, "No, no, a Yemenite woman doesn't need to know how to read or write." But her mother-in-law gave permission for her to go. And so she entered the first grade, at the age of seven, already married.

This practice led to bitterness on the part of women. Their protests can be heard in song and story. This song was sung to me by Ziporah Sibahi Greenfield, who learned it from her mother, Nadrah, who died in Israel in July 1992, at the age of 101, and who was twice betrothed, in Yemen, to grooms she did not want to marry. But each time she ran away, until finally her parents consented to let her have a say in the choice of her husband; her actions were signs of great protest and independence for a woman at that time. She and her husband were married for over sixty years and had five children.

The song was widely sung among women throughout Yemen, and, thus, passed from one generation to the next. Women of each district sang a different melody.

# 23

# *A Yemenite Woman's Protest*

Oh, my mother,
Oh, my father, why did you sell me?
Sell the cows and the goats
and ransom me.
Oh, my mother,
you who gave birth to me,
can it be
your heart has forgotten me?
Is it because of the distance?
Is it because you have other children to care for?
Oh, you who have given birth to me,
if you knew of my tears,
if you knew what is happening to the child you raised?
Oh, my father,
Oh, my mother,
if it rains at night,
it is not really rain.
It's my tears turned into a mighty flood.

## *The Hungry Bride*

### INTRODUCTION

"Did you hear the joke about the mother-in-law who. . . ?" Every one of us has heard such jokes and told them.

New brides, all over the world, and mothers of the groom, all over the world, enter into their new mother-in-law/daughter-in-law relationship with some amount of trepidation and fear. And so, stories which deal with relationships between mothers-in-law and daughters-in-law have an important place in folk literature.

Many of these are jokes. Others deal with the theme of how to tame a bad mother-in-law. In these stories, as in this one from Yemen, the taming of the mother-in-law is not a reflection of reality, of the real mother-in-law/daughter-in-law situation. Instead, it is a fulfillment of the secret wishes of the often very young bride who, as was the custom in Yemen, went to live in the home of her husband. There, as we can see in the story, the mother-in-law was the ruler of her matriarchal roost; the new bride was expected to be obedient and servile.

The two IFA versions of this tale were both told by women from Yemen. This one was related to Rachel Seri by her sister-in-law, Yonah.

# 24

# *The Hungry Bride*

nce upon a time there was a rich woman who had an only son. And, when he grew up and reached the age of marriage, his mother sought a gentle girl from a respected family, so that her son would have a refined and polite wife who would fulfill the wishes of her mother-in-law. And after some time she did, indeed, find such a wife from a good family, a girl who was gentle, beautiful, polite, and soon there was a wedding with such beauty and luxury as befits royalty itself. The joy in the family was great.

After the wedding the mother-in-law instructed the bride on all their customs and procedures. The bride listened in silence and respect.

All their meals were served for three; the husband, bride, and mother ate together. But, as soon as they began to eat, the groom's mother would pinch her daughter-in-law under the table until the girl was in pain. This too she endured in silence, but she could not eat.

All this time her husband knew nothing of his mother's actions. He would urge his wife, "Eat something. Eat something." But the moment she put food to her mouth, her mother-in-law would pinch her again. And so the girl stopped bringing food even as far as her lips. She said nothing and suffered in shame.

Day after day the girl grew thinner. Moving about the house in sadness, she did not smile or utter a word to anyone. Her husband grew worried. "Perhaps she's sick," he thought.

When he mentioned the matter to his mother, she answered, "Yes, your wife seems to be of a different sort than we're used to. She's very strange." Still the husband remained anxious and sad, as he cared deeply for the welfare of his wife.

One day his good friend asked the reason for his sadness, and the husband told his friend all the bitterness that was in his heart. "If your wife is so thin," said the friend, "it is a sign that she is hungry."

"What! Our house is full of good food. How could she be hungry?"

Then the friend advised the husband to try to make the wife laugh. He told him to give an order that a hen be slaughtered. Then, when the hen would jump up and run away, the wife would laugh and overcome her muteness. The husband did as his friend advised. But still the wife was silent.

The husband took his wife to a doctor. But the doctor found no illness and said only, "Your wife is hungry."

So again the husband pleaded with his wife, "Please, eat something, anything you like." But again, when the three sat around the table, and the bride began to put food to her mouth, she felt the pinches of her mother-in-law. The girl decided that, in order to avoid this pain, she would be silent. And so the secret was kept from her husband.

The husband became more worried than ever, and went to seek the counsel of his friend. "I have an idea," said the friend. "Invite me to your home for three days. At meal time I will come and see what is happening. There must be a secret, there must be some reason for this problem."

And so it was done. One evening the friend arrived and sat between the mother-in-law and the wife. Suddenly the wife began to eat. She laughed, smiled, and spoke in a happy mood. The same thing happened on the second and the third day. Her face grew fuller, she gained strength and weight, and, on the last evening, burst out into laughter. To this her husband asked, "Why are you laughing so much?"

His wife replied, "Oh, I remember the way the hen was jumping. It was so funny." And she began to laugh again.

On the fourth day, after the friend had left, the mother-in-law spoke to her son, "My son, your wife is not well. At first she was shy and sweet. But now she talks too much and has become very nervy. You must divorce her."

The poor husband loved his wife. But his mother's nagging, day and night, began to sway him. So again he went to his good friend to ask him what to do.

His friend told him, "Pretend that you are getting a divorce and that you are seeking a new wife. After a few days I will come, disguised as the new wife, with the permission of your mother."

The husband took his friend's advice and sent his wife back to her parents, who were people of dignity and importance. He "remarried," with the permission of his mother, who liked the "girl" very much. The mother taught the new bride how to keep the house, and to honor her and fulfill her wishes. The bride listened in dignity and silence.

One day the bride announced to her mother-in-law that she was pregnant, and that she wanted two peas to eat. The mother-in-law saw that the girl was a good wife who honored her and gave her respect.

"Why not?" she answered. "The entire house is yours. Take what you wish and do what you wish."

And so the bride took an enormous pot, filled it with water, put wood into the oven, and put the two peas into the pot.

"What are you doing?" cried the mother-in-law. "Why do you need such a big pot for two peas? It would hold enough food for a wedding."

The bride answered quietly, "You said I could do as I wish."

The mother-in-law said nothing.

The next day the bride took a sack of wheat, a sack of rice, and a sack of lentils and put them in the big pot. This time she asked no permission.

"What are you doing?" shouted the mother-in-law.

The bride answered, "You said I could do as I wish."

The mother-in-law suffered in silence.

The next day the bride announced, "Today I want the broiled liver of a bull."

"Why not?" answered the mother-in-law. "Take a liver from the *mahsan*, where the meat is cured." But the bride went to the barn, slaughtered a live bull, broiled its liver, and ate it.

The mother-in-law was angry in her heart. "Why did you do such a thing? It's a shame to waste an entire bull."

"But you said I could do as I wish," replied the daughter-in-law, in an innocent voice.

One day the son happened to ask his mother, "Mother, what do you think of my new wife?"

And his mother answered, "She's fine, fine." How could she tell her son about her new troubles?

Soon afterwards the new bride told her mother-in-law, "My dear mother-in-law, you need to rest. Go and stay at the home of your friends for a few days." This the mother-in-law gladly did.

But what did the bride do? She loaded the donkey with sacks of wheat, rice, and lentils and took them, with a cow as well, to the house where her mother-in-law was staying.

"Dear Mother-in-law, see what I have brought you. Sacks of wheat, rice, and lentils for you to sort. And take good care of the cow. Don't forget to take her to graze."

The mother-in-law was shamed in front of her friends. Her

lips were silent, but in her heart she thought, "Oy, how terrible this daughter-in-law is. How sweet the first wife was."

Another day the bride declared to her mother-in-law, "Come, dear Mother-in-law, come with me to the river. I will wash you because you are dirty." And, despite the mother-in-law's protests, the wife dragged the woman to the river and washed her hair.

"Oy, Mother-in-law, how many lice you have in your head." And one-by-one she began to pick the hair out of the older woman's head. Then she scrubbed her scalp until the woman screamed in pain. The woman could bear this treatment no longer, and she ran to her son and said, "My son, divorce this woman and return to your first wife who was so sweet, so good."

And so the son gladly dismissed this wicked "wife" and called back the one he loved. This time his mother did not dare to pinch her or command her.

The daughter-in-law was so happy. Now she would be the lady of the house, independent, with no one to be cruel to her, or to tell her what to do.

## The Lost Princess and the Lost Prince

### INTRODUCTION

This story was told to Rachel Seri by Rivka Brami of Tunisia. In this tale there is a polarity within the heroine herself, but here it is not a polarity of good and evil. Rather, it is a polarity of princess and slave. The young woman sacrifices herself and sells herself into slavery in order to find, and eventually rescue, the prince. The system of being sold into slavery, both among men and women, was well known in biblical times.

This story belongs to a tale type in which the hero usually ransoms a princess from slavery and marries her. In this story it is the princess who goes on the quest to free the prince. This is reminiscent of a Libyan tale, IFA

5528, about the princess Zohara, who must fulfill several tasks before being worthy of marrying the prince.

The heroine, here depicted as a strong woman with the fine qualities of perseverance, cleverness, and beauty, is aided by other women as well: the young daughters of the ministers, and the old woman who takes her in. This help and friendship is not forgotten by the princess. This, in itself, is a woman's message.

The story relies on her finding the prince because of the fragment she has of his coat; the fragment alone is enough to characterize its owner as her beloved. This may be in keeping with the hasidic theme, found in hasidic literature, that one is characterized by one's clothing. Certainly, the biblical Joseph was known by his famous coat of many colors.

Also, the seven days and seven nights of the wedding feast are typical of the Jewish wedding.

# 25

# *The Lost Princess and the Lost Prince*

nce there was a king who had an only daughter whom he loved dearly. But the girl became ill and grew thin and pale, and the king worried endlessly about her health. And so he consulted his ministers, who advised him, "Send your daughter to a faraway orchard with our daughters for company. Let them dine, dance, and play together for one year's time. Perhaps, during that year, your daughter will regain her strength."

The king agreed and sent his pale daughter, with the daughters of the ministers, to that faraway place. There they lived, secluded and happy, surrounded by beautiful trees of every description, and feasted on delicious fruits of every kind.

One year passed, and the king paid a visit to the orchard.

There, when he saw his daughter, plump, healthy, and beautiful, he was very happy.

"Oh, Father," begged the princess, "let us remain here for another year."

Again the king agreed. And so the girls sang, ate, laughed together, and when they grew tired, each one chose a place to sleep. One day the princess lay down on the sands of the beach, and there, under the light of the sun, fell into a deep sleep.

Now, in that country lived a certain prince who loved to fly his pet pigeons. One day one of the birds flew away to that very orchard, and the prince, running to catch it, came upon the sleeping princess, looking radiant and beautiful. What did he do? The prince cut a piece of his coat and placed it on her face. "I wish you to be my wife," he said aloud. And then he left.

Several hours later the princess awoke. How frightened she was when she saw the piece of coat! "Girls, girls, tell me, who came into the orchard?"

"We were all asleep," they said, "and saw no one." The princess was quite annoyed. "Then I will go to search," she said. "If, by the end of one year, I do not return, know that I am dead. Weep over me, and tell the king that you could not find his daughter." And so the princess, taking with her food and clothing for the journey, set out on her quest.

Soon she came to a strange city where she came to the house of an old lady and asked for rest. "Gladly," said the lady, "you're welcome to stay. But I have no money for food." Thereupon, the princess gave the lady her gold ring, her only possession. And so, with the money from the sale of the ring, the two bought food, ate, and slept well.

The next morning, after they had put the house in order, the princess said, "Please buy me some black paint." And with the paint the princess colored herself all over, disguising herself as a black servant. "Please," she said to the old lady, "take me and sell me in the market as a slave to a rich master."

"Why, my daughter? You are so beautiful." But the princess entreated the old lady who, at last, took her to the market to be sold. There she was bought by the minister of the king to take care of his daughter, who had suddenly been struck by a strange illness. "I hope that you will bring me good luck," he told her, and instructed the slave girl to tend his daughter day and night.

When night fell, the slave saw that, before her very eyes, the minister's daughter was suddenly turned into a horse. Then, as she watched, the girl became a cow, then a camel, running here and there, from one place to another. The slave, in fright, dropped her candle, putting out the wick. She left the room to find new matches or something with which to light her candle when she heard a low moaning, very much like a prayer: "Here now, minister's daughter, turn to a horse, turn to a cow, turn to a camel. Run here, run there." Then it was that the slave girl realized that the voices belonged to two people, practicing witchcraft, in order to annoy the minister and make his daughter suffer.

She approached these witches, saying, "Please, I need some matches. The minister's daughter is getting married, and some children playing nearby put out the candle."

Now a young man standing near the house overheard her words, and, pulling out a sharp knife, he quickly killed the two witches. "Why—why did you do that?" the slave girl asked.

"I wanted to marry the minister's daughter," said the young man, "but when I asked her parents for her hand, they did not agree. And so I sent these two witches to force her to come to me. But see, they deceived me, for now my beloved will marry another."

The slave girl approached the girl's parents, "Your daughter is cured," she told them. "But, if you want her to remain healthy and free of illness, you must give her in marriage to that man who has already asked for her hand." Overjoyed, the parents ran to see their daughter, and remained with her for an entire night, to assure themselves that she would not become transformed into another beast. Then, thanking the slave girl, they released her from her bondage, and married their daughter to the man who loved her.

The slave girl returned to the old lady's house. There she remained for two weeks' time. Then, once again, she announced, "You must sell me again as a slave." The old lady refused. But the girl entreated her until she agreed.

This time she was sold to another minister of the king to take care of his daughter, who had suddenly become mute. "I hope you bring me good luck," the girl's father said. And so, the slave girl sat at the daughter's side until nightfall, when the mute girl gave her a drink of black coffee in which she had mixed a sleeping potion. The slave girl fell into a deep sleep.

Then the mute girl punched her to see if she were truly sleeping. Convinced that the slave girl would not awake, she took, from behind her ear, a tiny key, opened a nearby door, and threw into that nearby closet some bread and water. "Will you marry me, or die?" she called out. A man's voice answered, "No, I will not marry you. I will marry only the girl on whose face I placed a piece of my coat."

"If so, remain here until you die," screamed the girl. And, with those words, she locked the door and went to bed.

The next morning the slave girl, tired from her sleep-like stupor, worked all day tending the "mute" girl. When evening fell, the girl once again asked her to drink a cup of coffee into which she had mixed the sleeping drug. But, this time, the slave girl poured out the coffee and only pretended to be asleep. So this time, when the mute girl opened the secret door and asked the question of the voice behind it, she heard everything. And when the voice once again answered, "I will marry only the girl on whose face I placed a piece of my coat," she knew that she had found the young man she had been looking for.

In the morning, the slave girl spoke harshly to the girl pretending to be mute. "Either you speak or I will tell your parents what happened here last night." And so the girl decided to speak. The slave girl approached the parents. "Your daughter is cured," she told them. In disbelief and with great joy, the parents ran to see for themselves, after which they released the slave girl from her bondage.

Once again she returned to the old lady's house, where she remained for two weeks. Then again she said, "Please sell me in the market." The old lady refused. But the girl entreated her until she had no choice. This time she was sold to the king's slave. "I hope you are good luck for my master's son," he said.

When they approached the king's house, the girl found everyone in mourning. The house was dirty; the walls, covered with creeping spiders; and the king's belongings, in a state of neglect. "Why is everyone mourning?" asked the slave girl.

"Our son is lost. Our son is lost," the parents wept.

"Stop mourning. Perhaps he will return," the girl declared. And slowly, slowly she described the house of the minister and his "mute" daughter and told of the key behind the girl's ear, which opened a secret closet where their son could be found. The parents did as she instructed and soon found their beloved son, almost dead from hunger. They took the boy home, where he was washed, fed, and dressed.

Meanwhile, the slave girl, while arranging the boy's room, found his coat, with a piece missing. This piece she retrieved from her own pocket, for she had kept it with her all that time, and placed it in the young man's bed. That night, as the prince slept, he felt that something, some rough fabric, was disturbing him, and, in the morning, came upon the piece of coat. How it reminded him of the beautiful princess sleeping in the sun!

"Who arranged my bed?" he asked his mother.

"The slave girl," answered the queen.

"Then I want to marry her," the prince declared.

"But, my son, how can you be married to a slave?"

"No, Mother, she is a princess."

The slave girl was called before the queen. "Are you a princess?" asked the queen.

"Yes," she answered and then proceeded to tell all of her story and all that had happened.

A royal wedding was arranged, which lasted for seven days and seven nights, as a wedding should. All the people of the city were invited, as were the girl's family, the old lady who had helped her, and the ministers' daughters, who were her friends. One and all rejoiced with the lost prince and the lost princess, who continued to live in the palace, had many children, and lived happily ever after.

## *Lanjeh*

### INTRODUCTION

This story, told by a Jewish woman from Morocco, deals with the theme of mother-daughter conflict. From a Jewish point of view, it is an outgrowth of the story of Solomon's daughter being locked in the tower (*Midrash Tanhuma*); from a universal viewpoint, it is a reflection of "Rapunzel."

The story shows us that even a female monster can be a good mother; the mother's devotion, which she carries out even after being rejected by the ungrateful daughter, continues until the last possible moment. (A female message!) The daughter later suffers because of her rejection of her mother. (Another female message!)

However, there is no reunion of mother and daughter. Perhaps the message is that each must remain forever in her own realm; the daughter did what she had to do: Every daughter must grow up and leave the parent. The mother's naming the child, Lanjeh, which, in Arabic, means "God will keep you well," is a kind of mother's gift or message in itself.

The overt Jewish element, the harsh edict against the Jews, is one that is well-known in Jewish history and, therefore, in folktales. The community's being saved by the wisdom of the rabbi is well-known in Jewish folklore as well.

# 26

# *Lanjeh*

Once there was a monster who, every day, would go off into the forest to hunt for food, and there devour plants, animals, anything it could.

Now, this monster had a home, set deep in the forest near a grazing pasture, as large and luxurious as the home of a wealthy person. It lacked for nothing. And, upon arriving home each day, the monster would chant a certain spell, then to be transformed into a beautiful woman, and, thus, enjoy the luxury of her palatial home, while, outside the house, it remained a ferocious beast.

One day, while rummaging about in some ancient ruins hidden in a deep cave in the forest, the monster came upon a cradle, shaped like an egg. From the cradle came a weak, thin voice. "Please, please don't eat me."

Greatly frightened, the monster asked, "Who are you? Where do you come from, the land of demons or the land of humans?"

"From the land of humans," squeaked the voice.

So then the monster slowly opened the cradle, and behold! There within lay a beautiful girl, whom the monster took home and adopted as a daughter. The girl was called Lanjeh.

Now, when the mother went out to hunt, she locked the girl in the last and highest room of the many rooms in that house, so that Lanjeh was out-of-sight, should anyone by chance come upon that house. And, every morning, before leaving, the monster would wash and clean the girl's lovely black hair, which seemed to become even more beautiful as she grew. In the evening the mother would check and count the girl's lovely hair to make sure that no one had touched it but she. Thus the days and years passed until the girl reached the age of ten. And her sparkling beauty grew even greater with time.

One day, when the king's shepherd had brought his flock to the pasture to graze, his own horse lifted its head and beheld an amazing sight. There in the window of a huge house was a young girl of radiant beauty. "How can God bestow so much beauty upon one person?" thought the horse. And every day, as it grazed, the horse looked up at that window. Soon it could think of nothing else, not of grass, not of drink, until it became thin and gaunt.

Now it so happened that one day the king himself came to inspect his flock and inquired about the reason for the horse being so thin. "May my soul live, I know only one thing," replied the shepherd. "Every day, when the horse grazes, it lifts its head and stares intensely at a nearby house."

"Silly shepherd," retorted the king, "you too must lift your head and see what the horse sees." The shepherd, greatly embarrassed, begged forgiveness for his foolishness, and did as the king bade. And when he saw the face of the beautiful girl, he too wondered, "How could God bestow so much beauty on one person? Why, she is surely fit for no one other than the prince."

And, before long, the king had received this suggestion, and sent his son to the forest to look upon the girl. The prince stood beside the shepherd's horse, and when the animal lifted its head, the prince did likewise, casting his eyes at the radiant girl. His heart went out to her at once, and, the very next day, determined to speak to her, he approached the walls of the house and whistled—one long, shrill sound.

"What is that?" asked the girl as she looked out the window, and, seeing the face of the youthful prince, she fell in love with him as well.

"Can you, perhaps, give me some water?" asked the prince. "My journey has been a long one and I am quite thirsty."

"Oh, I gladly would," she answered, "but I have no way to get it down to you."

"Well, you have a long braid," advised the prince. "Tie the water bucket to your hair and, in that way, lower it down." This the girl did, but soon afterwards, she became worried. "My monster mother will soon be home. Leave at once, or your end will be bitter." And soon afterward, upon her return, as the monster mother counted the girl's hair, as usual, she did indeed find one missing.

"Who has been here?" she demanded in an angry voice.

"No one, Mother. As I looked out, the passing birds must have plucked one hair from my head." Thus the girl told her mother a lie.

The woman was quiet, but the girl spoke deviously. "Tell me, Mother, how could a person succeed in escaping from an enemy?"

The mother's heart sank. She took these words as a bad omen. "Lanjeh," she asked, "are you planning to leave me?"

"How can you think such a thought? Where would I go, Mother? Who has even seen me here?"

So the monster mother answered the girl's question. "You

would take with you a comb, a mirror, and black *kahal* for the eyes. When the enemy approaches, throw down the comb. At once the road will be covered with thorns. As the enemy succeeds again, throw down the mirror. At once the woods will be filled with water. And if the enemy succeeds again, throw down the *kahal*. At once the road will be clouded in darkness, and you will be able to make your escape." The girl listened and remembered the words of her mother in her heart.

The very next morning, after the monster mother had brushed the girl's hair and left on her daily hunt, the prince came for the lovely girl. Lowering herself down on a rope, Lanjeh was sure to take with her a comb, a mirror, and a small quantity of *kahal*. Then the prince mounted his horse and rode off like a thundering storm. But the monster, hearing the great noise, dashed through the forest to overcome them.

"Lanjeh! Lanjeh! Lanjeh!" she called. The girl did not stop. "Lanjeh! Lanjeh! Lanjeh!" the mother begged, cried, pleaded. She almost came upon the horse, when the girl threw down her comb, and, in an instant, the entire road was covered with thorns. The monster, in her anguish, made her way through this obstacle and almost came upon the horse once again, when Lanjeh lifted the mirror and threw it down upon the road. Deep lakes filled the road. But the monster mother made her way through these as well, and just as she was about to overtake the horse, Lanjeh threw down the *kahal*, black as coal. In an instant the fog and darkness blocked her way. The monster mother, unable to continue, cried and wept at the loss of her daughter.

As loudly as she could, she called, "Lanjeh, Lanjeh, listen to my words, which I tell you for your own good. Heed my words and no harm will come to you, I promise. At the crossroads you will find two spools of thread: one white; the other, black, and where the white spool rolls, take that path. Remember, Lanjeh, don't take the black road. Farewell, Lanjeh, farewell."

Soon Lanjeh and the prince came to the crossroad, and Lanjeh did as her mother's words told her. She prepared to follow the path of the white thread.

"No, no, no," objected the prince, "your mother means only

to trick us. If she told us to follow the white path, it is there that she will catch us. It is the other road we must take."

And no amount of the girl's pleading would dissuade the prince. So, putting spurs to the horse, they rode off down the path of black. There, in front of them, swooped a powerful eagle of enormous size, whose feathers were a palette of color as if they were enchanted. "Who wants my special feathers?" it cried. "Come forth and pluck them!" The colors were so beautiful that at first the girl was tempted, but then she thought, "No, no, we don't need them."

But the prince insisted, "I must have those feathers," and so he dismounted and put his hands on the eagle's back. At that moment he felt himself lifted up, up, up as the eagle swept away into the sky. "Lanjeh, Lanjeh, ride to my parent's palace. The horse knows the way," he cried. And so, as her beloved prince was carried away, out of sight, she rode to the palace, where the whinny of the horse brought the king and queen at once. "And where is our son?" they asked, as they recognized the horse. The girl was thrown into a prison room. "This is my punishment," she thought, "for the way I treated my monster mother, who adopted me and cared for me with great love."

That night the eagle descended to the roof of the prison, the prince upon its back.

"Lanjeh, Lanjeh, where did you sleep tonight?" he asked.

"In a warehouse of straw," she replied.

"Lanjeh, Lanjeh, what did you eat tonight?"

"Only water and crusts of bread."

"My God," thought the prince, "this is my bad luck for not heeding your voice."

On the second night the eagle reappeared, the prince again upon its back.

"Lanjeh, Lanjeh, where did you sleep tonight?"

"In a warehouse of animals."

"Lanjeh, Lanjeh, what did you eat tonight?"

"Crusts of bread from dishes filled with dirt."

"My God," thought the prince, "why did I not heed your voice?"

Meanwhile the people of the house were awakened by the

voices. "Whom were you speaking to?" they inquired of the girl.

"Only to your son, the prince."

Upon uttering these words, the girl was taken to the palace, there fed and garmented, as befits a royal princess.

That night the eagle and the prince descended again.

"Lanjeh, Lanjeh, where did you sleep tonight?"

"In the palace in a warm bed."

"Lanjeh, Lanjeh, what did you eat tonight?"

"The finest of foods on dishes of gold."

"Be happy, my heart," called the prince, "for at last you are in the trusty hands of my parents."

At all this talk the king and queen were most alarmed, and quickly summoned the most trusted advisors to find a way to rescue the prince.

"Only the rabbi, the teacher of the Jews, can help you," they were told.

And so the rabbi was summoned. "Find a way to save our son or your people will be expelled!" The king's demand was curt and clear.

"The solution is simple," stated the rabbi. "Order your servants to bring forth a wide, deep bowl filled with boiling tar. Spread this on the roof on the very spot where the eagle lands."

And so the rabbi's advice was carried out at once. That night when the eagle landed, its feet indeed stuck to the hot tar, and the prince, weakened and almost dead from thirst and hunger, was rescued.

Of course, he was quickly nursed back to health, after which preparations were made for a wedding feast of great luxury, never before seen in that kingdom.

And the prince and his bride lived together in health and in wealth all the remaining days of their lives.

So may we as well!

# Motherhood

Every week my mother-in-law, now in her eighty-sixth year, who lives thousands of miles from our Jerusalem home, sends a wonderful, chatty letter of family and personal news. Recently the entire first page of one such letter told of a seventyish-year-old woman who was busy running between a nursing home, where her husband had just made residence, and two different hospitals, where her grown children lay seriously ill. My mother-in-law's concluding statement to these details was, "A mother's work is never done."

Such is the message in these tales told by Jewish women. In fact, the message is even stronger: a mother's sacrifice knows no limit.

The function of these tales is to give older women listeners the important message of the power of a mother's sacrifice, or to instruct young female listeners on the meaning of "Honor your mother," the words of the commandment.

# Honor Your Mother and
# The Bird and Her Three Goslings

## INTRODUCTION

The first story, "Honor Your Mother," was recorded by Aliza Shenhar, who heard it in her childhood from her mother, Malka Gutter, from Poland.

The second story was told by a Jewish man from Romania, Zvi Solomon, who heard it from his mother. The two stories are so similar that, at first glance, they appear to be the same. However, there are differences between the woman's telling and the man's:

1. The title of the woman's story, "Honor Your Mother," is a biblical injunction and an educational message in itself. The title of the male story has no such message.

2. The woman's version tells of the suffering and hardships endured by the mother in fulfilling her task, and explicitly tells us, the listeners, that she would do anything for her children's sake.

3. The message in the woman's tale is more educational, since the mother tells the surviving children what message they should learn. The third gosling's answer shows that he was ready to sacrifice himself for the perpetuation of his family. This is the lesson he learned from his mother, and for which he was saved.

Of the three versions in the IFA, one was told by a woman; the others, by men who heard them from women.

Both stories belong to the tale type, "Raven drowns his young who promises to aid him when he becomes old." This may allude to Proverbs 30:17:

The eye that mocketh at his father,
And despiseth to obey his mother,
The ravens of the valley shall pick it out,
And the young vultures shall eat it.

119

# 27

# *Honor Your Mother*

his story took place during the birds' migration to a warm climate. A mother bird needed to cross the great sea with her three fledglings, but the fledglings were small and did not yet know how to fly, and the distance was great.

What did the mother bird do? She took the three small birds on her back and thus flew with them across the sea. Yes, the burden was heavy, but the mother loved her fledglings and was prepared to do anything in the world for them.

And so the mother bird flew, one day, two. But, on the third day, when the mother was very tired, she said to the first gosling, "Tell me, my son, would you carry me on your back?"

"No, Mother," answered the little child.

The mother grew angry. "What! You are not ready to fulfill the *mitzvah* 'Honor your mother!' " she said, and, in her anger, she dropped the child into the sea.

Later on she asked the second gosling, "Tell me, my dear son, would you carry your mother on your back for such a long distance?"

"No, Mother," answered the second child.

Again the mother became angry. "You are not ready to fulfill the *mitzvah*, 'Honor your mother!' " she said, and, in her anger, she dropped this child as well into the sea.

By now the mother's heart ached, for she was afraid of remaining with no children at all. So she turned to the third child and asked imploringly, "Tell me, my dear son, would you carry your mother on your back to get her across the great sea?"

And the third gosling answered, "Mother, I would not carry you on my back because I would have to carry my own sons. I would transport them across the great sea in the same way that you are carrying me now."

The mother bird heard her son's answer and did not reply. She continued on with her flight.

# 28

# *The Bird and Her Three Goslings*

 mother bird had three goslings. When the season for migration arrived, she took the first gosling and carried him on her back, to bring him to a warm land. When they were over the sea, the bird asked her gosling, "My son, when you grow up and are strong, and I am old and weak, will you take me to a warm country?"

"Of course, Mother," answered the gosling. The mother bird snatched him from her back and sent him to the sea.

She returned and carried the second son. And when they were over the sea, she asked him, "My son, will you take me to a warm land when I am old and you are strong?"

"Of course, Mother," answered the second gosling. He too was taken from her back and dropped into the sea.

Then the mother bird took the youngest gosling from her nest and carried him on her wing. And when they were over the sea, she asked him, "My son, when you are big and strong, and I am old and can no longer fly under my own power, will you carry me on your back and deliver me to a warm country?"

"No, Mother," answered the third gosling, "I will not be able to carry you, for then I will have to carry my own goslings."

The mother was happy with her son's answer and delivered him to a warm land.

## *A Mother's Love—1*

### INTRODUCTION

What wouldn't a mother do for a child? Are there any limits to a mother's sacrifice and devotion? The answer to these questions are the subject of this tale.

The story was told to me by my friend, Simha Shemesh, who heard it from her mother, Dina Elbar. Simha and her siblings were all born in Morocco, where they listened to their mother's stories in Moroccan Arabic. Upon telling me the story, Simha said, "I heard this story many times from my mother, when she told me all the trouble she went through to have children. She had a condition called pregnancy fever, and many children were born dead. Then, when the French invaded Morocco, they brought modern medicine, and Mother was taken care of properly so she could have live babies. This story was told to show that there is no limit to a mother's devotion."

Simha, a skilled storyteller, uses several techniques during the telling to make the story more realistic to the audience, and to allow them to participate in it: (1) she begins the story with facts of geography and family background; (2) she explains cultural and linguistic details; (3) she leaves place for the audience to fill in their own words, thereby allowing them to express their feelings about the character's action in the story.

This story is called "K'be'dah Um," which in Arabic means "love of a mother." The story relies on a wordplay; the letters k-b-d can mean either liver, or heavy, or honor, as in "Honor thy mother," the biblical commandment. This double entendre was not missed by either the storyteller or the listener.

The story includes the following plot: the child stabs the mother, the child stumbles, and the mother calls, "Can I help you my child? Are you hurt?" This motif, originally found in *The Decameron* of Boccaccio, can be found in several IFA tales.

# 29

# *A Mother's Love—1*

Once there was a family who had only one child. The father died young, and the mother was left alone to raise her son. She loved the child dearly and worked very hard to bring him up as best she could. The boy had the best education, and the mother provided everything he needed.

The woman yearned, waited until her son would marry. How she longed to see grandchildren! So she urged him to take a wife.

"No, Mother, I don't need a wife," he said. "I love you. You have done so much for me. A wife would only come between us."

"But you must marry, my son, and have a family. I'll find you a good wife."

"Well, my mother, I'll do anything you say."

So the mother found her son a good wife. The two were married, and they all lived together happily.

But, as time passed, the house seemed too small. The new wife did not feel that she was the lady of the house. She felt that her husband honored his mother more than he loved *her*. And, with time, her envy grew stronger. So, at last, the wife urged her husband to get rid of his mother.

"But how can I do that?" he protested. "My mother gave up her life for me. I must honor her."

"Then you must choose between your mother and me," shrieked the wife. "As long as she is here, I am not the lady of the house."

Thus the wife spoke day after day, until the husband could bear it no longer.

The mother saw that her son seemed ill. "What bothers you, my son?" she asked.

"Nothing, only casual problems."

"No, you must tell me, my son."

And so the son told his mother the truth.

The woman thought for a moment and said, "I understand your wife, my son. She wants to feel free. She wants to be the mistress of the house. It's all right. Take me to the forest and leave me. Live happily with your wife and children."

At first the son refused. But between the nagging of his wife and the willingness of his mother, he was finally persuaded to do as his wife asked.

At the forest his mother said, "My son, I ask you for only one promise. After you kill me, take my liver and it will care for you."

Now, the word for liver in Arabic is *kebed*. In Hebrew it's *kaved*. As the heart is the center of feeling, so the liver is the heart of parental love, devotion, and care. And *kaved* can also mean "Honor your mother," as the Bible tells us.

So the son did as he was told. He killed his mother, and put her liver in a bag. But on his way home he stumbled and fell. Suddenly, he heard his mother's voice, "Oh, my son, are you hurt?"

"No, Mother, I'm fine. I'm fine."

And so the son continued on his way. At the edge of the forest he was stopped and arrested by the king's guards. Thinking he was a robber, they brought him to the palace, and he soon stood before the king for judgment.

"And what were you doing in the forest?" asked the king.

"Hunting for animals."

"Do you have anything to show?"

Of course, the son didn't want to show what was in his bag, so he said nothing. Soon he was sentenced to be hanged.

Just then his mother's liver began to pulse, for she was worried about her son.

"What's in the bag?" asked the king.

"Nothing, nothing."

But the king insisted. And when he opened the bag, he found the liver, and made the young man tell the whole story.

"How dare you!" screamed the king. "You are a complete _____." (You finish the sentence.) "How dare you! Your mother gave you life and cared for you. Now you shall be hanged, and not for walking in the forest."

And so it was done.

# The Mother

### INTRODUCTION

The opening lines of this story are the storyteller's way of making this story special and believable. She is saying, "This is not ordinary speech or events. I am going to create a story for you. It is a story that really happened."

In this story, told by Flora Sasson of Lebanon, the woman's message is clear. In this tale, unlike stories about confronting the Angel of Death, the mother is unaware that she will be sacrificing her own life. But in this tale of a mother's bravery and cleverness, she is ready to meet the elements, however harsh, in order to save her child.

This lovely theme was adapted by the author, O. Henry, in a story called "The Last Leaf."

# 30

# *The Mother*

his story took place in the north of Lebanon in the village of Hamadin. And the happening, as told, goes like this:

In the village lived a widow and her beautiful daughter, an only child. One day the girl became ill and was ordered to rest. And so she lay on her bed near the window and looked out at the only tree in the yard. Thus, days, weeks, months passed, and the autumn came. But the girl's condition didn't improve. On the contrary, she grew worse. And so, one day, as she looked at the tree, she said weakly, "You see, Mother, see those leaves. When the last leaf falls, I will die." The mother's heart grieved, and she watched anxiously as the leaves fell.

One cold night the wind howled, and the mother's heart was full of despair, as she saw the wind taking the last leaves. With every leaf her heart sank even deeper. At last there was only one leaf left. What could she do?

So the poor woman ran outside, unaware of the cold, the gusts of wind, and the storm. She approached the wall in front of the tree, and there she painted, on that wall, a picture of the last leaf. So good, so accurate was the drawing that it looked like the real leaf itself.

When the girl awoke, she looked out the window, and there she saw one lonely leaf. Days and weeks passed. From time to time she looked out, and always she saw that last leaf, still hanging on to the branch of the tree. A new spirit entered the girl. Slowly, slowly she recovered, and at last she got well.

But the mother, by going out on that windy night, had caught cold. She developed tuberculosis, and soon died.

When the girl was able to leave her bed, she went outside to see the miracle that had occurred: Why had that leaf not fallen?

And what did she see? The painting, done by her mother, which had cost her her life for her child's sake.

Then the girl realized her mother's great love, and grieved greatly for her mother who, in her own death, had given life to her.

# Aging

"Who will take care of me in my old age? Will my husband or my children provide for me?" These questions, asked over and over again by aging women, express their deep concerns.

Tales told by these women send messages to their listeners and, sad but true, sometimes that message is, "Women, your children are ungrateful. They can't be depended on." These tales instruct young female listeners how to behave toward their aging parents and older listeners how, *while they are still alive*, to behave toward their children. The intention of the tales is to instill proper behaviors—or to change those that need changing.

### The Experiment

#### INTRODUCTION

This tale, told by Bella Haviv from Russia, is typical of
tales told by the aged. The message here is: Children are
ungrateful. A parent spends years caring for children, but
they do not return the care.

The heroine in this story realizes that the aging mother
must be independent of her children, should not give her
wealth to her ungrateful children, and should remain
healthy enough to care for herself. Here, also, we see the
message that a loving husband is a treasured gift.

# 31

# *The Experiment*

Once there was a mother who worked very hard,
and all that she earned she divided amongst her
children.

One day her neighbor scoffed at her, "You
foolish woman! Why do you give your money
away? You are growing old, and if you fall sick, your children
will neglect you."

At this the woman laughed. "Not *my* children!" she answered.

"Then," said the neighbor, "perform an experiment. Pretend to break your leg, and cover it with a sheet, so that people
will think you have been injured. Hire a wagon and go to the
home of each of your children. See who will accept you."

And the old woman did as her neighbor advised.

She arrived first at the home of the eldest daughter. "Oh
Mother, what happened to you?" cried the daughter.

"Oh, my daughter, I fell and broke my leg. Now I cannot
walk, and so I have come to you. . . ."

"But, Mother," interrupted the daughter, "you know that I have my own child and that I am so busy taking care of her that I have not the tiniest bit of time left. How will I be able to care for you?"

The mother left and went directly to the home of her son. Her daughter-in-law greeted her at the door.

"Dear Mother-in-law, what happened to you?"

The mother repeated the story of how she had broken her leg and had come to her son's house for care.

"But, Mother-in-law, you know that my husband is a doctor and that all day long patients come to see him. Where would I be able to put you?"

And so the mother left and went to the home of the youngest child. There she told the same story—and received the same refrain.

At day's end the mother went home, lay on her bed, and groaned. A short time later her husband returned from work. "My dear wife, what happened to you?"

"I fell and broke my leg—and cannot walk," groaned the woman.

The husband lifted his wife, put her in bed, and made a cup of tea. "Lie quietly, and I will run and fetch the doctor."

At these words the wife could no longer pretend. "Do not run for the doctor," she said, and she told her husband about the experiment and all that had happened to her that day.

"From now on," she said, "whatever money we earn will be ours to use."

And so no longer did the woman go to visit her children.

A week passed—two—then a month. And when the children saw that their mother did not come, they ran to her. "Dear Mother, how are you?" they asked sweetly.

"Ah," said the woman, "I have already seen how you accepted me, and so decided to remain home happily with Father. As long as we do not need your kindness, we will have enough money for all our needs."

# The Grandfather Who Was Thrown
# Out of the Sukkah

## INTRODUCTION

This story presents one of the mysteries in folklore research. All versions have an old grandfather as the persecuted person; a male child is the one who teaches the educational moral; and the woman, in our Jewish versions, is harsh in her punishment of the old man. Yet, the story is told by women; of twenty versions in the IFA, eleven were told by women.

One of these women's tellings is the story presented here, told by Flora Cohen of Egypt to her daughter. Here she turns the tale into a story for Sukkot; perhaps it was told in a *sukkah*, where, traditionally, many stories have been told. Her version has been published in Israel in educational magazines for children, probably for their educational message.

Another IFA version was told by a woman, Aliza Anidjar of Tangiers; she comments that she heard the story as a little girl, when she would care for her grandmother, washing the old woman's face and eyes.

Grandmother would call out, "Oh God, how she makes my face like a mirror!" and would add, "May your children and grandchildren do for you what you do for me — not like in the story of the wooden spoon." And then Grandmother would tell the story. Aliza also comments that when she herself told the story to her own granddaughter for the first time, the child hugged her and promised never to behave like the son in the story.

This story is divided into several subtypes:

1. AT 980C. In this type a father tells the son to put the grandfather in a cart and carry him to the forest. The child returns home with the empty cart, which he will need for his own father. This type may refer to the custom in ancient times, before Moses ordered the honoring of one's parents (Exodus 20:12, Deuteronomy 5:16), of transporting old parents to the forest, putting them on a cart, and leaving them to perish. Of four such IFA versions, only one was told by a

woman. The reason for this is anyone's guess. Perhaps the thought of putting a parent out to die is too unbearable for women to perpetuate; perhaps men feel that they are better able to survive in the forest, or are better able to understand the reason for the custom. What do you think?

2. AT 980 B. In this type, the grandfather is given a wooden bowl or spoon to eat from, after which the child carves a similar bowl for his father.

3. AT 980 A. This third type, called the half-carpet, which we see in this folktale, presents the old man being covered with a mat or small carpet.

In all three types the educational message learned by the father is the same. Because the child's action actually changes the father's behavior, the message is a powerful one. The child's wisdom reminds me of the biblical quotation: "Out of the mouths of babes and sucklings hast thou founded strength" (Psalms 8).

# 32

# *The Grandfather Who Was Thrown Out of the Sukkah*

here once was an old man who lived at his son's home, with his son, his daughter-in-law, and his grandson. Once, on the holiday of Sukkot, the old man sat at the head of the table, but while he was eating soup, his hand shook slightly, the spoon fell, and some of the soup spilled on the cloth.

The boy's mother, the daughter-in-law, was very angry at the old man, and shouted at her husband, "What is this? Do you see how your father dirties the tablecloth? It's impossible for him to remain in the *sukkah*. Any moment we are expecting guests, and what will they say if they see such a dirty cloth?"

Said the husband to his wife, "But this is my father, and where will I take him now?"

"I don't care," screamed the angry woman. "Do whatever you do. But in this *sukkah* he cannot remain." And she did not wish to speak to him any longer. The son had no choice. He took his father, and put him under the stairs, and covered him with a mat.

But behold! The grandson was walking down the street. And what did he see? His grandfather sitting under the stairs, shaking with cold. The boy asked, "Grandfather, why are you sitting here with only a mat to cover you?"

Answered the poor grandfather, "Your father, my son, gave me this mat. I was sitting upstairs in the *sukkah* but my hand shook, and I spilled a little soup on the cloth. And your mother didn't want to sit with me. She commanded your father to send me down here, and he fulfilled her request."

The boy replied, "Grandfather, give me half of the mat. I need it."

The old man began to protest. "Aren't you ashamed, my child? This mat is too small for me, and you want to take half of it?"

"Never mind," said the boy, "give me half of it." The old man had no choice. The boy took half the mat, rolled it, and went into the house. And as soon as he entered, he turned to his father and said, "Father!"

"What is it my son?"

"Father, please save this for me."

"Why?" wondered the father.

"Because when you grow old, Father, I will cover you with this mat. And I will build a *sukkah* just for you, so that you will not dirty our *sukkah*. That would be a disgrace for our guests."

The father was angry. "I am your father, I spent a great deal of money on you, and you, you won't want to sit with me, and would cover me with such a mat!"

The boy asked, "And your father? Didn't he spend money

on you? And you, didn't you throw him out of the *sukkah*? And didn't you cover him with this mat?"

The father fell on his knees, and thanked his small son for the lesson he had taught him. He sought forgiveness from his old father for all that he had done. He brought him to the *sukkah* and sat him at the head of the table. The old man forgave his son and daughter-in-law, and all were happy for the holiday.

And from that moment the sons of the house respected the old man until his last day.

# Death

Is there anything stronger than death? When God has decreed that your time has come to go to the next world, and when He sends the Angel of Death to fetch you, is there anything you can do to change the Angel of Death's mind? The answer, according to Jewish folklore, is, "Yes." The giving of charity will save you from death.

The idea that charity saves from death, or, in Hebrew, *tzedakah tatzil mimavet*, has become one of the most important precepts in Jewish life, and has influenced Jewish tales and customs. The thought that charity could have such a tremendous influence led people to give food to orphans, to give money at funerals, to arrange a trousseau for a needy bride. This idea also made its way into folktales, where the strong message, in turn, then encouraged people to give charity.

Included here are several types of these widely told tales, in which the woman, by virtue of her wit, righteousness, or good deed, saves her own life or that of her husband. Sometimes the mother, instead of the bride, saves the life of her son.

The idea that charity saves from death has biblical (Proverbs 10:2, 11:4) and postbiblical foundations. Much talmudic and midrashic lore tells of charitable deeds saving one from a sinking ship, from deadly snakebite, or from other clutches of the Angel of Death.

These stories give visual expression to the biblical verse (Proverbs 10:2) upon which they are founded: "Treasures of wickedness profit nothing; but righteousness delivereth from death." What is common to all versions is that *the one who gives charity is saved because, and only because, of the giving. Tzedakah* came to mean not only giving money, but also giving real help, doing good deeds, for others. Inherent in this giving of charity is that *the giving brings more good to the giver than to the receiver.* As *Midrash Vayikra Rabbah* 34:10 tells us, "More than the house lord helps the poor, the poor help the house lord."

### INTRODUCTION

Tales about charity saving from death are told almost equally by both men and women, but there is a difference between the two. My examination of twenty-five tales in the IFA showed the following pattern: Where men told the tale, the stories were almost entirely about a stingy man who is about to be bitten by a snake. Convinced at the last moment to give charity, the man, via his charitable deed, thwarts the power of the snake. This tale is based on an almost identical postbiblical legend about Rabbi Meir, and a similar story in the Jerusalem Talmud *Shabbat* 6:8.

Where women told the story, the tales were almost entirely about a woman whose good deeds save her from the clutches of the Angel of Death. Such is the plot in this story from Yemen. It was told by Sa'ada Seri, born in Yemen in 1852, and was told to her granddaughter, Rachel Seri.

The overt message of such a tale is: "What is stronger than death? Charity!" The covert message is: "What is stronger than death? Woman!"

The tale also reflects the storyteller's (and the society's) ideas about the virtues of women. A strong message is that women should not gossip or mock others. As the Book of Proverbs (11:13) tells us: "A tale bearer reveals secrets; but he that is of a faithful spirit conceals the matter."

In addition, this tale reflects the teller's (and the society's) belief in the power of dreams.

# 33

# *Charity Will Save from Death—1*

 nce there were a husband and wife who lived peacefully together. In the morning the husband would go to his business in the matters of trade, and in the evening he would return. His wife would remain at home where she would clean and cook and launder and climb to the roof to hang her clothes.

137

And so their life was peaceful and quiet. The wife was innocent and righteous, never spoke in public, or dealt with foreign people. This was in order not to spread gossip, or mock others, God forbid. May God save us from the evil tongue! The husband was righteous as well. He kept his tongue, and avoided the company of clowns and people whose heads were empty. Every day he went to work and promptly came home.

One night, in a dream, the husband saw his wife falling from the roof to her death. In a fright he awoke, and warned her, "Today do not wash or hang the laundry." That day he went to work as usual with a heavy heart, and prayed in his heart for the dream not to come true.

The wife cleaned, cooked, laundered, and went to the roof, as usual. But suddenly she heard a knock at the door. Leaving her bucket of laundry on the stairs, she descended and opened the door. There before her stood a poor man, asking for bread. And so the woman cut off one-third of the only loaf she had in the house, and handed it to the stranger. He thanked her and left.

Once again she went to the roof, but she heard another knock at the door. She descended and found a second beggar standing before her. And so, willingly and with love, she sliced another third of the loaf, and gave it to the stranger.

The woman climbed to the roof. Once more she heard a knock at the door. There was a third beggar in need of bread. And so the woman took the third and last part of her loaf and gave it to the stranger, leaving nothing for herself. The man left, satisfied and happy. The woman, who had not eaten all day, returned to hang her laundry.

In the evening the husband returned, anxious, worried, and prepared to see the disaster that had befallen his wife. But his wife was happy, healthy, unharmed. And so he understood that a miracle had occurred.

"What did you do all day?" he asked.

"Nothing. I remained at home as usual."

But the husband asked repeatedly, "What happened today? What did you do today?"

And so, finally the wife told him of the poor strangers who had come to ask for food.

Then the man understood that the *tzedakah* his wife had given had saved her life. He told his wife of his dream and encouraged her to give *tzedakah* to remove dangers. May God save us!

## *Charity Will Save from Death—2*

### INTRODUCTION

One of the greatest joys in Jewish life is the wedding of a bride and groom. It is a time for dancing, feasting, and expressions of joy. But the time of the wedding is also fraught with many dangers. And why?

There is a belief, among all Jewish ethnic groups, that demons are particularly alert on the wedding night of the young couple. These demons seek to thwart the happy alliance, and try to harm either the bridegroom, the bride, or both.

So how can one thwart these demons? Is there nothing to be done to protect the bride and groom? The Jews of Russia closed doors, windows, and chimneys during a wedding, so that demons could not enter. Egyptian Jews dressed the bride as a man and the groom as a woman, in order to confuse and deceive the Angel of Death. Such customs arose throughout the Jewish world.

Soon, methods of defeating demons became intertwined with the idea that giving charity can thwart the Angel of Death. A famous talmudic story, *Shabbat* 156b, tells about the daughter of Rabbi Akiva, who, on her wedding night, took a brooch and stuck it to the wall; by chance it penetrated the eye of a snake that was about to kill her. It was later determined that on the wedding day she had given her portion of food to a pauper. This single act of charity had saved her life.

These tales, based on the story of Rabbi Akiva's daughter, reached the ears and mouths of the folk, and such tales are usually told by women.

However, the tale I have chosen to share with you here was told by Yechiel Dan, a male teller from Yemen. In this tale the woman is still the strong heroine, for even a male teller cannot destroy the strong woman's message associated with the story. However, the male teller turns the father of the girl into a hero: *He* is one of the thirty-six hidden saints scattered throughout the world; *he* prays for his daughter; *he* suffers for her ("What would a father not do for a daughter?"); *he* worries about her; and, *he* remains at her side until the very end.

Notice that the mother is absent in this story! A female telling would probably include a mother, who might share in the decision about the daughter's fate.

# 34

# *Charity Will Save from Death—2*

nce there was a very righteous man who kept all the *mitzvot*. Truly he was one of the thirty-six saints for whom the world exists.

Now, the man's wife was barren and the couple had no children. Day and night he prayed for a child until, at last, Heaven heard his prayer and answered, "You shall have a daughter, but when she reaches the time of her wedding night, she will die. If you agree to these conditions, so it shall be. If not, you will have no child."

Since the man had no children, he agreed. What else could he do?

And so a daughter was born to them, a girl of wisdom and beauty, who grew up as tall and graceful as a date tree. But when the matchmakers came and spoke of different suitors, the father rejected them all. How could he give his daughter in marriage, knowing that on the night of her wedding she would die?

Thus many years passed, and at last the daughter resented the life of an unmarried woman. So she chose a handsome young man and approached her father. "Father, I love this man and it is he I want to wed." And although the father tried to dissuade the girl, his pleadings were in vain. She insisted that, without marriage to the young man, life was not worth living.

Well, what would a father not do for a daughter? And so, although he knew that she would die on the night of her wedding, he agreed. The time of the wedding was announced and it was celebrated with great joy.

Only the poor father, knowing what fate awaited his daughter, couldn't close his eyes. And so he stood guard at the entrance to her room, constantly reciting from the Book of Psalms.

In the morning, as dawn rose, the father knocked on the door. He was curious. What had happened during the night?

"Praise the lord. Thank God for He is good," muttered the old man. And then he asked, "My daughter, what was the good deed you did yesterday, or, perhaps, the day before that?"

"I did nothing unusual," answered the girl.

"Still, think hard. Try to remember. Perhaps there is something."

The girl thought, and then she remembered that on her wedding night she and her new husband were given the special soup served to a new bride and groom. This was the soup of pigeons, eaten so that the new couple may live in peace like a pair of doves. Such was the custom that the groom would eat the soup of a male pigeon while the bride would eat the soup of a smaller, female bird.

"And so," the girl related, "just as I picked up my bowl to drink the golden soup, I heard someone crying in the street, 'Give me a slice of bread. I'm so hungry, for I haven't eaten for two days.'

"I looked around and there was a pauper begging for food, but no one paid him any mind, for everyone was busy with the wedding feast. And so I took my own bowl of soup and gave it to the beggar. Then I took the empty bowl to my room. That is all."

At once the father entered the room to check. And where the girl had put her hair pins into a hole in the wall before going to bed there lay the body of a poisonous snake. Yes, the pins of the bride had killed the snake who had come to claim her.

And so the bride received her reward for the *mitzvah* she had done. By giving her food to the hungry she had performed an act of charity, and that one act saved her from certain death.

# The Fate of a Son

## INTRODUCTION

In the Babylonian Talmud (*Yevamot* 64a) we find the following riddle: "Why is the prayer of the righteous compared to a pitchfork?" The answer is: "As a pitchfork turns the sheaves of grain from one position to another, so does the prayer of the righteous turn the dispensations of the Holy One, blessed be He, from the attribute of anger to the attribute of mercy." Prayer and supplication also have the power to save one from death.

This story, told by a Jewess from Morocco, is one of many about the bride saving the bridegroom from death. Here we see that it is the girl's piety and devotion to Torah that bring her to appeal to God, and thus to save her groom. In these tales the bride is usually nameless, while the name of the groom (R. Reuben the Scribe, Matanyahu, etc.) is given.

Sometimes the bride outwits the Angel of Death by using the reasoning from Deuteronomy 24:5: "When a man taketh a new wife, ... he shall be free for his house one year and shall cheer his wife whom he hath taken." How could the Angel of Death argue against such a defense?

Sometimes, because of the wife's clever argument or her supplication based on her devotion to God, the Holy One grants her husband additional years of life. In IFA 6868, told by another Jewess from Morocco, the husband is granted ninety years. Could there be a stronger Jewish women's message than this?

In still another tale, IFA 8608, told by a Jewish woman from Libya, Elijah promises a childless couple that they will have a son, on the condition that the child be placed under the guardianship of the Prophet. When Elijah does eventually come to claim the child, the mother's implorings are so strong that Elijah gives up his right.

A version of this story was told to me in October 1992, in Delhi, India, by Elizabeth Galiker, a member of the Jewish congregation. She heard the story from her grandmother:

Many years ago my grandfather was ill. One night there was a knock on the door, and when my grandmother opened it, she saw a man whose face was covered with a white veil. He asked for my grandfather by name.

"He's not here," Grandmother answered, and she closed the door. Grandmother was an illiterate woman.

That night my grandfather died.

The story was related to me twice, and the tellings were virtually identical. Each time Elizabeth was sure to stress that her grandmother was unschooled.

The message, the reason, for this statement is unclear to me. Is it possible that Grandmother recognized the Angel of Death but that her lack of knowledge of the Bible or Torah rendered her incapable of imploring or convincing the Angel to rescind his decree? Grandmother's attempt to fool the Angel, while sincere, was ineffective—since she did not act in a knowledgeable way (that is, from a Jewish point of view).

In the tale told here, the parents receive the news about their child's birth via a question asked of God, and answered by Him, in a dream. The belief in dream questions is found among Jews all over the world.

# 35

# *The Fate of a Son*

nce there was a great rabbi who had no children. He prayed to God for others who were barren, and these prayers were received in Heaven. One day a woman appeared at the door.

"How can I help you?" asked the rabbi's wife.

"My husband is threatening to divorce me, for we have no children. I wanted to ask the rabbi to intervene for me in

Heaven, and to ask God to send me a child." The rabbi's wife
promised to deliver the message.

But when her husband came home, she rebuked him. "You
pray for others, but you do nothing for us."

"If it were our luck to have children, God would have sent
them," replied her husband.

"No, no," cried the woman, "I want a son or a daughter. You
must do something."

"In that case, let us make a dream question," said the
husband.

And so, that night they asked God to send them an answer
in their dreams.

The rabbi and his wife both dreamed the same frightening
dream. They would have a son, a wonderful boy, but on the
night of his wedding, he would die.

"Oh, what shall we do?" wailed the couple. "What shall we
do?"

"We will give *tzedakah*, make *bar mitzvahs* for orphans, and
do other good deeds." said the wife. "Perhaps, this will undo
the fate of the decree."

"Maybe God will help us," said the husband.

Nine months later a son was born, and great was the joy in
the town. The boy studied Torah. Soon his wisdom was even
greater than his father's, for what other boys took years to
study he learned in only hours. All this time the mother
watched with outward joy, but cried in secret, knowing the fate
that awaited him.

When the boy reached eighteen years of age, he approached his father. "You know, Father," he said, "it is written
in the Torah that the time has come for me to marry." The
rabbi, with tears in his eyes, said, "Well, my son. . . ," but he
couldn't continue.

Now, next door to the rabbi lived a woodcutter who had a
wise daughter. And one day, when the rabbi had a dispute with
another *hacham*, they posed a question for the girl to answer.

"Father, why are you asking our neighbors' daughter for the
answer?" asked the son.

"My son, she knows more than you. She is a *hajwa*, a wise
girl, who never sees the sunlight, but who studies Torah day

and night. She answers questions by passing the answers through the window. To her you will be married."

The girl's father agreed, for everyone loved the rabbi's son. As for the girl, whatever her father said she considered holy. And so, the son of the rabbi and the daughter of the wood-cutter were wed.

But suddenly, soon after the wedding, as the son entered the bridal chamber, he noticed a shadow that seemed to be following him. The shadow spoke to him, "The time has arrived for you to die!"

"Why, why is that?" cried the groom.

"God has made an agreement with your parents that you will die on your wedding night."

"But what can be done? Is there nothing to be done?" answered the groom.

Upon hearing these words, the bride began to speak, "What happened? Whom are you talking to?"

And so, the groom told her what the shadow had said.

Then, with great sorrow, and with her hands raised toward Heaven, the girl beseeched, "Oh God, I was closed up inside my home all my life. I studied Torah and thought only of you. So now I ask you, are you going to do this to me?"

And the girl was answered by the voice of God, like the voice that spoke to Rachel when she gave signs to Leah and when the fate of Rachel's barrenness was canceled. It was the very same voice that the bride heard: "Strike your foot three times upon the ground and then open the door. Your husband will not die." And so the girl did as she was told. And when the door was opened, there was a giant snake lying dead upon the threshold.

The next morning, to his parents' great surprise, the husband was found alive and well, and the bride was laughing. Her mother-in-law hugged her and kissed her. "The decree has been canceled, the decree has been canceled," she shouted again and again.

And so the bride and the groom lived happily ever after, and had many children, all good sons and daughters of Israel.

## By Right of His Wife's Charity

### INTRODUCTION

In yet another tale about charity (from Yemen), we see
that the giving of charity can be of benefit in matters
relating to death, in this case the death of a well-known
rabbi. Since proper burial is so important in Jewish
tradition, getting the man out of the house is a particular
*mitzvah*. Here again the woman is the one whose deeds
bring the miracle about.

# 36

# *By Right of His Wife's Charity*

n a small city there lived a rabbi who was very
rich but who was also a miser. To his young wife
he would give portions of food, measured out
according to the scale, and to this he would not
add even a drop. His wife always told him, "My
husband, give food to the poor as well," but he would scold her
when she spoke like this.

Now, when the wife prepared food for herself or for her
husband, she would take off a tiny amount and put aside this
food or soup in a small bowl for the poor, without her husband's knowledge. And how did she do this?

In the kitchen was a small window, and through it she would
pass the food that she set aside for the poor. And always, one
poor person, knowing there would be some food, would go
and take it, blessing the woman who gave it without her
husband knowing.

One day a dreadful thing happened in that house. Her
husband arrived from work, and the moment he sat in his
chair, he fell to the floor—and died.

The woman wept. Soon all the officials of the government
and the rabbis arrived—for the husband had been the most

famous rabbi in the city. They placed him in his coffin, and proceeded to take it out through the door, but they could not. The coffin would not fit. Then they tried to take it out through the window, but could not. The coffin simply would not fit. Then the wife spoke: "Take it out through the small window in the kitchen."

"What! If we couldn't fit the coffin through the large doorway or through the large window, how will we fit it through this small space?" they laughed.

But the wife began to cry and to shout until the men relented. "Very well, we will try and we will see."

And when they came to take the coffin through the small window, behold! The window widened—and widened—until the coffin could fit through.

Everyone wondered at this miracle.

The next day, after the rabbi was buried, they called the wife and wanted to hear, from her mouth, how this great miracle could have occurred. She did not know what to tell them, but after an entire hour passed, she finally spoke:

"My husband was a stingy miser, and gave me food only according to the scale. Every day I would steal from his food and from mine, and give a third of our portions to the poor, and pass it through this very window. Perhaps, because God saw this deed for the poor, He sent me a miracle, allowing my husband's coffin to pass through this space."

The woman returned home, where she became very rich. And day after day she would give food to the poor, for now she had great warehouses, filled with enough for all the days of her life. In this way God gave her luck.

# A Mother's Love—2

## INTRODUCTION

This story, too, deals with outwitting the Angel of Death, but here it is due to a mother's love. The universal type

is called Alcestis because it is based on the story of
Alcestis in Greek mythology: Seven days after the birth
of a little boy, the Fates appear in the palace to predict
the baby's fortune. They prophesy that the boy will grow
up to be a mighty king but will die on his wedding day.
When that day does come, Death (personified) arrives and
says that he has come to take the prince, or anyone else
who will die in his place. Despite the imploring of the
prince to his father and mother to save him, they decline
to do so. Only the young and faithful wife agrees to
sacrifice her life for that of her husband. Later, the queen
of the underworld convinces her husband to restore the
young woman to life.

A Yiddish ballad tells of a young man about to be
snatched away by the Angel of Death. His parents agree
to die in his place but when they see the Angel of Death,
they change their minds. As in the legend of Alcestis,
only the bride agrees. This same plot and group of
characters appear in some IFA versions.

But, according to Haim Schwarzbaum, a scholar and
researcher in Jewish folklore, in Jewish oral versions the
negative aspect of the selfish parents is not usual.
Instead, as in our story, told by Aliza Anidjar of Spanish
Morocco, the *Yiddishe Mamme* sacrifices her life for the
sake of her sick son.

As you can imagine, this love story, which gives the
woman a halo of glory, is transmitted by women. Of the
nine versions in the IFA, almost all were told by women.

The number of Alcestis stories in the IFA are but a few
of the many stories in which the bride saves the
bridegroom from death. This may be because most
Jewish stories do not take for granted that the Angel of
Death will be ready to relinquish his "catch" merely
because a substitute can be found for the bridegroom.
Rather, the bride saves her groom because of her
cleverness and skill. (See story no. 35.)

# 37

# *A Mother's Love—2*

nce there was a couple who had an only son. The boy took ill, and then his condition worsened. And the parents saw that their beautiful child would soon die.

The father, unable to bear this news, ran to the city's garden, where he began to weep. Suddenly there appeared before him an old woman, dressed in black. She was none other than the Angel of Death. "What is the matter?" she asked.

The man retreated, for he knew who the woman was.

"Don't be frightened," she said. "Tell me, what is the problem?"

"My son is going to die. Oh, I would do anything to save him."

"Well, then, the remedy is in your hands," said the woman.

"In my hands?"

"Yes, you may die in his place."

Upon hearing these words, the father became frightened and began to run. He ran, ran, ran until he reached home.

"And how is our son?" he asked, upon entering.

"The same."

Now the mother needed to rest from her bedside vigil, so she went out to the same garden. And, as she sat sitting so sadly, the same old woman appeared.

"What is the matter?" she asked.

"My son is sick and is about to die."

"And do you want to save him?"

"Yes, yes, of course."

"Then you may die in his place."

"All right, yes, I agree," said the mother. "But just give me a moment to kiss him good-bye."

So the woman went home and kissed her son. "You will live," she said. "It doesn't matter what happens to me."

Then the husband realized what had happened. "No, no, no!" he cried aloud.

"Yes, yes!" his wife answered, "I must save the boy's life." And she kissed her husband, and left.

At the garden she sought the old woman but couldn't find her. Instead, there appeared another old woman, dressed in white, holding a bouquet of flowers in her hand.

"Where is she?" asked the mother.

"Who?"

"The Angel of Death. I want to die in my son's place."

"I am the Angel of Death," said the woman, as she handed the flowers to the mother. "I only wanted to see how far a mother's love would go. Go back. Your son is healthy. And you will all live in happiness and peace."

May we all have the same decree.

III

THE NATURE
CYCLE

# The Week Cycle: *Shabbat*

"Remember the Sabbath day and keep it holy," the commandment tells us. The festival of *Shabbat* (or *Shabbos*, if you come
from Eastern Europe) represents a basic element of Jewish
belief: the Sabbath day is a symbol of contact, of covenant
between God and the children of Israel (Exodus 31:16, 17).

So important is the *halachah* of *Shabbat* that the Talmud
says: "Jerusalem was destroyed only because the Sabbath was
desecrated" (*Shabbat* 119b). But there has always been a
conflict, especially among poor Jews, between wishing to
keep the festival and actually being able to do so.

Also, special festival foods, songs and dress developed in
Jewish homes across the world. My own mouth waters at the
memory of my mother's freshly baked *hallah*. And how I
remember the special sense of lovely peace on Friday nights
when, dressed in white, we sang a song of welcome to the
Sabbath Queen: *Bo'i, bo'i, hamalkah, Bo'i, bo'i, hakalah.*
("Come, come, oh queen, come, come, oh bride.")

Little wonder, then, that many stories about this conflict
and these customs have been created! Little wonder, also,
that, on *Shabbat* or *Shabbos*, women, meeting together in
their special places in the synagogue or at home, created tales
for each other and their children. These were wonder tales, full
of magic, which began, in Yiddish, *"Amol is geven"* ("Once
upon a time") or the equivalent in other Jewish dialects, and in
which Elijah the Prophet appeared as fairy godmother. They
were religious tales, the purpose of which was to teach the
listener proper conduct. Family life played a prominent role;
generosity and hospitality were emphasized; stinginess and
pride were punished.

And where did these women get ideas for the heroines of
their tales? From the stories they heard of postbiblical
women.

153

## The Miracle of Elijah the Prophet

### INTRODUCTION

This story, told by Esther Alfasi from Morocco, is based
on a famous talmudic legend (*Taanit* 24, 25) about the
wife of Rabbi Hanina ben Dosa. In order not to indicate
need of help or mercy from the community, she, too,
pretended to be baking *hallot*. She, too, was the recipient
of a miracle. But in the talmudic story it is the neighbor
who goes away in shame. As the Bible tells us: "None
who believe in thee shall be ashamed." (Psalm 25:3) The
wife of Rabbi Hanina ben Dosa became the prototype,
the model, in stories where poverty needs to be hidden.
Thus, in such Jewish folktales, it is the wife who does
so.

In another version of the tale (IFA 6042) told by a male,
the details of the wife's piety (her prayers, her blessing
of the *Shabbat*) and the opening statement about the
greatness of God are eliminated.

In this story Elijah the Prophet, the most frequent
acting character in Jewish folk legends, resolves the
confrontation between two women; one rich (evil) and the
other poor (pious). This reflects the polarity between Lilith
and Eve. Or, it may be a reflection of the conflict between
good and evil within each one of us.

# 38

# *The Miracle of Elijah the Prophet*

God has been everywhere and nowhere. There is
no place from which His light is missing.

Once there was a poor Jew who had many
children and whose meals consisted only of
black olives and bread. But they said, "May God
be blessed. It is good that we don't need the gifts of others."

155

For the proverb says, "He who needs to take from the table of others, for him the world is dark."

One Friday the poor family had no money for flour to bake *hallot*. So what did the woman do?

That night, while her husband and children were at the synagogue, she placed two stones on the table in place of the *hallot*. Then she covered them with a white cloth, and set the candles near them. And she repeated three times, "Blessed be the holy *Shabbat*." Then she continued, "Thank the Lord for His kindness. His kindness is forever. God is true, Moses is true, the Torah is the true Torah." With great enthusiasm she pronounced the word "true."

Suddenly her neighbor appeared. "And why is there no smoke from your oven?" she asked. The poor woman continued her prayers.

But the neighbor didn't settle for the silence, and sent her hand wandering over the white napkin. Aha! She burst out laughing and ran to tell the neighbors what the foolish woman had done.

The poor woman, filled with shame, began to cry bitterly. As she did so, her husband and children returned from prayers, and with them was a guest, dressed in ragged clothes. At once the woman wiped her tears, and received her family and the guest with a shiny face.

The guest was asked to recite the blessing over the bread. He took the knife, lifted the napkin, and behold! How astonished the woman was to see two beautiful *hallot*!

And in the kitchen the pots were full of delightful and delicious *Shabbat* foods. For it is said that God rested on that day and took pleasure.

When *Shabbat* was over and the guest had gone on his way, the woman told her husband what had happened. Then it was that the couple understood that God had given them the privilege of sharing their *Shabbat* with Elijah the Prophet. May he be remembered for good!

## *The* Shabbat *Candles*

### INTRODUCTION

This Polish story has a clear and wonderful chain of female transmission: The wife of the *shohet*, herself, who was privileged to have this "revelation" with the Prophet, told the story in Yiddish to Nehama Salz. She related it to her daughter, Esther Weinstein, who told it to her daughter, Judith Gut, who gave the story to the IFA. During the process of this transmission the East European *Shabbos* changed to the Hebrew *Shabbat*.

In this tale, set in Safed, home of the sixteenth-century kabbalists in Israel, we see the utmost of piety in the Jewish characters: a *shohet*, a woman of valor, a family happy with their lot. For the woman's strong wish and intention to fulfill the *mitzvah* of lighting candles, she is rewarded.

In another IFA tale from Russia a mother leaves her family to live with a Christian. Yet she continues to light the Sabbath candles. The light of these candles eventually saves the life of her son, lost in a snowstorm in the forest. The message here, then, is that the lighting of the Sabbath candles is a stronger deed than any misdeeds she might have committed.

In both stories there is a clear Jewish women's message: "She who lights Sabbath candles receives a reward. You should do the same."

# 39

# *The* Shabbat *Candles*

 n Safed there once lived a poor family that had many children. The father was a *shohet* and, in addition to his wife, Leah, who was a woman of valor, there were his parents, who lived with them as well. All were humble and happy with their lot—and so they lived a quiet life.

One Friday Leah went out to buy the needs for *Shabbat*: flour for *hallot*, fish for the meal, wine, and other things, and when she returned, she began to prepare the finest foods for the Sabbath meal. The kitchen was filled with smells of *gefilte* fish, *tzimmes*, rich soup with noodles, *ruggelach*. Later she spread the table with a fine white cloth, on which there were two *hallot*, a bottle of wine, glasses for *kiddush*, and—Disaster of disasters! There were no candles! She had forgotten to buy them. But now the shops were closed. What could she do? How could it be that she and her elderly mother-in-law would not fulfill the commandment to light the candles for *Shabbat*?

Leah started to cry and to pray and to ask mercy from God, "*El Rahum Vehanun*," as one asks on Yom Kippur. "Help us. Help us. The holy Sabbath is approaching."

Suddenly she heard a strange voice from the street, calling loudly: "Candles! *Shabbat* candles for sale! Come and buy!"

Leah hurried outside and, behold! In the street stood an old Jew and in his hand was a suitcase; inside the suitcase were a few candles. "Hurry up, woman," he called. "There is no time to spare. Here, take the candles and light them. As for money, pay me next week. And may peace be upon Israel."

The peddlar hurried and put the candles in Leah's hands. She wanted to thank him—but, suddenly, he disappeared.

Only when she told the story to her husband and when the family saw that no one came to claim the money did they realize who the old man was: none other than Elijah the Prophet, may he be remembered for good.

"Ah," they sighed, "what a pity that we didn't know it was Elijah right away. Why, we could have asked him for a blessing for the children and all Israel."

# By Right of Observing the Sabbath and The Rabbi Who Would Not Mourn on Shabbat

## INTRODUCTION

My name in Hebrew is Beruriah, and so, as a child, I was repeatedly told of the bravery of the woman named Beruriah, heroine of a midrashic story (*Mishlei* 31), whose sons died on *Shabbat* but who refused to mourn on *Shabbat*. And so she kept the event hidden from her husband until after *Shabbat*. Then, upon showing him the bodies of their children, she told him, "The Lord has given and the Lord has taken, blessed be the name of the Lord" (Job 1:21).

Not mourning on *Shabbat* is one of the 613 commandments, but is it possible for a human being not to mourn the death of a child? Understandably, keeping this commandment is very difficult to do. The next two stories were created by their tellers to encourage keeping the *mitzvah* of not mourning on *Shabbat*; these stories clearly show that one who does keep the *mitzvah* is rewarded.

These two tales (both from Morocco) are obviously based on the midrashic story about Beruriah. In the midrashic story the sons do not return to life. But in folk versions, such as the ones we see here, the boys are revived; it is possible that the folk cannot accept the death of the children, and so they reward the brave parent by having the children brought back to life.

The first story was told by a woman; the second, by a man. In the woman's story, as in the postbiblical legend, the heroine is a woman; in the man's story, the hero is a man. In the woman's version, the death of the child is made even more poignant because of the couple's longing to have a child. Here they used the device of the dream question. This is based on a belief among many Jewish ethnic groups that one can ask a question of God and receive the answer in a dream. Also, in the woman's version, but not in the man's, many years were added to the child's life because of the virtue of the mother. What a wonderful message!

# 40

# *By Right of Observing the Sabbath*

In a certain city lived a rabbi and his wife who were childless. The wife was often very sad, and when her husband would ask the reason, she would answer, "This is the truth. My heart is sad because we have no children."

So the rabbi suggested, "Come, let us make a dream

question, a special prayer before we sleep, and perhaps we will receive our answer in the dream."

At this the wife grew happy, and, on the very same night, before they went to bed, they asked God to send them a son. God received the request and sent an answer: "Yes, you shall have a son."

And so, nine months later, a son was born, a child who was like the rays of the sun. He grew quickly, studied well, and had words of Torah on his lips.

Years passed, and it was time to prepare for his becoming a *bar mitzvah*. Every son in town took part in the event, and great was the joy in the home of the rabbi.

But one morning, on *Shabbat*, the mother went to wake her son, and found him dead.

What could she do? This was the Sabbath, and it is forbidden to mourn.

So the woman wrapped the body in a sheet, covered the bed, so as not to reveal anything, and said nothing to the rabbi. And when the rabbi asked, "Where is our son?" she answered, "Oh, perhaps he has gone to the synagogue or to Grandmother's house. He will soon return."

The rabbi said nothing, but there was no quiet in his heart. He went to the synagogue, but his son was not there. And after prayers, when he returned home, he again inquired, "Where is our son?"

"Oh, he was here, but he said that Grandmother has been feeling sad, and he decided to eat with her."

"What! How could you let him go? You know that I can't sit at the table without my son at my side!"

"Ah, but what could I do?" cried the wife. "This was his grandma's request. No matter, come and eat. Surely he will come soon." But the rabbi refused to eat until their son returned.

"Look," said his wife, "this is not a daughter who must be bound to the house. This is a son. Let him wander from home for one day."

And thus, on the Sabbath day, at noon, they finished their meal in the peace of the Sabbath.

Later the rabbi went back to synagogue for evening prayers.

Still his son was not there. So he returned home to make *Havdalah*. But as soon as the prayers for the close of *Shabbat* were finished, the wife led her husband into their son's room. Tears began to fall from her eyes.

She approached the bed and lifted the sheet. And, behold! Her son sat up in bed.

The rabbi was alarmed. "What happened here?" he cried.

Then it was that his wife told him how she had found their son dead, but that since she didn't want to disturb the Sabbath or to take the joy of *Shabbat* from the room, she had not revealed the secret.

The son also was alarmed. "I don't know what happened, Mother," he said. "I was far, far away from here when an angel came to me and said, 'Twenty more years have been given to you because your mother didn't desecrate the Sabbath.'"

And, then, great and complete was the family's joy!

# 41

# *The Rabbi Who Would Not Mourn on* Shabbat

 here once lived a rabbi who spent all his days sitting at prayer and study. Every day his wife would beg, "Go and work and bring home money. The children need food and clothing, and in this house there is nothing."

But the rabbi would answer, "God will help." And, daily, the rabbi went to synagogue to sit and study.

Once his wife said to him, "The children have no food. Take them with you to the synagogue, for I cannot bear to see them weep from hunger."

The rabbi was silent and gave no answer.

But again it happened on a Friday that there was not even a penny in the house with which to buy provisions for *Shabbat*.

The wife implored her husband, "Take the children with you to the synagogue today."

The rabbi had no choice. He took his two children, one, eight years of age and the other, ten. On the way to the synagogue stood a house, old and decrepit. And as the rabbi passed with his children, the front of the house suddenly collapsed. The children were buried beneath it; no breath of life was left in them. But the rabbi behaved as if nothing had happened. He went to the synagogue and returned home in the early evening in time for *Shabbat*.

"Where are the children?" his wife asked.

"With their aunt," answered the rabbi.

The next day, on *Shabbat* morning, the woman asked again, "Where are the children?"

"They are playing outside with their friends and won't return until nightfall," answered the rabbi.

Evening approached and the rabbi left his house to go to pray *Minchah* and *Maariv* in the synagogue. And behold! On his way he saw his two children, well and whole, playing beside the house that had collapsed! He went to pray as usual, and then returned home with his sons.

Curious, the mother asked the children, "Where were you all *Shabbat*?"

The children wanted to answer, but their father interrupted and told his wife all that had happened.

It was clear to all that the two sons had returned to life because their father had not wanted to mourn for them during *Shabbat*. By virtue of fulfilling that commandment, the rabbi had received a great reward.

# The Gifts of Elijah the Prophet— A Woman of Valor

## INTRODUCTION

This tale, told by a woman from Tunisia, is basically a story about Elijah, whose deeds in the tale bring about the message: A woman is the best gift of all. In another IFA version, the wife's virtue, rewarded by Elijah, is that she accepts a dirty, tired, hungry stranger (Elijah, of course!) and treats him with utmost respect and hospitality.

Here, in our story, the wife's virtue refers to the post-biblical legend about Beruriah, which served as the basis for the last two stories. So valued was this theme in the heart of the teller, Ora Prigon (as heard from her mother, Miriam), that she fused it into this Elijah story. And, so valued is the heroine of the story for keeping this *mitzvah* that she is called, in the title, a woman of valor. A higher honor cannot be given.

# 42

# *The Gifts of Elijah the Prophet— A Woman of Valor*

nce an old white-bearded man was seated in the shade of a large tree. He was none other than Elijah the Prophet, and, as he sat, he noticed three men coming across the field toward the tree. The men sat down to rest, and, as they did so, began to chat.

"Ah," said the first, "if only I were a rabbi, I would teach Torah to the poor children of our city. And I would become a *hazan* as well, so that our children could learn the melodies, the traditions, of our forefathers."

"If I were rich," continued the second, "I would feed the poor folk of our city without charge. Yes, I would open a restaurant, from which no poor person would be turned away."

"And I," piped in the third, "wish only to marry a woman of valor, an *eishet hayil*."

No sooner did the third man finish his words than the white-bearded stranger spoke up.

"What would happen if your wishes came true?" he asked. "Would you really fulfill your promises?"

Then each man gave assurance that he would indeed fulfill the promise he had expressed.

And so to the first man Elijah handed a book. "Here, take this book," he said. "From it you will gain great wisdom."

To the second man Elijah handed a rounded, shiny stone. "Take this stone," he said, "and from it you will gain riches."

To the third he said, "Upon you I bestow a blessing: May you find your future wife, a woman of valor!"

And so the three men separated, each going his own way in great joy. And each began to bring to fruition his own request.

The first began to study. He became a rabbi, led prayers in the synagogue, and learned the melodies of *hazanut* as well. Then he opened a great school to which he invited orphans, poor children, and anyone who wished to learn.

The second became wealthy, opened a restaurant to which all the poor of the city were welcome, and even gave coins to needy travelers to help them on their way.

The third had no sooner returned home when he found a beautiful girl waiting at his door. She told him that she was a relative and asked if he would marry her. And so, before much time had passed, the two were wed. And, although they had little money, they were the owners of a cow, which gave enough milk for them to sell and from which to earn a meager living.

Thus, several years passed. One day Elijah decided to visit the three men, to see how each had fulfilled his promise. And so he approached the school built by the first man. But by this time the man had tired of being a rabbi, of teaching young children and receiving no payment in return. And so, when Elijah, this time dressed as an ordinary man, arrived at the school, accompanied by a young child, the man drove him out. "What! Do you think of bringing me another student without tuition? Enough of this!" he cried.

At once the school disappeared, leaving a gigantic empty hole in its place. And, as Elijah and the small boy walked down the road, Elijah carried in his hand the book he had once given the first man as a gift.

Then Elijah approached the restaurant belonging to the second man. But by this time the man had tired of feeding the poor, of sharing his wealth with travelers and receiving no money in return. And so when the stranger approached, the restaurant owner was most unpleasant. "What! Do you think I can afford to feed a stranger?" he shouted.

And so Elijah left. At once the restaurant disappeared, leaving in its place an enormous gaping hole. And, as Elijah walked down the road, he held in his hand the shiny stone he had once given the second man as a gift.

Finally, Elijah arrived at the home of the third man. And when Elijah approached, he was welcomed most kindly. "Come in, weary traveler. Rest yourself, eat and drink with us." And then Elijah was invited to spend the Sabbath with the man, his wife, and their three sons. A new young calf was slaughtered in honor of the guest, and before the beginning of Sabbath, on Friday night, Elijah and the husband left for synagogue to pray.

While they were gone, the children played a game. Picking up the sharp knife used to slaughter the young calf, they played as if they too were about to kill a calf, and, while so doing, one child, by accident, slew his brother. Their mother, overcome by shock, by grief and great sadness, nevertheless realized that she must hide the boy before her guest returned, in order not to spoil the holy feeling of the Sabbath. And so the boy was placed under the bed.

The men returned. Elijah, of course, knew at once what had happened.

"Where is your other son?" he asked.

"Oh, he has gone to the neighbor. Surely he will return soon," the wife replied.

A short time later the guest asked again. "Where is your son? Surely we should wait for him to join us in our Sabbath meal."

"He is at his grandmother's. Often he visits her for Sabbath," was the reply.

And after the meal Elijah questioned, "Where is the boy? I wish to see him."

Again the wife made some excuse, but soon she could hide the truth no longer, and led her guest to the room where her son lay.

At once Elijah recited a very special prayer, and behold! Before the woman's eyes her son was returned to life! Her joy knew no end.

Then her husband understood his wife's *mitzvah.* "You are truly a woman of valor," he exclaimed. "And I am truly blessed to have you as my wife."

The stranger spent the Sabbath day with the family, and, at the close of Sabbath, rose to go. But before he left, he handed the couple two objects, a book and a rounded, shiny stone. And from these gifts they were able to obtain the wisdom and riches they needed for all the days of their lives.

## Grandmother's Last Shabbat

### INTRODUCTION

Often, in my storytelling travels, people say, "Those folktales were told in countries long ago. Do people tell stories these days, in the United States?" The answer is, "Yes! We tell stories all the time, in our families, in a *sukkah*, at *Pesah*, etc." And here is one such story, told to me in 1985 in Illinois by Yael Weinberger, of Laguna Beach, California, who heard the story from her aunt, Ruth Goldman.

The story tells of a courageous heroine (in this case, her own grandmother), who, like the grandmother in the midwife story, performs a great *mitzvah*. Here we see the message of the previous stories: The Sabbath must not be desecrated!

Also note that the storyteller builds up to the performance of the *mitzvah* by including details of grandmother's other good deeds as a Jewish woman. Why, even the president of Israel heard of her fame! As Ecclesiastes 7 tells us, "A good name is better than precious oil."

# 43

# *Grandmother's Last* Shabbat

**M**y grandmother, Haya, was a very proud woman and very jealous. She came from an Orthodox family but married a salesman, Mr. Gorich, who was not religious at all.

Since he traveled, he would, from time to time, visit other women as well. Grandmother, being proud and jealous, did not handle this too well, and, after some time, they were divorced. This all happened in Germany shortly before World War II.

Grandmother left Germany in 1939 with her daughter, my mother. Somehow she got to England, to London. There, after a few years, she married Mr. Hass, who had no less than seven children. He was very Orthodox.

Now, this new husband was very old, and he did not tell her that he was also very sick. Believe it or not, from the night of their wedding until the day he died, she nursed him.

From that time on Grandmother was extremely Orthodox in all her ways. She kept a kosher home for people who needed a meal for *Shabbat*. People came from all over to her *hatzeir*, to her courtyard.

Grandmother had high standards. If she felt that things were not done the way she wanted, she wouldn't let people come. Once the prime minister of Israel, Levi Eshkol, wanted to spend the *Shabbat* at her home, but she refused because she wasn't feeling well. Nothing could convince her to change her mind. Yet, Grandmother was known for her charity, her *mitzvot*, her warm house.

In 1968 Grandmother became ill. It was clear that she was not going to live much longer. It was the Sabbath, and Grandmother called her daughters, in turn, to her bedside. All the family was around her. And, as the day wore on, it became clear that Grandmother would not live through *Shabbat*.

"What time is it? What time is it?" she kept asking.

The doctor was astounded. "By all means this woman should be dead. Her body has no strength. How can she be hanging on?"

Toward afternoon Grandmother kept whispering, "When is *Havdalah*? When is *Havdalah*?"

Someone went to call the rabbi. The rabbi saw that Grandmother was suffering, that her life was hanging by a thread, that she continued to breathe only because she didn't want anyone to desecrate the *Sabbath*. So—he decided to do an unheard of thing. Even though *Shabbat* had not yet ended, he called for the *Havdalah* mirror. Then he went into her room and made *Havdalah*. And, as soon as his words were finished, my grandmother, Haya, died in peace.

# The Observance of the Sabbath
# and
# A Disloyal Woman Honors the Sabbath

## INTRODUCTION

Many stories are told to praise women who refuse to desecrate the Sabbath, despite the physical inconvenience of doing so. These two stories are such examples.

The first story was told by Miriam Kort from Afghanistan. I, myself, heard the story told at the *shivah* (period of mourning) of an Afghani woman in Holon, Israel. The purpose for telling the story was to glorify the piety of the dead woman, and to transmit, to the women listeners, the following message: This is the way Jewish women should behave.

The second story was told by Aliza Anidjar of Spanish Morocco. The message here is: Every woman, even a woman held in ill repute, keeps the *mitzvot* of the Sabbath. You should too.

# 44

# *The Observance of the Sabbath*

he Jewish women of Hurath are very pious and observe all the laws. Once, on the Sabbath day, a woman took her baby's cradle to the courtyard and placed it in the sun. When the afternoon passed, she wanted to return the cradle to its room, but the edge of her scarf had caught in the straw of the walls, which were plastered with a mixture of straw and asphalt. So the woman stood on the place, with the cradle on her back, until Sabbath was over, because of the possibility that the straw would be loosened from its place and that she might, God forbid, desecrate the Sabbath.

# 45

# *A Disloyal Woman Honors the Shabbat*

nce there was a woman who was disloyal to her husband. She worked as a prostitute, and since she owned her own house, it was there that she conducted her business.

Now, on Friday at noon, she would lock the door for *Shabbat* and would not open it for customers until Sunday.

One *Shabbat* morning someone knocked at her door. The woman went to the window to see who it was, and drew the curtain. A man stood near the window.

"I don't receive anyone until after *Shabbat*," she said. But, as she spoke, her fingernails got stuck in the curtain. If she moved her hand and tore the curtain, it would be as if she had done work on the Sabbath, and since she did not want to desecrate the Sabbath, she stood still, without moving her hand. Thus she stood all day until evening came and *Shabbat* was over.

It happened, after some time, that people did not see the woman for many days. So, being worried, they opened the door, and found the woman dead. The woman was buried, and on her grave grew a lot of grass, and to that very spot came many birds, both large and small. People went to the *dayan*, the judge of the city, and told him, "On this certain grave a large bird chased away the smaller ones. Someone special must be buried in that place. Who is it?"

"I don't know. I will go to see."

So the judge went to investigate, and was told by the woman's neighbors that she was a prostitute. But he was also told that the woman had a daughter, and he went to find her.

"All week long Mother didn't let me stay with her, for she didn't want me to see what she was doing," the daughter said, "but on Friday she would let me in."

"And why?" asked the *dayan*.

"Mother always said that *Shabbat* is the holiest day of the year, even holier than Yom Kippur and Pesah."

And then the daughter told him about that Sabbath day when her mother held her fingers in the curtain all day long.

# The Young Girl from Poland
## and
## the Baron de Rothschild

### INTRODUCTION

This tale was told in order to praise the good deeds of Baron Edmond de Rothschild. A descendant of a prominent European banking family, he himself gave generously to Jewish and Zionist causes during the late nineteenth and early twentieth centuries. His philanthropy is the subject of twenty legends in the IFA. In this story, the baron appears as a real-life Elijah, thus providing a realistic, rather than a supernatural, solution to the conflict of the tale. The generosity of the baron is intended, not for the girl alone, but for others as well, so that they may all live as proud Jews.

But, according to the woman teller, Esther Weinstein from Poland, the Jewish girl also becomes the heroine. Her determination to observe the *mitzvah* of keeping the Sabbath, even at the cost of losing her livelihood, is rewarded.

# 46

# *The Young Girl from Poland and the Baron de Rothschild*

aron de Rothschild, the famous philanthropist, used to live in France. And there he was known for his many good deeds.

Once a young Jewish girl came to Paris from Poland. Her parents had remained in Poland, and she herself began to work as a seamstress in a factory that manufactured clothing. She was most satisfied with her work, as was her employer, a Jew.

But one day the factory was sold to a Christian. All the workers remained in their jobs but were ordered to work all the days of the week except Sunday. Up to the time of the selling of the factory none of the workers worked on *Shabbat*.

The employees agreed to the new conditions, except for the new girl, who did not come to work on Saturdays. One day the new boss sent for her. "If you do not agree to work on Saturday, there is no work for you here. Consider yourself fired."

Bitter was the situation of the young girl. How was her soul to continue? The amount of money left to her was very small.

The girl thought and thought until she found a solution. She wrote a letter to Baron de Rothschild, the philanthropist, and in it related all of her story. With the letter in hand, she waited on the street where the baron, in his horse-drawn carriage, was to pass with his family.

And when she saw the carriage approaching, she stood in the middle of the road, requesting to deliver her letter to the baron himself.

The carriage stopped. The baron took the letter and asked her to remain for a moment, awaiting his reply. He read what she had written, pressed a small sum into her hand as a loan, and promised to take care of the matter. And so the young girl returned home, while the baron and his family continued on their way.

A short time later, what did the girl receive but an invitation to appear at the home of the baron! Great joy filled her heart, and she dressed herself nicely and went to the baron's house.

There the baron greeted her with great respect. "I have purchased the factory where you work," he told her. "Return, and from this moment on, you shall be its supervisor. And, from this moment on, neither you nor your employees shall work on *Shabbat*."

On the very next morning a clerk arrived at the girl's home, and delivered into her own hand the keys of the new factory of Baron de Rothschild.

From then on the girl directed the work at the factory, and everyone was happy with her decisions.

And on Saturdays the work ceased.

## *The Taste of the Sabbath Meal*

### INTRODUCTION

Stories in which the "flavor" or taste of the Sabbath is known only to Jews stem from a talmudic legend

(*Shabbat* 119a), in which the Emperor complains to Rabbi Joshua ben Hanania about the taste of the food. The latter answers, "We have a certain seasoning called the Sabbath, which we put into it, and that gives it a fragrant odor." A similar story is found in *Bereishit Rabbah* 11:14.

The idea that Sabbath comes in the form of a bride, or queen, comes from the sixteenth-century mystics of Safed. Dressed in white, they would go outside the town on Sabbath eve to welcome the Sabbath bride with prayer and song. This led to the custom of *Kabbalat Shabbat*, turning to the west to welcome the spirit of Sabbath.

This folk version was told by Ziporah Rabin from her memories in White Russia.

# 47

# *The Taste of the Sabbath Meal*

In a certain village lived a Jew named Mushke, and on a farm near the village lived the lord himself. Mushke and the lord were friends and did business together.

Once Mushke invited the lord to a meal on Sabbath eve. The house was alight with candles, burning in silver holders in the middle of the table, upon which was spread a fine white cloth. Over everything hovered the spirit of the "Sabbath Queen." Around the table sat the family and their honored guest. The Sabbath food was served: *gefilte* fish, chicken soup, and noodles; after that, a plate filled with chicken, *kugel*, and other good things. All were joyous as they sang the Sabbath songs.

After the meal the guest said, "I thank you for the great pleasure. Never have I eaten such tasty food! I, therefore, ask your permission to send you my cook, so that you can teach him to prepare the dishes that I ate here tonight."

And so it happened! The very next day the cook came and learned what he could. But when he returned to his home and served the meal to the lord, the latter tasted the food and screamed, "You didn't learn correctly!" In great anger he went to Mushke with the complaint that the Jew had fooled him! "The food that my cook served didn't have the taste of the Sabbath meal."

And Mushke answered quietly, "My dear lord, ingredients and cooking alone cannot make a Sabbath meal. The taste of the food depends as well on the spirit of the Sabbath Queen, who accompanies the people of Israel in all their wanderings."

# The Year Cycle: Hanukkah

Hanukkah is the festival of religious freedom, recounting the heroism of the Maccabees against the overpowering army of Antiochus in 164 B.C. It is not surprising that, for women, the festival is imbued with stories of heroic Jewesses, who, according to history, stand out as prototypes, models, because of their bravery. Indeed, stories told at Hanukkah have more female acting characters than do stories of any other festival.

The first of these heroines is the daughter of Mattathias, sister of the Maccabees, who in some texts is given the name Hannah. History tells us that the Greek rulers, seeing they could not win over the people, passed an ugly law: Every Jewish bride, on the first night of marriage, was to be sent to the local ruler, with whom she was to spend the bridal night. The sources tell us that for three years and three months the Jews felt helpless against this decree but that, on the night of her marriage, the daughter of Mattathias rose, ripped off her robes, and stood naked before the crowd. Her brothers, ashamed and appalled, wanted to slay her for this dishonor, whereupon she exclaimed, "Do you not feel shame for a daughter of Israel? Why do you not act like the brothers of Dina?" (See story no. 16.) Upon these words, her brothers held council and decided to kill the Greek who would defile their sister. Thus, according to this women's version, the rebellion of the Maccabees began! Here we see, in story, the inflammatory power of a woman's words!

The second heroine is Judith, a young Jewish widow, whose brave deeds are recounted in the apocryphal Book of Judith. The story tells how Judith, reminiscent of Yael (Judges 4:17–21), seduces the enemy, the Assyrian general Holofernes, weakens him with drink, and bravely beheads him. Thereupon, the enemy retreats, and the women rejoice in a psalm before God.

Judith's brave actions have so captured the folk imagination and are so strongly associated with Hanukkah, the holiday of bravery, that she is depicted on many *hanukkiot*

175

(special Hanukkah candelabras) in many parts of the Jewish world. So too does her bravery act as a model for folktales told by women during Hanukkah.

The third Hanukkah heroine is a mother of seven sons, who lived at the time of Antiochus, and who was willing to see her children sacrifice themselves rather than have them bow down to the god of the non-Jewish king. Her story is found in the Book of Maccabees II, chapter 7, as "Seven Brethren with Their Mother." Her name, in later tradition, became Hannah, and that story became known as "Hannah and Her Seven Sons." The story of her bravery is told at this time of the year.

In legends where the sanctification of God's name (*kiddush hashem*) is carried out, not by an individual, but by an entire family, the woman (daughter, wife, or sister) plays the dominant role.

For this reason the story is associated with Hanukkah.

# The Cossacks and The Brides

## Introduction

Here we have an insight into two tales, based on the story of Judith and Holofernes, from two communities which could not be more different from each other.

The first tale, "The Cossacks," IFA 1935, was told by David Ha-Cohen, originally from Russia and one of Israel's greatest storytellers. The tale refers to the period in Russian Jewish history (seventeenth century) when the cruel Chmelnitski marched with his Cossack armies, ruthlessly murdering one hundred thousand Jews, and destroying three hundred communities.

The story has been turned into an etiological tale, that is, a tale explaining the name of a river in Russia. But its similarity to the apocryphal Judith is unmistakable — although, in the apocryphal version, Judith does not die.

The second tale, "The Brides," gives us insight into the history of Ethiopian Jewry and into the storytelling of Ethiopian women. It is one of the latest tales in the IFA, number 14687. The story is not usually known to women outside of Ethiopia, yet it contains many similarities to Jewish women's folktales told in other communities. The story reflects a historical event in the annals of the Ethiopian Jewish community: Zar'a Yaqob was a Christian king who, during his reign between 1434 and 1468, exterminated *Beta Israel*, the House of Israel.

Women told this tale during the week of menstruation or following the birth of a child. At such times they were isolated in the company of other "unclean" women in huts set aside for this purpose (as prescribed in Leviticus 15). What better time than this for telling women's stories!

Usually, fighting is an affair between men, but in this tale we see a different kind of fight. Here we see the message that *kiddush hashem*, dying for the sanctification of God's name rather than being defiled by a non-Jew, is a powerful Jewish female weapon. We see that a Jewish woman has a choice of living in a non-Jewish manner or dying proudly as a Jewess.

In both tales women do not die as victims. Instead, they cause the death of their enemies.

177

# 48

# *The Cossacks*

n the days when the murderer Chmelnitski, may his bones be ground to powder, sent his Cossack army to raid the forests and villages of the Ukraine, when they destroyed Jewish communities by fire and slaughtered Jews with swords, there came to a faraway and isolated town a group of such Cossacks to rest. Tired of robbing, tired of killing, they swore peace to the townsfolk, and so the Jews fed the soldiers and cared for their horses as well.

Now, one such Cossack soldier fell in love with the rabbi's daughter, a girl of great beauty—perfection herself—who was already betrothed to another groom.

But the Cossack repeatedly approached her—to no avail. And so, when the Cossack saw that he could not win her in a pleasant way, he threatened to burn the entire town and to slaughter the Jews, the first of whom would be her father, the rabbi.

There and then the faces of the Cossacks changed. Rumors spread amongst the Jews that great evil was about to befall them, these rumors being fostered by the Cossack himself, who burned with love for the young girl.

Now, when this pure virgin saw the danger that would befall the town because of her, she remembered the deed of Judith against Holofernes, and she decided to do the same.

And so, when, one summer night, the Cossack again approached her, she turned to him smilingly. "Wait for me at midnight on the mountain near the town and I will come to you," she said.

So the Cossack awaited her, his passion burning, and as she approached, he opened both arms to embrace her. Then the girl reached under her dress, drew forth a double-edged knife, and plunged it firmly into the breast of the soldier. The girl approached the river, slowly, slowly letting herself into it. There she drowned.

In the morning the Jews found the body of the dead Cossack, hid him, and buried him on top of the mountain.

Some days later the river brought up the body of the rabbi's daughter, who was then buried according to Jewish custom.

And unto this very day, the mountain where this event took place is called "Cossack."

This legend is an etiological tale, explaining the name of the mountain near the village of Vahlini on the banks of the river Styr.

# 49

# *The Brides*

 n the days of the emperor Zar'a Yaqob there was a bitter war against *Beta Israel*. The king's soldiers killed many, many Jews in the mountains of Semien, and finally only the women were left.

The women had no weapons. What could they do?

They wove for themselves a large basket—that was indeed so huge that many people could fit inside—and tied it to a rock just above the edge of a cliff. Then they climbed inside the basket, and when the soldiers of Zar'a Yaqob approached, they called, "Come take us. We will be your brides!"

The soldiers quickly, gleefully climbed into the basket, expecting to take the women. But then, suddenly, one woman drew forth a knife and cut the rope that held the basket. And the basket plunged down—down—down the cliff—with the women and the soldiers still inside it.

## I Don't Kneel

### INTRODUCTION

When I was a little girl of about seven, my mother, then a teacher at the Bais Yaakov School in the East Bronx (in New York), would take me to the school's festival celebrations: the Purim contest, the Pesah *seder*, and so forth, but the most lasting impression, which has remained with me until this day, was the Hanukkah play, put on by the children of the school, of "Hannah and her Seven Sons." This was my first introduction to the idea of *kiddush hashem*, dying for the holy name of God. I remember being frightened by the cruelty of the story and by the nagging possibility that such a fate might await me. On the other hand, I was absolutely struck with admiration for the mother and her brave children who preferred to die rather than bow down to a pagan god.

The following story is based on the feeling, among Jews, that bowing or kneeling is equivalent to accepting another god (as in the story of Hannah). Dying for God's holy name rather than accepting another god is one of the three reasons, in Judaism, for which one is permitted to die, and this concept has been inserted by the folk into their tales in almost every location in which Jews have lived. Unfortunately, these cruel edicts have been a sad reality in many parts of the Diaspora.

The tale I share with you here, one of the most poignant I have ever collected, is a tale of *kiddush hashem* in Auschwitz. It was told to me by Tillie Farkash, originally from Transylvania and now a resident of Jerusalem, who survived several concentration camps during World War II.

One night, after sharing this story by reading it aloud at the home of a friend in Jerusalem, I was told by another guest, a woman sitting next to me, Rose Bilbul, that she heard the same story from her sister, Gisella Pearl, a former inmate at Auschwitz; Rose then related the story to me. The very next morning, another guest at the gathering phoned to say that, after hearing my reading of the story, he related it that very same evening to his wife and child. The fact that the story was told by at least several women and then transmitted to others attests to both the power of the incident and the power of the tellers.

# 50

# *I Don't Kneel*

 was nineteen when we were taken to Auschwitz. On that first day I wanted to go with my mother, but the Germans gave me a blow, and I couldn't follow her. I know that she was killed on that first day. And my father, too, with my brother beside him. We were nine children. So many died there, so many. Also in Bergen Belsen.

In every place there were stories. At Auschwitz there were so many stories.

We were kept in the *Richtenslager*, one thousand women in one barrack. We had no beds—just the floor to sleep on, with a pile of stones dividing the barrack like a long table.

Every morning we were called outside for roll call—to see if anyone was missing, if anyone had tried to escape to—where could they go? We had to stand outside between the barracks in rows of five—five, five, five. We had no coats, no warm clothing, nothing—and we had to stand outside in the cold rain or the snow. It was forbidden to move from the row.

Mengele would come—or Grayze. Did you ever hear of Grayze? She was a type like Mengele, but a woman, a German—in charge of the *lager*. She was very beautiful, very elegant, dressed in the uniform of the Germans—and when Mengele didn't come, Grayze would come.

Everyone feared her like—I don't know what!—even more than we feared Mengele. She was very cruel, and she always came with two big dogs. Every morning we stood in the rows, outside, while she watched as the rows were counted.

But one morning it was discovered that two girls were missing from the camp—two girls—and we were ordered to fall on our knees and to wait until the camp was searched. We fell on our knees.

But one girl, a woman of 30, the daughter of the rabbi of Budapest, refused to kneel. She was standing on the end of her row, and she just refused to kneel. "I am a Jew," she cried out. "I don't kneel to anyone." In Yiddish she cried (we all knew Yiddish), *"Ich bin a Yood. Ich k'nee nisht. Ich bin a Yood."*

So Grayze ordered the dogs to devour her, and the guards to beat her. And they tore her apart in front of our eyes. And the girl cried one thousand times, *"Ich bin a Yood"* until she died.

I didn't know her name. How could I know it? We were one thousand girls in one long barrack, and we called each other by first names. There were so many with the same name—Leahs and Rachels and Miriams. No, I didn't know her name. But I know she was the daughter of the rabbi of Budapest, and she refused to kneel, and she cried out, *"Ich bin a Yood"* ("I am a Jew"), a thousand times until she died.

# A Hanukkah Guest

## Introduction

This story was told to Ilana Cohen Zohar by her mother, Flora Cohen, originally from Egypt, who was a prolific and captivating storyteller in Israel and with whom I had the privilege of sharing many storytelling evenings. The story is similar to "Two Women Washing on Passover," for which the model is the pious and humble wife of Rabbi Hanina ben Dosa, whose humility and piety are rewarded. However, in this tale the woman has seven children, reminiscent of Hannah and her seven sons, whose story is told on Hanukkah. Also note the triple miracle, befitting a Hanukkah tale, at the end of the story: Money that does not get used up; pancake batter that does not run out; and a small jar of oil that lasts for eight days (à la the Maccabees).

The woman's message, then, is that honoring guests is a *mitzvah* that even the poorest woman must do and for which she will be rewarded. The tale has a similarity to the story of Elijah and the widow (1 Kings 17:16); in both tales the widows are recipients of miracles; in our IFA tale the hidden hero, although not mentioned by name, is none other than Elijah.

# 51

# *A Hanukkah Guest*

here once was a widow with seven children. On the eve of Hanukkah, the children begged, "Mother, the holiday is approaching and you haven't made pancakes. Won't you make us some this year?"

The mother's heart ached that her orphaned children should have no pancakes, for there was no money in the house—but how could she tell them the truth? "Very well," she said, "I am going to the river to rinse the pots and bring the flour for pancakes."

And so the widow went to the river, racking her brains all the way: "Where can I find the money? I promised the children that I would buy them flour for pancakes." Lost in thought, she suddenly saw an old man standing beside her. The man addressed the widow: "Peace to you, good woman. I am a stranger in this region and I wish to celebrate the holiday here. Would it be possible for you to take me in?"

The woman answered, "Gladly. Our home is ready for a guest."

Suddenly the old man disappeared and the woman could see him no longer. She began to grieve in her heart: "How could I have promised the man that he could celebrate the holiday with us, when we have nothing in the house?" Thus, she worried all the way until she reached her home.

There she saw her seven children, standing in the doorway, shouting with joy, "Mother, Mother! An old man came by and gave us Hanukkah money. He also asked me to tell you to take this oil and use it for the Hanukkah lights. And he gave us a big bag of flour for pancakes."

The widow rejoiced. She took the money and said, "The month of *Kislev* is the month of miracles. The Lord has performed a miracle for me so that I could prepare holiday treats for you."

They spent the holiday happily. Although they bought many, many things, the money did not run out. And although they made many pancakes, the batter was not used up. And the little jar of oil was enough to keep the candles lit for a full eight days.

# The Sabbath of Divorces

## INTRODUCTION

This story was narrated by Simha Shamaka, who heard it from her mother, Idriya, in Mesilata (Husbat), Libya, where the event took place.

The narrator commented, "My mother used to tell me this story on Friday, on the eve of *Shabbat Hanukkah*. She would say 'Hurry and finish what you have to finish; otherwise the *Shabbat* will become Divorce *Shabbat*.' When I heard her say this for the first time, I wondered and asked, 'But I am not yet married. How can I be divorced?' Then she answered, 'It can happen when you grow up,' and she told me this story. Since then she repeated it many times."

The story has an important covert Jewish message: the pancake (*levivah* in Hebrew) is prepared from grated potatoes for Hanukkah. The Hebrew *levivah* is of the same root as *lev* — heart, and so the Hanukkah pancake is often heart-shaped. Thus, the women's *intention* to fry pancakes for their husbands (upon their return from the synagogue) has a sexual connotation, especially when it is *Shabbat* night (prescribed for conjugal sex), and this night occurs at Hanukkah, which is full of sexual symbols and, as we have already seen, has more female heroic and rebelling characters than any other Jewish festival. From a woman's viewpoint, the reactions of the men are tragic and the intentions of their wives are misunderstood.

In this story we see that it is the woman's duty to serve her husband and that her fate is determined by masculine whim. Remember that the Libyan Jews were influenced by Moslem culture, in which a man could repeat three times, "You are divorced" — and the deed was done! Women telling this story might be reflecting their husbands' wishes to do the same, but in actuality the Jewish divorce is a long and complicated procedure.

The story begins with the women trying to capture the sun in a pail. This is akin to the famous Helm story, wherein the "clever" Helmites try to capture the moon so that it can serve the community of Helm for the monthly blessing of the moon on a cloudy night.

# 52

# *The Sabbath of Divorces*

ne day, the day before the Hanukkah Sabbath, the women of Kusbath decided to gather for drinking tea, eating *levivot*, and exchanging gossip. Still they began to worry that maybe there wouldn't be enough time to prepare for Sabbath. They didn't know what to do. Finally, one said, "Let us capture the sun in a pail of water, and in the evening we will take the cover off. In that way the sun will continue to shine, and we will be able to prepare for Sabbath properly."

The women of Kusbath were very happy with the wise advice and quickly captured the sun in a pail. Then they closed it securely with rags, tied it with ropes, and sat down to spend their time in pleasure.

As the day wore on into evening, the women hurried to remove the sun from their pail. Alas! The pail was full of water, but there was no sun to be found. Meanwhile, the day grew on, and the men began to return from synagogue. Everything was covered in darkness.

The men became angry. "Where are the candles? Where are the *hallot*? Where is the wine for *kiddush*?"

The women answered, "We wanted to spend the day drinking tea and eating *levivot*; therefore, we captured the sun in a pail, so that when we finished relaxing, we would be able to prepare for Sabbath by sunlight. But, alas, when we opened the pail, we saw that the sun had fled!"

On the day after that Sabbath, all the men of Kusbath divorced their wives!

And from the time of that story on, which took place before the Hanukkah Sabbath, the Sabbath before Hanukkah is called instead the "Sabbath of Divorces."

# The Year Cycle: Passover (Pesah)

When I was a little girl, Passover (Pesah) was always my favorite holiday. The hustle and bustle of preparations for the holiday, the making of *haroset* (which was my job), the beauty of the *seder* itself, the special melodies sung by the whole family, the finding of the *afikoman*, were things I waited for all year long. But not until I grew much older did I realize that this festival, so special to me, required so many special needs, and how much work the holiday was for mother.

Pesah, indeed, is one of the most difficult holidays to keep. From a halachic point of view, the entire house must be rid of *hametz*, and new clothing must be purchased—for it is forbidden to wear old clothing, lest a piece of *hametz* might be stuck to it. For Jews in many parts of the world the economic difficulties of buying new clothing and necessities for the *seder* were, and still are, a reality. (Not everyone can go to Waldbaum's—or another local supermarket—to buy *matzah*.) And so, the economic difficulties at Pesah time are the subject of many folktales in many countries. In these tales the woman is often the heroine, rescuing the economic situation via her piety or cleverness. These tales are told by women.

Other types of stories are told at Pesah as well. A small number are historical tales about the biblical story of Moses, Pharaoh, and the parting of the Red Sea. Others are tales of blood libel, in which Jews were accused of killing a non-Jewish child in order to obtain his blood for use during the Passover festival. Blood libel accusations were a sad reality in both the Christian and Moslem worlds, and often they ended in severe punishment of the Jewish community. But in the tales the Jew was always found innocent. Neither the historical tales nor those about blood libel are about women, nor are they told by them.

# Two Washerwomen on Pesah Eve

## INTRODUCTION

This religious tale was related by two sisters, Jenny and Shoshana Elmaleh, from the city of Tunis. The story is from the type called "Let it be as you say" and is one of the most popular Passover tales in the IFA collection (over twenty versions), told almost entirely by women. Two Ashkenazi versions in which Elijah gives help at Passover are 2965 and 3016.

In this story we see women as keepers of the Passover festival, and the responsibility they have both for themselves and their families at this time of year. The story is simple in structure, and the Jewish female message is clear: Women who are pious, humble, and who adhere to the *mitzvot* of the festival are rewarded; jealousy, greed, and lying are punished. These traits of constant faith in God and hiding one's poverty are based on the actions of the wife of Hanina ben Dosa, a postbiblical sage, and they have become a model of behavior for all Jewish women.

Elijah the Prophet, who solves the conflict in this tale, is the most popular hero in Jewish folk legends; he appears in hundreds of tales from every corner of the globe in which Jews have lived. Elijah is a miracle worker, sent by God to do His will. Elijah knows who is stingy or greedy. He also knows who truly believes in God. He rewards those who are pious and humble and in financial need, so that they may raise a Jewish child or celebrate the Sabbath or other festivals.

Since many customs of the Passover celebration involve Elijah (we open the door for him, fill a cup of wine for him, sing a song for him), it is only natural that stories of Passover include Elijah as the one who solves the tale's conflicts. In some tales from Jewish communities where Jewish children were kidnapped or killed by cruel rulers at Passover time, Elijah becomes aggressive and murders the enemies of his people.

By now you may be asking, "If Elijah is the one who solves the conflict, isn't this a man's tale?" The answer is "No!" In Jewish folk tradition Elijah is not considered to be a male in the sexual sense. According to the Bible, he never married, and so, in matters of family life, he is a neutral figure.

As in the story of the Sabbath *hallot* (no. 38), this tale is about the conflict between good and evil, and the potential for both good and evil within each one of us.


# 53

# *Two Washerwomen on Pesah Eve*

 here once lived a woman who didn't have money with which to celebrate Pesah. She could not prepare her house for the holiday.

The day before Pesah arrived, the poor woman had ten children, and in her house there was nothing. The woman decided to go to the river and wash her children's clothes, for there was no money with which to buy new ones, and on Pesah it is forbidden to wear dirty clothes. Perhaps a piece of *hametz* might be stuck to them.

While she was washing, an old man approached. "What are you doing, my daughter?" he asked.

"I am washing my children's clothes," she said.

"And is your house clean for the holiday?"

"Yes," answered the woman.

"May this be His will," said the old man. "And do you have a sheep for the holiday?" he continued.

"Yes."

"May this be His will," the old man said again.

Afterward, the old man gave the woman money with which to buy the needs for the holiday. The woman went home, and what did she see? A sheep tied to the side of the house, the house clean and in order, and the closet, that had been empty, filled with clothes!

Now, this woman had a rich neighbor who had a sheep tied with a rope, and who was able to buy clothes for her children and to prepare her house for the holiday. When the rich neighbor saw the sudden riches of the poor one, she was jealous. "Where did all this come from?" she asked. The woman told her story: "At the edge of the river, while I was doing my wash, an old man came to me and blessed me."

And what did the rich woman do? She found old torn clothes and ran with them to the river, as if to wash them. The old man came to her. "What are you washing, my daughter?" he asked.

"My poor children's clothing," answered the woman with a cry.

"Is your home already clean for the holiday?"

"No, may this be His will," the woman cried.

"And do you have new clothes for the holiday?"

"No, may this be His will!"

The woman went home. And, behold! All the riches and goods that she had in her house were gone.

It is understood that the old man was none other than Elijah the Prophet, of blessed memory. His actions came to teach us that he who thanks God is given wealth by Him; however, if one is not satisfied with his lot and wants even more, God takes away from him even what he has, and he loses all.

## *The Passover Dress*

### INTRODUCTION

I was told this story by Judith Zuckerman Kaufman of Wisconsin at the Conference on Alternative Jewish Education (CAJE), in De Kalb, Illinois, in the summer of 1985. She, in turn, heard it from her mother-in-law, Nehama Granzitsky, who told it at a family reunion for the holiday.

Before telling me the story, Judith pointed out the importance of her mother-in-law's stories in their family's tradition, these stories being a Jewish educational link between the old world (Europe) and the new (America).

Here again we see the importance of new clothing on Passover. In this tale, however, there is no miracle from Heaven. But reward for honesty does come, via the intervention of a woman, even if she is the mother of a thief — for, as we see here, even among thieves there is a code of honor.

The storyteller points out the importance of the good ethical reputation of the heroine's father. This refers to Proverbs 22:1: "A good name is rather to be chosen than riches."


# 54

# *The Passover Dress*

y mother-in-law, Nehama, came from a little town called Myshagal, not far from Vilna in Lithuania. It was a small village of, perhaps, a few hundred people, perhaps more.

When she was twelve years old, Nehama owned two dresses, one for every day and one for *Shabbat*. Her grandmother, whom she loved very much, would buy her a new dress for Rosh Hashanah and another for Pesah. How she looked forward to the holidays and her new dress!

But one year her grandmother died, and Nehama knew that that year there would be no new dress for Pesah. But as the days of the holiday approached, as she walked in the tiny square at the center of the village, why, there she found a purse lying on the ground. Here was the money for her new Pesah dress! In great excitement she raced home.

"Look! Look what I found!" she burst out as she entered the house.

Now, Nehama's father was a wood turner, greatly respected by Jew and Gentile alike. His workmanship was of the topmost quality, and he was known for miles around as an ethical businessman as well.

"Nehama-le," he answered, as his daughter entered, "we cannot keep this purse. The true owner will be looking for it."

And so her father put out word that a certain purse had been found, and that whoever could describe it could come to claim it.

Nehama hoped and hoped with all her heart that no one would come forward, and as the days of the holiday grew nearer, no one came. Perhaps she would have her new dress after all!

But then, just before Pesah, the owner appeared. And who was it? Of all people, none other than the mother of the town's chief crook, leader of the *ganovim*, the thieves of Myshagal.

Nehama had to return the purse. There was no new dress for Pesah.

Not long afterward fighting broke out. World War I had started, and the people of the village had to evacuate to Vilna, where they would be safer. And there they remained for some time.

But when they returned and entered their houses, they found that every house, every house in Myshagal, had been looted.

Only Nehama's house was intact, just as she had left it. And why? The head of the crooks had watched over this house and had seen to it that, from this family, nothing was taken.

# The Year Cycle: Purim

The story of Purim, the joyous festival which celebrates the miracle of the Jews being saved from their oppressors in Persia, is the story of an assertive and self-sacrificing Jewess, Esther by name, whose actions brought about the rescue of her people; in other words, her assertiveness was "good for the Jews." Here we have an "out-of-the-mode," self-acting woman who, unlike Lilith, becomes a positive, to-be-admired heroine in Jewish legend. Indeed, as the story of Purim is traditionally read each year from the biblical Book of Esther (*Megillat Esther*), women identify with her. Also the many *midrashim* (*Esther Rabbah*) give women an outlet for telling the story from many points of view.

It would seem natural, then, that other tales would be created in which a strong, brave Jewess saves her people or improves their lot. Two such (recent) IFA tales are numbers 17168 from Poland and 17463 from Tripoli. In both stories the heroine is named Esther. Coincidence? I would suspect not.

Both stories were told to the IFA by men, but it is possible that, because Purim is a holiday with which women identify so strongly and because, for women, it is a time to tell stories of strong women, the tales were originally created by women.

Throughout Jewish history, when Jews, in plights born of edicts and harsh decrees, were miraculously saved, stories would arise about these miraculous rescues; such stories are called "Second Purim" or "Small Purim" stories, and they are traditionally told on the anniversary of the date on which that particular rescue occurred. Hundreds of such tales exist from many places in the Jewish world. (My good friend, Eli Marcus, whose doctoral thesis at the Hebrew University involved tales of Jewish–non-Jewish relationships in folktales of Moslem lands, has over one hundred twenty such tales in his possession; one-fourth of these come from Italy.) "Second Purim" stories are based on the structure of the Esther story: a Jewish community saved at the last moment. But since the stories are based on historic happenings, they rarely include a Jewish heroine, nor are they necessarily told by women. One exception is the story of Goar of Meshed (Mashad in Persian), who did rescue her people during the late nineteenth century in that community. Another is about a Jewess on the island of Rhodes who likewise saved the Jewish community, during a war between Turkey and France. These may be found, respectively, in Raphael Patai's comprehensive works on the Jews of Meshed and in the doctoral dissertation of Eliezer Marcus on folktales of Jews in Islamic countries.

IV

THE WOMAN IS
CLEVER,
LOYAL, AND
STRONG

# The Woman Is Clever,
# Loyal, and Strong

This *potpourri* of tales makes clear the messages that women are clever, loyal, and strong, both spiritually, via their faith, and physically, via their perseverance, and that these attributes give women control over the world of men. And how are these messages made so vivid?

The women in these tales are those falsely accused of adultery or those over whom the male world, in some other way, has a sometimes frightening hold. But the solutions to these tales show these women to be "super loyal," "super clever," and "super strong." *Their* wisdom leads to richness and wealth. *Their* magic powers, or piety, can save the welfare of a family. *Their* faithfulness, despite the suffering caused by unfounded accusations of adultery, leads to power over the world of men.

Thus, often fortified by biblical passages, these tales express strong Jewish messages, strong female messages, and strong fulfillment of women's wishes often suppressed.

# Love Like Salt

## INTRODUCTION

For thousands of years salt has played an important part in Jewish life. As the Bible tells us: "It is an everlasting covenant of salt before the Lord unto thee" (Numbers 18:19). In biblical tradition the newborn was rubbed with salt before swaddling (Ezekiel 16:4).

Because it doesn't spoil, salt is a symbol of the eternal, the everlasting. For this reason, among Oriental peoples, salt was used to ratify agreements. And, perhaps, it is for this reason that my mother-in-law, upon entering my first home when I was a newly-married bride, tossed salt (and pennies for *parnasah*) into the closets. The Friday night custom among some Jews is to sprinkle salt on the *hallah* before eating it. This signifies that love (for which *hallah* is a symbol, especially on Friday night, prescribed for conjugal sex) is eternal.

And salt has always been valued as a seasoning for food. I absolutely love the ending of this tale, comparing life without Torah as being tasteless, without *tam*, to life without salt, life without taste. What a beautiful bit of Jewish folk wisdom! This ending comes from an IFA version, told to Rivka Kaspo by Bluma Rodinick of Romania. The ending would be more logical and even more poignant were it part of the following plot:

1. A father refuses to let his daughter study Torah.

2. The daughter teaches her father the lesson of food being tasteless without salt.

3. The girl associates life without Torah to be equivalent to life without salt.

4. The father realizes his daughter's wisdom and allows her to study.

This particular folktale is thought to be the basis for Shakespeare's *King Lear*, in which the king asks his daughters, "Who loves me the most?" The truth, as in our story, lies in the answer of the third daughter. In folktales it is usually the third child who is the hero or heroine.

This IFA version, told to Sarah Haimovitz by her mother, Esther Rochfeld of Poland, is structurally one of the simplest versions in the IFA. Usually the daughter is expelled from the house. Thereafter, she is either married to a poor man or simpleton, or wanders until she finally marries a king. Her father, unaware of his daughter's new identity, is then invited for dinner, which she herself cooks without salt. The father learns his lesson and the two are reunited.

In one of the tale's subtypes, the girl is expelled because she says that woman is more important than man. She then proves this to her father, as does the woman in the *cherchez la femme* story, no. 56, in this book.

Written versions are found in Gaster and in Cahan, where all variants (told in Yiddish) were told by women. Thirty-six versions, including subtypes, are found in the IFA; most were told by women.

# 55

# *Love Like Salt*

 king had three successful daughters whom he loved very much. But the youngest, who was the most clever and most talented of the three, the king loved most of all. Is it a wonder, then, that such love awakened the jealousy of the sisters? They sought every opportunity to take revenge against the youngest sister. Their opportunity came one day when the king asked the three daughters this question, "Tell me, my daughters, how much do you love me?"

The oldest said, "Father, I love you like the brightest diamond."

The second answered, "Father, I love you like a necklace of pearls."

The third said, "Father, I love you like salt."

The king grew pale. How could his daughter answer that she loved him like common worthless salt? And the two older daughters seized the opportunity and began to incite their father against the youngest daughter. The king ordered her thrown in prison.

When this became known to the queen, she ran to the prison and asked her daughter why she had spoken such nonsense.

"No, Mother," answered the girl, "this is not nonsense at all." And she asked the mother to convince the king to hold a big feast and to invite the most respected guests and dignitaries in the city to come to partake of delicious foods. And then she instructed her mother to tell the chef to cook all the food without salt, and then to serve it on a long table and to see what would happen. The queen did as her daughter asked. When the food came before the guests, they dipped in their spoons, just once out of politeness, and ate no more.

The king was furious and called the chief chef. "Is this how you cook for the king? Do you know what fate awaits you?"

"Yes, my lord, the king," answered the chief chef, "but I am not guilty. The queen gave me strict instructions on how to prepare the food, and I followed her instructions exactly."

The queen did not even wait for the king to turn to her. "My dear king," she said, "I too am innocent. It was your daughter, your youngest daughter, who told me not to put salt in the food."

And then the king realized that no pearls, no diamonds, and no dear possession in the world could be exchanged for the taste of salt. And so he ordered that his daughter be released from prison. Hugging his daughter he said, "Where salt is missing, everything is missing."

"Yes, Father," she answered, "food without salt has no taste, and life without Torah is like life without salt."

## *The Woman Will Humiliate and the Woman Will Raise*

### INTRODUCTION

This story from Morocco was told by Miriam Atar. The title is a paraphrasing of the prayer of Hannah in

I Samuel 2, "The Lord bringeth down to the grave and bringeth up." The women's message is found in its title, as it is in another IFA version, 6501, from Tunisia, called, "Everything Comes from the Woman." Most IFA versions were told by women and the women's message is clear. In this version the wife is portrayed as an *eishet hayil*, as described in the Book of Proverbs. The piety of the woman gives this international tale a Jewish flavor.

# 56

# *The Woman Will Humiliate and the Woman Will Raise*

nce there was a good king who loved justice and was kind to his people. This king had a wise wife who was really an *eishet hayil*, as is written in the Book of Proverbs. And not only that, her beauty was beyond compare. So great was the king's love for his wife, so dear was she to him, that legends about their love spread throughout the kingdom.

One day the royal couple went for a ride in their chariot, for it was their habit to visit different parts of the kingdom to see how their people were faring. And when they reached a distant place, in a dry *wadi*, they came upon a hut, so shabby that if not for a few logs that supported it, the hut would have collapsed. Surrounding the shack were weeds and thorns, dried from the summer sun. No tree or bush for shade, no bit of green was to be seen.

The king stopped and looked at the barefoot children playing near the hut, who seemed so sweet. "See those beautiful children," he said. "If only some industrious hand would take charge, these children would be in better condition."

"Woman will humiliate and woman will raise, my lord," said the wife.

"What do you mean?" asked the king.

"As I said, 'Woman will humiliate and woman will raise,' " said the queen.

"You mean nothing depends on the industriousness of the husband?"

"No, the woman is the one who determines the situation."

"No, my dear, I think it is the man," said the king.

"If so, my lord, let me remain here for seven years and prove that I am right."

After some hesitation, the king replied, "Very well, it will be difficult for me to live without you. But, for the sake of these poor peasants, you may remain." And so the king returned to the palace.

The queen shed her royal garb and donned, instead, clothing of rags.

She entered the hut, and, therein, saw the mother preparing dough, which the children, from time to time, threw into the oven to eat as *pitot*.

In the evening the husband returned, an axe and rope upon his shoulders. "And may I know what this aunt is doing here?" he asked.

"I'm a poor wanderer, and the heat is so strong. May I take shelter?"

"Welcome, aunt. I am a poor woodcutter and have just sold a pile of logs. With the money, I bought flour and vegetables. Come and eat with us."

And so the queen sat and watched as the children, with poor manners, snatched their bread before it even reached the table, leaving little for the grownups to eat. Soon all went to sleep, still hungry.

In the morning the queen took the children to a faraway stream where the waters were as clear as crystal. There she washed their clothes and combed their hair. With some flour she made a dough and promised each child a roll for lunch. From the dough she shaped round loaves, which she then covered to let them rise. She arranged the oven and continued to move from one job to another until the day passed. In the evening, when the father returned, he found the children clean and the table laid, as befits the table of an *eishet hayil*. The smell of fresh bread filled the hut. All ate and were satisfied.

And so, day by day, the woman's work continued, and the queen taught the wife the secrets of efficient work. The woodcutter too worked diligently and gave his money to the aunt, who was able to save. With these coins she bought wool, and, with the logs fashioned for her by the woodcutter, she made looms. When the wool was washed, she wove it into rags, while all the while the wife studied this new profession. And so, as time went on, the family grew even more success-ful. Their savings became greater each day, and soon they were able to buy clothing and shoes for the children, who were sent to the nearby school. Some years passed, and, in this manner, their savings became so great that the family was able to build a large house.

After seven years the king returned to the *wadi*. Imagine his surprise when before him stood a house as large as a palace! Its windows were of glass and its bells were of gold. And surrounding the house were gardens filled with trees of every description.

The queen appeared in royal clothes. The king greeted her with these words: "Indeed, my dear, you were right. 'Woman will humiliate and woman will raise.' I have felt this in my flesh for the long seven years of your absence." And, so saying, the king took the queen back to the palace.

When the woodcutter returned that evening, he looked for the aunt but could not find her. "Perhaps," he told his wife, "she was a good angel sent to us by God." And so, he and his wife, and the children too, thanked God for this special gift.

## *The Daughter Awaits the Gift of God*

### INTRODUCTION

This story, told by Flora Cohen of Egypt, is also a subtype of the previous story, "Love Like Salt." Many of the common elements can be recognized: the girl's expulsion, her marriage to a poor man, the reunion with the father. However, the girl's awareness of the greatness of God gives it its Jewish element and turns the story into a religious one. Again it is the woman's faith and wisdom that are proven to be true.

Note the inclusion of the pomegranate, which symbolizes fruitfulness, as in the story "The Pomegranate Girl," no. 19.

# 57

# *The Daughter Awaits the Gift of God*

nce there was a rich merchant who had three daughters. And when he went abroad, he asked each girl what gift she would like. The eldest asked for a white dress, embroidered with diamonds. The second requested a gold watch, embellished with ornaments. And the third said, "Father, just come back healthy and well."

"But what gift would you like for yourself?" asked the father.

"There is no present but the present from God."

Upon hearing these words, the father was angry, but he kept the anger in his heart.

Some time later the merchant again went abroad and again asked his daughters what gifts they would like. The two eldest asked for clothes and jewels, but the youngest replied, "I want only the gift of God."

Nevertheless, to make her happy, the merchant brought his youngest daughter a dress and a watch. "Give this to my sisters," she said. "I want only the gift of God."

This time the father was really angry. "Go then. Go from this house. Go and get the gift of God." And so the father married the girl to their servant, a poor man who swept the floors and carried water, and threw them out upon the road.

The girl was not angry. "This is a good gift if it is the gift of God," she said. And, thereupon, she and her new husband went to live in a shabby hut.

One day, on his way to do some menial work for the people of the forest, the husband met three people who begged for water, for they had had nothing to drink for several days. The husband, a kindhearted man, replied that he would fetch water from a nearby well, and bade them wait. But what he did not tell them was that the well was fraught with danger, for no one who had ever gone down into it had ever returned.

The kindhearted husband lowered himself to the bottom of the well, and, behold! There in front of him sat a giant Negro, at whose right hand sat a beautiful white girl with lovely golden hair and sparkling blue eyes. At his left hand sat a black girl whose hair was curly and whose bulging eyes were dark and black.

"*Shalom Aleichem*," said the Negro.

"*Aleichem Shalom*. I have come to fill my bucket."

"Very well. But only on the condition that you answer a question. Tell me which girl is prettier, the white or the black?"

The husband did not hesitate. "Why, your beloved, the one you love, is the prettiest, even if she be as dark as coal." The Negro was pleased with this answer. And so he gave the husband a gift, a kettle with which to give water to those who are thirsty, and he handed him also three large pomegranates. "Open these only when you are near your wife," he said.

The husband thanked the Negro, left the well, and drank from the kettle. But, to his surprise, the kettle did not empty. No, not one single drop was missing! And then, to his greater surprise, when he shared the water with the thirsty travelers, the kettle remained as full as before.

Upon returning home, the husband told his wife what had happened. The two opened the pomegranates, and behold! The fruits were filled with dazzling jewels, precious stones, colored gems of all sizes. "Thank God. There is no gift like the gift of God," said the wife.

The couple built a fine house, even larger than the house of the merchant. They bought clothing, furniture, fine carpets, and all manner of costly goods.

And, at the entrance to the house, they posted a large notice: "Whoever is in need of clothing, food, or drink is welcome—if he will tell his tale!" And soon all the poor of the city came and partook of the couple's offer—and so, many stories were told and heard in that house. The wife, disguised as a man, listened with great interest.

One day one of the merchant's daughters passed that house and saw the sign. She ran home, crying, "Father, Father, there is a house in the forest even richer than ours, and there all who are poor may come and eat." The father, curious and quite surprised, donned the clothes of the poor and entered the house. And when it was his turn to tell his tale, he told of his daughter who always said, "There is no gift like the gift of God" and whom he had expelled.

The daughter, in her disguise, recognized her father at once, but he, of course, did not know her. "And aren't you sorry that you expelled your child?" she asked.

"Yes," he answered, "but I am sure that she will come back and ask forgiveness."

"Oh, no, Father, she won't because she received God's gift," cried the girl, and she showed her face. Upon seeing his daughter, the father wept, fell on her neck, and begged her forgiveness. "Yes, you were right," he said. "It is better to make a request of God than of people. It is God who gives all gifts, to rich and poor alike."

And so the father and his daughter were reunited, and their faith in the gift of God remained with them all of their days.

## *Three Hairs of a Lion*

### INTRODUCTION

This story was told to me by Rafi Israeli, a Jerusalem friend, who heard it over forty years ago as a child in Fez, Morocco. At the time, the story was being told to his mother, Ruhama Israel, by her mother-in-law, Zohara Israel.

According to Rafi, his grandmother, Zohara, was a wonderful storyteller. On winter nights she would gather

her grandchildren in her big bed and, night after night, in the dark, would transmit stories, sayings, rhymes. "She was an illiterate woman and, thus, via this oral tradition, made sure that her family retained their heritage."

The setting of this particular story is important in understanding its women's message which, although not explicitly stated, is easily deduced: a woman's own resources (wit, courage) can overcome even the most dangerous and seemingly insurmountable obstacle. In this sense, the story reminds me of "The Treasure," AT 1645, known geographically from Native Americans in North America to storytellers in the Far East, and in the Jewish world as well. In that story a man travels far and wide to find a treasure shown him in a dream; the treasure turns out to be in his own house. Here, in this tale, a woman seeks advice for an answer to a problem; the solution is within her all the time.

As Rafi relates, "After one of the numerous fights between my mother and father, who was a rough person, Mother, as usual, went to seek consolation from my grandmother. She was the only person my father feared; she had authority over him. (We too ran to Grandmother for protection from Father.) Well, one day Mother ran to Grandmother and told her again, 'Father did this' or 'Father did that.' This time Grandmother answered, 'Let me tell you a story.'" And the story she told is the story I share with you here.

# 58

## *Three Hairs of a Lion*

A married woman was on bad terms with her husband, and often ran to the rabbi to seek advice, as Jews have always done. The rabbi would advise her, to no avail.

But one day the rabbi said to the poor woman, "I have a remedy for you but it's risky, and you have to follow my instructions exactly."

"Rabbi, I will do anything you say. My life is involved and anything you say will be worth trying. There is no other way."

So the rabbi said, "Listen carefully. If you can pluck three hairs from the mane of a lion and bring them to me, I'll give you the remedy."

So, frightened but excited, the woman went to the forest, and there carried on daily observations of the comings and goings of the animals. And one day, as she observed a lion approaching in her direction, she pulled from her bag a big piece of meat she had prepared for him. She threw it on the ground, and ran for her life. But, as the lion slowly ate his meal, she crept back and came closer to the beast. The same thing happened the next day and the day after until the woman became acquainted with the lion, and the lion felt familiar enough to come closer to her. And after the two had achieved this familiarity and while the lion was eating his meat, she gathered up her courage and plucked a handful of hair from the lion's mane. Then she quickly ran to the rabbi, and, with a cry of victory, burst in uninvited. "Rabbi, here they are. Now, where is the remedy?"

The rabbi turned to the woman. "You fool!" he answered. "If you have learned to tame a lion, you can certainly learn to tame your husband."

# The Clever Daughter of the Poritz

## INTRODUCTION

In this story from Lithuania, the clever woman is the daughter of the *poritz*, a rich landowner upon whose estate many people were employed, and where the Jew was traditionally the keeper of an inn. In this story we see that the *poritz* was kind, and his daughter, both kind and wise.

This tale, known in *The Decameron* of Boccaccio, has Jewish literary variants, as well as oral versions in the IFA. Most of these come from Islamic countries (Syria,

Yemen, Iraq, Morocco), where intoxicating drinks are
forbidden to the Moslems. In these stories the wine is
replaced by eggs, all of the same color. In a Hebrew
version, told among Arabs in Israel, King Solomon is
asked to differentiate between 1,001 boiled eggs.

# 59

# *The Clever Daughter of the* Poritz

Near a large forest stood the mansion of the rich
*poritz*. He was not an evil man. On the contrary,
he paid his workers well and was respected by
all.

Now, the *poritz* had a clever and beautiful
daughter, who was loved and desired by the boys of the
village. But none dared speak to her. After all, they were but
simple villagers and she, the daughter of the *poritz*!

The girl realized quite well the feelings of the young men,
but she pretended not to notice. And so, time did its own
thing: the young men married, had children, and concerned
themselves with their own families.

One such young man worked in the stables of the *poritz*. He
had married and was the father of three. But his old love
flamed, and when the beautiful young woman came to claim
her horse—for she dearly loved riding—the young stable hand
appeared as one walking in a dream.

Now, the young daughter knew that the stable hand was a
devoted worker. But she knew also that he cared little for his
family, that often he was sad, and that he spent his nights
sleeping at the stable. There was little his family could do to
mend his heart.

And so, what did the daughter of the *poritz* do? She waited
until her father was away. Then she set a fine table, upon
which she placed three glasses, filled with wine. To this meal

the stable hand was invited. He was most astonished, especially when asked to sit opposite the beautiful girl.

"Do you love me?" she asked.

"Yes," he answered, and simple words poured from his heart.

Then the daughter pointed to the three glasses of wine, and had the young man drink all three. "Which wine was the best?" she asked.

"Each glass had a good taste," he answered, "but the wine in the last glass was best."

The girl smiled. "All the wine was the same," she said, "but, while drinking, you thought they were different. As it is with wine, so it is with the nature of women. Go back to the bosom of your family."

And then the young stable hand realized how he had neglected his wife and his children. He mended his ways and lived with them in great joy. And never did he forget the wise words of the daughter of the *poritz*.

## The Magic Power of a Woman's Curse

### INTRODUCTION

This story was told to me by my dear friend, Haya Gavish, a doctoral student in folklore at the University of Haifa, who heard it in 1987 from Haya Gabai, a housewife from Zakho, Iraqi Kurdistan. Almost all Jews from Zakho left Iraq for Israel in the early 1950s. The teller is the sister-in-law of the head of the Jewish community in Zakho.

At the time of the interview, Haya Gavish asked the teller about the economic situation of the family in Kurdistan. Now, in Israel there is a Kurdish family, the Ella family, whose members are famous building contractors. How did they become wealthy? People say that, via some magic powers, they found a treasure in Israel. To counteract this story, the teller related this personal narrative. According to Haya Gavish, the story belongs to

a genre of stories (there are many of this type) which
explain how the family became rich.

We see here the conflict between two minorities (Jews
and Armenians) who usually were on good terms. But
here, when the Armenian threatened the economic future
of the family, it was as if they were being threatened by
death. The situation, in the eyes of the Jewish matriarch,
called for the utmost of magic power (in this case, the
curse of death).

According to Haya Gavish, who has been studying the
Iraqi Kurdish community for more than ten years, the
woman in Kurdistan was in the lowest of positions. There
was almost complete physical separation of men and
women; the woman had little or no education, and was
usually confined to the house. A young girl could be sold
at her father's will. But, as we see here, there were some
unique women who had magic powers. To me, the
message, sent by the Jewish Kurdish woman teller, is
that a woman (on the lowest rung of the socio-economic
scale) could save her family from economic failure; a
woman could do what men could not. What wonderful
wish fulfillment! What an ego booster for women!

# 60

# *The Magic Power of a Woman's Curse*

t's not true that we were poor in Zakho. In fact,
we had a store in Mosul and another in Zakho.
About the Zakho store I have a story:

The Armenians became rich in Zakho. One
Armenian named Karo wanted to rent the store
of Ephraim Ella's father, my nephew. The Ella family rented
the shop from Chazan Beck, the head of the richest family in
Kurdistan; the rent was seventy *rupees*.

But the Armenian went to Amram Ella, Ephraim's father,
and said, "I will offer Chazan Beck one hundred forty *rupees*,

double what you are paying, for the shop." And the Armenian did go twice to speak to the owner about the matter.

Now, I used to sit in the house of Ephraim's father. Ephraim was not only my nephew; his father is also my cousin. So then Ephraim Ella called to his mother, "Mother!"

"What?"she asked.

"I'm losing my shop because Karo, the Armenian, will rent it."

Mother answered, "No, a *kapparah* on you. (A scapegoat will go in place of you.) Don't be afraid. You'll see. If, after three days' time he remains alive, you may cut my hand. I will curse him. He will not live."

Believe me, this was on Thursday. She came and said to her son, "Don't be afraid. No one will take your shop."

On *motzei Shabbat*, the end of Sabbath on Saturday night, it was the custom for men to sit and drink together in the coffee house. On that Saturday night the coffee house collapsed. Nine were killed: he (Karo) and eight other Armenians. Many others were seated there but only the Armenians were killed.

Then people came to Ephraim Ella. "Oy, Karo was killed, and with him eight more. His sin is going with him."

And Amram's mother said, "Didn't I tell you that someone instead of you would be killed?"

Then Chazan Beck, the owner of the shop, himself, came to my cousin. "Amram, I ask you to tell your mother that even if someone offered me four hundred *rupees* for the shop, I wouldn't give it to them. This is your shop. Let your mother not put a curse on my son."

Ephraim Ella, son of Amram, is alive in Israel today. And he is a rich contractor in Israel.

# The Glass of Water

## INTRODUCTION

One day, as I was hesitating about whether or not to splurge on a certain item for myself, I shared my hesitation with a Jerusalem neighbor, Naomi Sapir. She promptly told me this story, which she had heard from Leah Moser, who had related it from her family tradition in Iraq.

To me the message is a woman's version of the teaching of Rabbi Hillel, one of our great sages: "If I am not for myself, who will be for me, and if not now, when?" This is a centuries-old Jewish slogan about the need for personal responsibility. In this case, however, there is an additional message, one of socio-economic overtone, for here we see that even a lowly servant should care for herself. "If not," as Naomi stated, "she will lose her human existence."

# 61

# *The Glass of Water*

ne night the lady of the house, the employer of a certain servant girl, heard the servant calling from her mattress bed, "Jar, jar, please roll over to me. Jar, jar, please roll over to me."

At that moment the woman called the servant. "Marjana, bring me a glass of water."

At once the servant jumped up and brought the water as she was bade.

Then the lady asked, "Marjana, why did you call for the jar to roll to you?"

"Because I am tired and haven't the strength to get up, and I wanted a drink."

The employer was confused. "Then why, when I asked for water, did you get up at once and bring it to me?"

"For you I work, and I must do as you ask."

Then the lady gave the girl the water she herself had brought, and forced her to drink.

"Never lose the power to do something nice for yourself," the lady told her. "Always remember to get up, not only because you must do so for others, but also because you must take care of yourself."

# A Good Friend

### INTRODUCTION

What would you do if your father married you to a fearsome creature? or sent you to a forest, there to be chased by an evil demon? The heroine in this story has this problem.

The title of this tale, told by an Ethiopian woman, gives its general message: Friends are often more loyal than family.

But the story is an important one for Ethiopian women: According to my "Ethiopian connection," Ina Ruth Sarin, who has been collecting tales of Ethiopian Jewry for many years, the usual tale of child-parent conflict involves a son and father, while the girl is generally a "good girl," always obeying and helping her father. In this tale, she also obeys her father's request, despite her personal fear. *But* she quickly changes her actions when she sees how she has been betrayed. The telling of this tale, then, sends female listeners many messages:

1. Beware of your own family. Men will lead you to trouble and women will not support you.

2. A woman, when abandoned by family, must think and act for herself.

3. Never forget who befriended you and who did not! To those who helped you, remain loyal and generous! Those who injured or abandoned you should not be forgiven. Instead, they should be punished.

This story is number six in a collection of Ethiopian stories housed in Tel Aviv University. They were collected in the early twentieth century by Jacob Faitlovitch, one of the first pioneers in the collecting of Jewish-Ethiopian stories, and a scholar of Jewish-Ethiopian culture and history. His library on the Jews of Ethiopia was donated to the Municipality of Tel Aviv.

# 62

# *A Good Friend*

 man and a demon were friends for a long time. One day the demon asked his friend to give him his daughter as a wife.

The man answered: "Any other wish I can fulfill, but this one is impossible—and even if I were willing to marry my daughter to you, she wouldn't agree."

But the demon wouldn't leave the matter alone. And so great was the friendship between the two men that the father finally promised his daughter to the demon.

After a while the man met the demon again in the forest. The demon told him: "Leave your shoes here, and when you get home, tell your daughter you forgot your shoes at this place. Ask her to go and fetch them. And when your daughter comes here for the shoes, I shall catch her."

Since he had promised, the man saw no other choice. He left his shoes at that place, and when he got back home, he said to his daughter, "My daughter, I forgot my shoes on the way. Go and fetch them for me." And he described the place.

The sun was setting and the road became dark when the father sent his daughter. But although she was afraid of the dark, she went to do what her father had bidden.

She came to the place he had described, and began looking for the shoes, when the demon jumped up and tried to pounce on her.

At the sight of the demon, the girl was terribly frightened. She cried for help, and started running to her house. All this time the demon chased her as he spoke to her from his heart: "Your eyes shine like stars. Your teeth are white as milk. Your hair feels like silk!"

The girl continued running, and when she arrived at her father's house, she shouted: "A demon is chasing me. Open the door, my father!"

But her father and mother answered from within, "We cannot open. Go with him!"

The girl knocked on the doors of her uncles' houses. "A demon is chasing me. Open the door, my uncle." But no one opened the door for her.

In great distress, she suddenly remembered her best friend, and ran, ran to her house. On the way she collected ashes and coals, and each time the demon came near, the girl threw some of the ashes and coals behind her. And the demon stopped to pick them up and swallow them.

Finally she arrived at her best friend's house and shouted for help. "A demon is chasing me. Open the door." The friend recognized her voice. She got up from her bed, opened the door, and let her in.

The friend gave her water so that she could bathe her feet, spread a rug on the floor, and put the girl down to rest. When the demon arrived at the house, the friend's husband and all his male relatives were already waiting for him. They attacked him with axes and killed him.

For many, many days the girl stayed at the house of her best friend, who had helped her in her trouble and saved her from her pursuer—while the members of her own family had ignored her.

And when the time came, she married a wealthy man who built her a fine house.

When tales about her great wealth reached the ears of her parents and relatives, who, meanwhile, had lost all their wealth and were very poor, they decided to go to her and ask for help.

They forgot the evil they had done to her, but she did not forget.

When she saw her family approaching, she set her thirty dogs on them. And the dogs quickly devoured them.

Her best friend, too, became poor in those days and came to

her to ask for help. When she heard that her friend was coming, the rich woman sent slaves with mules to meet her—and when the friend came, she led her to the hall and bade her take off her ragged dress, and dressed her in a new embroidered dress and a new coat, and asked her to sit at the head of the table.

Afterward, she gave her friend a great deal of money and sent her back to her own house, escorted by slaves and mules, where she lived in great wealth.

# The King's Daughter and Her Seven Brothers

## INTRODUCTION

This tale was told to Rivka Par and Penina Resnick by Simha Shamaka, originally from Libya. The universal tale has the following plot:

1. Seven (eleven, twelve) brothers have a younger sister. Upon her birth, they flee, after having been erroneously warned that she is a boy and they will be killed upon his birth.

2. They are transformed into birds, cows, or other animals.

3. She sets out on a quest to find them. Despite many obstacles, she remains faithful to her task.

4. The brothers are eventually disenchanted, and all are reunited.

This IFA tale remains faithful to the universal plot. However, the teller's opening sentences give it a Jewish message. Note that the celebration at the end of the story (for seven days and seven nights) is similar to the celebration of a Jewish wedding.

Note also, from a female teller's point of view, the concern of the mother for her children, as contrasted to the harsh cruelty of the father.

The closing sentences are the teller's way of saying, "This story really happened. Believe it!" This technique brings the fairy tale into the realm of reality.

# 63

# *The King's Daughter and Her Seven Brothers*

here was and there wasn't a king and a sultan, and there is no king like our God. He who has troubles in life will be helped by God.

Once there was a king and also a queen who bore a new son each year, until at last she had seven sons. The king wanted a daughter. And so, when his wife became pregnant again he announced, "If, this time, you bring a son into the world, I will kill you, and your sons as well." The poor woman was frightened, not for her own life, but for the lives of her sons. How could she save them from the danger awaiting them?

And so she sent the boys to a faraway farm, which she had inherited from her parents. "Stay there and tell no one where you are," she instructed them. "In a few months one of you must return and look at the roof of the palace. If you see a red kerchief, know that I have given birth to a daughter. Then you may return. If you see a man's hat, know that you have another brother. Escape and run away to another land."

After some months a daughter was born. Good! *Mazal Tov!* The mother instructed the servant to hang a red kerchief high, high on the roof for everyone to see. But, instead, the servant put a hat on the roof, and the boys, knowing this, escaped to another land. No one knew where.

The sister grew up, an extraordinary child. Why, what an ordinary person learned in one year she learned in one day. She was lavished upon and spoiled with affection.

One day, as she played with her friends, she got into a quarrel. "Get away from here," cried the other child. "You are the curse of your seven brothers."

The princess went crying to her mother. "What does this mean? Do I have brothers?"

With tear-filled eyes the mother said, "Yes, yes, but they

were sent away." And she, thereupon, told the girl the entire story.

"Mother, prepare food, camels, and servants. I must go to find my brothers. I will not return until I have succeeded." The mother tried to prevent the girl from leaving, but to no avail.

For weeks the princess wandered with her camels until she reached her brothers, living in a foreign land. How happy they were to find each other, and decided that, on the very next day, they would return to the palace together. "Rest now," she told them, "and I will cook *couscous* for dinner."

Now, in that country lived a witch who was jealous of the brothers. And so, with a needle, she pricked the girl's finger, and a few drops of blood fell into the *couscous*. And the very moment that the boys put that *couscous* to their lips, they turned into oxen. The girl cried bitterly, but nothing was to be done. And so she tended the seven oxen as if they were human.

One day she stopped to give them a drink of water at a spring. While there, a handsome prince, who was watering his own horse, saw the girl and asked her to marry him. "Only on one condition," she replied. "The seven oxen must be taken care of as if they were my brothers."

And so the two were married, and within a year's time the wife bore a son. But their joy didn't last, for the same witch wanted to drive her away and marry the prince to her own daughter. And so, disguised as a servant, the witch came to live at the royal palace. One day she said to the wife, "Let's go out into the garden and I will comb your hair." And, as she did so, she stuck twelve pins into the head of the woman. As the last pin was stuck into her head, the wife turned into a pigeon and flew off to the rooftop.

No one knew what had become of her. Greatly saddened, the prince mourned for many days. Then the witch-servant said, "How long will you mourn? Your wife must be dead. Take my beautiful daughter as your wife." But the prince would not listen. He continued to raise his son and to seek his beloved wife.

Time passed and the young son grew up. One day, as he saw a flock of birds in the sky, he called, "Oh birds, birds in the sky, is Mother with you?"

And the birds answered, "Your mother is with the pigeons over the mountain. With her tears she cries for seven oxen." And, with this, one of the pigeons hummed about the boy, caressed him with her wings, and flew off again.

Now the prince, seeing this strange sight, put a delicate web of silk thread around his son. And so, on the next day when the boy saw the birds, he called again, "Oh birds, birds in the sky, is Mother with you?" Again they answered, "Your mother is with the pigeons over the mountain. With her tears she cries for seven oxen." Once again a pigeon landed at the boy's feet, but this time it became entangled in the silk web. The prince approached to caress and to calm her, when suddenly he felt a strange object protruding from her head. One by one he removed the metal pins that had been stuck there. And, upon the removal of the last one, there stood his beloved wife as beautiful as ever.

She told him of the evil witch, after which the prince ordered the witch and her daughter to appear before him. "If the life of your daughter is precious to you, tell me the secret of how to turn the oxen into boys," he demanded.

The witch realized she had no choice, for she feared for her daughter's life. "Go over the mountain," she said, "and find a cave in which there are seven jugs. Take the seventh, and run quickly from the cave. Then put one spoonful of the jug's liquid into the ear of each ox, and the oxen will be turned back into boys." So the witch said and so the prince did!

And so too did the witch's words come true! Great was the joy of the prince, the princess, and her brothers! And they vowed that, on the very next day, they would return to the palace. Said the princess, "I swore never to return without my brothers and I have fulfilled my oath."

The king and the queen declared a holiday. For seven days and seven nights there were to be no fires in the kingdom. And why? So that all the people of the land could come and eat at the palace and share in their joy.

I was there too. I rejoiced with them and left their house, happy and rich.

### Money Comes and Money Goes, but a
### Profession Lasts Forever

#### INTRODUCTION

The title, alluded to in Ecclesiastes 5:12, serves as the
overt message of the story.

This oicotype, AT 888*A, is popular in the IFA where
there are over thirty versions, almost all from Sephardic
countries (Syria, Yemen, Persia, Egypt, Tunisia, Iraqi
Kurdistan) and almost all told by women.

The version presented here is from Tunisia. Typically,
the woman's insistence on learning a profession saves
the life of a male. The overt Jewish message is: a
profession saves from death. The covert Jewish women's
message then becomes: woman saves from death!

(In one version told by a male, it is the mother-in-law
who is kidnapped. Wishful thinking, perhaps!?)

# 64

# *Money Comes and Money Goes,*
# *but a Profession Lasts Forever*

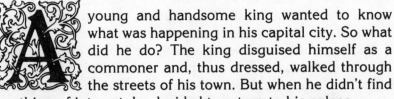 young and handsome king wanted to know
what was happening in his capital city. So what
did he do? The king disguised himself as a
commoner and, thus dressed, walked through
the streets of his town. But when he didn't find
anything of interest, he decided to return to his palace.

Suddenly, on his way, behold! The king found himself
standing next to a large and beautiful garden, whose flowers
gave forth a fragrance of unbelievable sweetness.

The king came closer—and behold! Three figures were

seated on the balcony: a couple who seemed to be middle-aged and a young and beautiful woman, undoubtedly their daughter, who sat embroidering a fine cloth.

"May I come in and rest?" asked the king.

"Please do, you are most welcome."

And so the king entered and was served coffee by the beautiful young woman. While the four were drinking, there was a lively discussion, and the young hostess asked, "How did you come to this place, and what is it that you wish?"

To this the disguised king answered, "I have come to buy diamonds and precious stones, as this is my business."

At this the young woman seemed to perk up her ears to listen more attentively, and so the king grew more confident. So, when the parents went to the next room for a moment and the couple was alone, the king spoke. "You have found favor in my eyes," he said. "Will you be my bride?"

Now, the truth is that the young woman had fallen in love with the handsome stranger, but she answered, "Money comes and money goes, but a profession lasts forever. I will not marry a man who has no profession."

"Then I will go and study a profession," decided the king, "but promise that you will wait for me and not marry another."

The young woman gave her word. And so it was that the king returned to his palace, called forth the finest carpet weavers in the land, and bade them teach him their craft, which was indeed work of true art. At last, when the king felt that his hands were skilled enough, he wrote to his beloved that he was ready to return, to which she replied by inviting him to her home.

On the way, being thirsty, the king stopped at a coffeehouse and quenched his thirst, but when he went to pay the bill, he suddenly felt the floor open beneath him, and he soon found himself in a deep, dark cellar. There he shouted for help. He was answered by a booming voice, "Don't move! Any attempt to escape will end in death. Only for a large ransom will you be freed!"

"I have no money to give you," the king replied to the invisible voice, "but do not kill me. I know how to weave carpets of unbelievable beauty, true works of art. These you will be able to sell for large sums of money."

"Very well, I agree," boomed the invisible voice, "but only on the condition that you begin your work at once. You will be locked in a room, given food and drink and all your needs for working, and there you will weave your carpets."

And so it was done! The young king was taken to a room, in the center of which stood a large loom—and he began to weave. After one month his hands had created a carpet of such magnificence that no human eyes had ever seen such beauty.

Needless to say, the captors were much pleased with this work, and one of the guards was sent to sell the carpet to a well-known merchant of the city. The merchant, as well, was pleased at the fine quality before him, and began to examine the carpet, running his fingers over the tightly woven threads. And, as he did so, he noticed that between the flowers on the carpet, in the smallest of letters, was woven: "The king is in trouble. Arrest this carpet seller!"

And so, while negotiating and trying to lower the price of the carpet, the merchant managed to inform the police, who came at once and arrested the carpet seller. At first the guard protested and denied any knowledge of the whereabouts of the king. But, when threatened with hanging in the town square, he quickly told the truth and led the police to the place where the king was hidden.

Soon afterward the owner of the coffeehouse was hanged, and the king and his beautiful bride were married. During the ceremony the king related what had happened. He finished his story by saying, "Yes, money comes and money goes, but a profession lasts forever. Thanks to my clever bride I studied a profession, and, thanks to my profession, I was saved from disaster."

And the king and queen kept the beautiful carpet in the palace all of their days.

꧂

# The Clever Wife

## INTRODUCTION

This story was collected by Sima Gabai, who heard it from Sima Hagoli in Baghdad, Iraq, where the story circulated.

Among girls of the lower social stratum, for whom tales of the marriage of a lowly heroine to a prince or king were common, this story represented the wishful thinking and dreams of these women.

In most of the parallel stories the clever acts come before the wedding, during the courting period when the girl has to "prove herself" as being a perfect future wife and mother. In this version the clever act comes *after* the marriage; its function is to change the behavior of the cruel husband (a "woman-killer"). This the clever wife accomplishes.

Note the strong concern of the mother—and the girl's happy reunion with her—at the end. These are women's messages.

In a male-transmitted version of the tale, IFA 7667, from Afghanistan, a snake (male symbol) leaps forth from the doll at the end of the story. The jealous husband seeks to slay the snake, as well as to stab the doll.

# 65

# The Clever Wife

nce there was a king who would marry a new bride only on the condition that, after the wedding, she break off relations with her parents and never see them again. Despite this harsh ruling many beautiful girls were eager to marry the king, and so, time and again, he chose from amongst them the one he liked most.

One, two, three weeks would pass. While the king was very busy attending receptions and audiences, his wife was always left alone at home with no one to speak to. After several months of suffering, the wife would pass away. The king would mourn his wife's death, and then, after a short time, would proclaim a contest for a new bride.

This went on for a long time. Queen succeeded queen, and not one was able to bear up more than a few months. At last there came a lovely, clever girl who wished to marry the king. Her parents, especially her mother, were against the match.

"My beloved and only daughter, it is difficult for me to throw you into the fire," she said. "The king is a woman-killer. At first he buries his wife in the castle and then in a grave. If you marry him, you will bury me together with yourself."

"Don't be afraid, Mother," the daughter consoled her. "The king will bury neither you nor me. I will settle everything, if you have patience."

At last the mother gave in. Her daughter was the only one to find favor in the king's eyes, and she won the contest. In due course she married him and was parted from her parents.

After two days, however, she became bored, as the king was always preoccupied with his duties. It was difficult for her to become accustomed to the silent house without anyone to talk to. So, what did she do? She took the skin of a goat, blew it up, dressed it in clothes, drew a face, and put a hat on its head. It looked like a man. Afterward she placed the stuffed doll on a chair and began telling it all the troubles that weighed on her heart.

One month passed, two months went by, and the woman did not change her habit. When her husband came home, she would talk to him cheerfully, and while he was away, she would talk to her doll.

Three months passed, four months went by, and the king could not understand how his wife had managed to stay alive. He decided to look into the matter. What did he do? He bored a small hole in the wall of her room, and lo, what did he see? His wife sitting with a stranger, talking to him. "Unfaithful one!" he cried in his heart. "She has been deceiving me all this time."

The king decided to take revenge and afflict his wife and her lover with severe and terrible sufferings. He behaved as if he knew nothing of the matter, but he gave orders to the watchman to be on the lookout for anyone trying to leave the palace. In the evening the watchman reported that not a single person had left. Then, after dinner, the king suggested to his wife, "Come, let us look around the house and inspect the rooms." At last they reached the chamber where the king had watched his wife conversing with a man. Suddenly the king stopped and drew out a dagger. "Where have you hidden your lover?" he cried.

The queen showed him the doll hidden in the cupboard. The king stabbed it with his dagger. Blood began to pour out.

"What is this?" the king asked. "If it is a doll, where is the blood coming from?"

"That is my sorrow and grief, oh, king. I told my doll all that was in my heart. Otherwise, I myself would have burst from suffering."

At last the king understood that he himself had caused the deaths of his former wives and that his present wife was the cleverest of them all. At once he revoked his decree and from that moment on allowed his wife to visit her parents. You can imagine the rejoicing of the mother and the daughter.

## A Woman of Valor—Crown of Her Husband

### INTRODUCTION

The title of this story combines two proverbs: "A woman of valor, who can find?" (Proverbs 31:10) and "A virtuous woman is a crown to her husband" (Proverbs 12:4).

According to this tale, told to Haya Bar-Yitzhak by Yahya Simhi from Persia, a "woman of valor" is one who is wise and resourceful. There is an obviously positive women's message: The woman is the mastermind, the activator, without whom her husband would never have left his lowly socioeconomic state.

# 66

# *A Woman of Valor—Crown of Her Husband*

n one of the cities of Persia there lived a porter, Hasan, who worked for others and, from his meager earnings, could hardly support his family. And so he would gather twigs and grass, which he sold to the townsfolk for heating, and from this small amount of money, managed to live. Still, at nightfall he had not even a single blanket with which to keep warm, and so he covered himself with the saddlecloth of his donkey. The merchants of the town looked down on this poor man, and treated him brusquely as he did their bidding.

Hasan lived on a small piece of land inside the yard of one of the richest merchants in the city. The merchant greatly desired this land, but Hasan's wife refused to sell.

Now, it was the custom in Persia for many merchants to gather together and go for an outing, a picnic, near a stream or spring on the outskirts of the city. There they would dance, feast, and make merry until the dark hours of the evening.

One night, on their way home from such an outing, the merchants passed the house of the porter, and thought to stop to refresh themselves with water. And so they knocked at the door.

"Does the porter Hasan live here?"

"Who?" answered Hasan's wife. "You must mean *Hawaja* Hasan, Master Hasan."

"No, we are looking for the porter named Hasan."

"How unkind of you to damage the name of my master by speaking in that manner! Wait here, and I will ask the lady of the house if he is here."

And what did the wife do then? She ran straight to the merchant and made him this offer: "I will give you my house, that you have desired for so long, on one condition. Lend me your house and all its contents for one week's time." To this the merchant readily agreed.

And so the wife returned to the waiting merchants. "My

master is not here," she said, "but the lady of the house invites you to rest, eat, and drink." And, so saying, she led the men to the home of the merchant, where the rooms were filled with costly treasures and the floor covered with the richest of carpets. "Where are we?" cried the merchants in astonishment. "Could this be the house of Hasan?"

After the men had finished their refreshments, the wife refused to let them go. "Master Hasan will be angry if he hears that you have been in his home and have not awaited him."

Thus, the men remained some time longer. Meanwhile, the porter's wife ran to find him at the bathhouse. Bringing him the fine clothes of the merchant, she instructed him to be shaved and washed, and, upon his return, to act in the manner of a master, not disclosing any sign of poverty.

And so, when Hasan returned, he found the men being entertained by musicians, invited by his wife. She had told them that Hasan did, indeed, from time to time, work in the streets as a porter—just to know the people better. "What!" thought the men with great regret, "and we treated him so badly."

Hasan continued to entertain the men, being directed by his wife to offer them the large pool and other luxuries of his home. And each time the men protested, "But our families will worry. We must return," the wife continued to delay them. Thus, for three days and three nights, the merchants remained. And with each passing day they regretted even more their brusque treatment of the porter.

Then Hasan's wife sat her husband on the donkey of the master and ordered the master's slaves to lead the two to market. "When people see you with so many servants, they will treat you with great respect," she told her husband. "Buy all sorts of goods in great quantity, and promise to pay in a few days," she told him. The porter did as he was instructed. The goods were sold, and so he was able to buy more merchandise, which he sold again. Soon he was able to buy more and more, and, not long afterward, became a rich man and built a big house not far from the home of the rich merchant.

And so Hasan the porter, who was the laughing stock of the city, became *Hawaja* Hasan, Master Hasan—and all because of his wife. A woman of valor is the crown of her husband.

### The Son Who Wanted to Be a Merchant

#### INTRODUCTION

This tale was told to Sarah Bashari by Bracha Chaser, a storyteller born in Yemen. The AT type, called "A Pound of Flesh," is found in many oral versions in Moslem lands; the IFA has nine Jewish parallels from Morocco, Syria, Yemen, Iraqi Kurdistan, Persian Kurdistan, Iraq, and Afghanistan.

In most of the versions the clever lawyer is the disguised wife of the accused husband. But in this version the couple is not married, and the plot ends in a wonderful wedding. Obviously, it is the young woman's wisdom that saves the young man and allows him to continue his life as a Jewish son and husband.

Note the support of the grandmother, who believes in the young man when his own father does not. This is a women's message.

In a Syrian version, IFA 9321, an Arab lends money to a Jew and demands the right to cut his flesh. In the end, of course, he is outsmarted by the clever reasoning of the judge. Thus, the tale fulfills the wishful thinking of its Jewish listeners to outsmart the non-Jewish majority that usually overpowers them.


# 67

# *The Son Who Wanted to Be a Merchant*

nce there was a very wealthy Jew who had an only son. When the boy grew up, he went to his father to ask permission to become a merchant. Upon hearing these words, the father grew worried.

"But you have no experience as a merchant, my son. And

the dangers on the seas are many. No, I cannot give my consent."

But the boy was determined, and went to ask permission of his grandmother, who lived in the upper part of the house. When the old woman heard her grandchild's request, she gave him a letter to present to the captain of one of the ships she owned. The captain, upon reading the letter, immediately gave the boy a ship full of expensive merchandise. "Can you sell all this merchandise?" he asked.

"Yes, yes," replied the young man.

And so, he soon set sail, and traveled on the open waters. After many days the ship arrived at a big and beautiful country. There he went ashore to seek a merchant who would buy his wares. After some seeking, the young man came upon a rich merchant, who bought all the merchandise, and offered a high price.

"No, no, I don't want money," replied the young man. "Instead, I want merchandise of great value. Give me the most expensive merchandise in the world."

"If that is what you want, the merchandise is in front of you," said the rich merchant. "Water is the most expensive merchandise in the world. Fill your ship with water and return to your own country."

The young man did as the merchant suggested and sailed back to his own land. There he told his grandmother what had happened and about the answer of the merchant.

This time the old woman gave him a bag full of gold and sent him to a goldsmith with orders to make him a golden glass as big as a heart, with a cover to close it.

Taking the golden glass with him, the young man once again went to sea. But, in the middle of the sea, the ship ran out of fuel. What could the young man do? He had no choice but to set anchor and, in a smaller boat, to sail to the nearest coast.

There he entered a small village, told of his misfortune, and asked for a loan of four hundred pounds. The head of the village, impressed by the serious manner of the young man, agreed. "I will give you the money," he said, "but only on one condition. The loan must be repaid in one year's time. If you are even one day late, then I may have permission to cut one kilogram of flesh from your body."

Again, what could the young man do? He accepted the condition of the loan, and sailed back to the country where he had sold his merchandise. Again he found the rich merchant, who bought all his wares. "I will give you anything you wish," he said. "Name your price."

So, taking out the golden glass, the young man answered, "In payment for the merchandise, I want your heart. Put your heart in this golden cup."

The merchant was shocked, and although he offered the young man money, precious metals, and dazzling jewels, the young man was persistent. The heart, and only the heart, would he accept as payment.

Now, this merchant had a daughter who was beautiful and wise. "I will give you my daughter as a wife," he said, "and three ships besides."

To this the young man agreed. He accepted the ships, the girl, and her servants, and set sail. But, way out in the middle of the sea, he remembered the loan he had received from the head of the village in that small country he had visited. Time was running out. The debt was almost due. So he set the ship's course at full speed for that distant country.

But when he arrived, he was one day late. A year and a day had gone by since he had received the loan.

The head of the village wanted his payment in full, including the right to cut the young man's flesh. The young man, as you can imagine, was in low spirits. And so, with saddened face, he went to the courthouse to appeal his case. Surely the *kadi*, the wise judge, would not allow his flesh to be cut.

Meanwhile, the girl, seeing the young man so sad and despondent, decided to disguise herself as the *kadi*, and hear the case herself. Soon the young man and the one who had granted the loan stood before the judge.

The man who had granted the loan spoke. "Your Honor, I lent this man money on the condition that he pay me back within one year's time, or else I could cut a kilo of his flesh. He agreed to the condition. Now he has returned to repay the loan, but the year is over and I wish to collect, according to the agreement."

Then the young man spoke. "But, your Honor, I have been traveling on the high seas and I came as quickly as I could."

The *kadi* thought for a while and answered, "This is my judgment: An agreement is an agreement. The young merchant was one day late and, therefore, must pay with his flesh. Call the butcher!"

And, when the butcher arrived, the *kadi* commanded the young man, now pale with fear, to stand upon the scale. "This is the young man's weight," the *kadi* said. "You are to cut from his body one kilo of flesh, not one gram more, nor one gram less. If you do not cut the flesh exactly, I will have the remainder cut from your body."

Upon hearing these words, the butcher was frightened, and refused to cut. Other butchers were called, but they too would not agree to cut the flesh of the young man.

And so the head of the village departed without receiving his kilo of flesh, and the young merchant was released.

Then the beautiful girl shed the clothes of the *kadi* and waited for the young man to return. "Did the *kadi* judge wisely?" she asked.

"Oh, yes, the *kadi* was very wise. If not for his cleverness, I would not have won the case."

The girl seemed angry. "Why didn't you invite the *kadi* to our house to thank him and give him a fine gift? Go now and fetch him."

So the young man went to invite the *kadi*, while the young girl changed back into her disguise. The *"kadi"* graciously accepted the young man's invitation and soon appeared at his house. And when the young man thanked him and offered a gift in appreciation, the *kadi* answered, "No, no, I don't want any payment. I want only to have your wife for one night."

The young man was shocked. "What!" he shouted. "I would never agree to such a thing."

At that moment the young woman shed her disguise and revealed herself. "If you had agreed to give me to the *kadi*, I would have left at once," she said.

So it was that the young man returned home, taking the beautiful girl with him. There he told his grandmother all that had happened. The old woman, in great happiness, praised the wisdom of the young man and of his bride-to-be.

The father too praised the boy's talents as a merchant, and arranged a luxurious wedding for the young couple. The two lived together in great happiness and continued to follow the laws of Israel.

# The Faithful Woman

## INTRODUCTION

This story was related by a young woman, Ida Alfassi, who heard it from elderly women neighbors in Casablanca. It belongs to the large group of stories about women who have been wrongly accused of adultery or other unfaithfulness. At the end of the tale, when her innocence comes to light, she is reinstated. The woman's sense of honor needs to be vindicated, and, in the story, it is. Both universal and Jewish versions of this tale type have been intensively studied.

The idea of women's unfaithfulness is not unknown in Jewish lore. One of the most widely known talmudic legends is about Beruriah, wife of Rabbi Meir, a great postbiblical sage. To test his wife's virtue, the rabbi sends one of his pupils to seduce her, and he finally succeeds. In another talmudic legend the same rabbi tests the chastity of his wife's sister by trying to persuade her to succumb to him; he fails. (Please note that legend often ignores historical truth.)

The overt women's messages of the story are: the virtue of faithfulness is rewarded; do not forgive the wicked.

The covert women's messages are: female beauty causes trouble; do not trust men, even relatives, even men who are pious and learned.

# 68

# *The Faithful Woman*

nce there were two brothers: one, rich, and the other, poor. The poor man had a very beautiful wife.

One day the poor brother came to the rich one to ask for a loan. But the rich man refused. Even when strangers tried to persuade the man to help his poor brother, he would answer, "Brother? I have no brother."

One day the rich man went for a walk in the town, and, in the course of his wandering, came to the poor quarter of the town. Through the window of one of the buildings he saw the face of a beautiful woman. "Whose wife is that?" he asked the people there.

"That is your brother's wife," he was told.

And so the rich man fell in love with the woman and desired her greatly. Day and night he thought of how he could obtain her.

One day the rich man sent for his poor brother. He gave his brother money and invited him (and his wife, of course) to his house, and did them many favors. After some time he gave his brother some goods with which to trade and, thus, to earn money in a far country. At first the poor man refused to leave his wife, but the rich brother promised that she would remain under his protection. So the poor brother set out on his journey with a quiet heart.

The very next day the rich man sent his sister-in-law vegetables, fruit, and meat, and told her that in the evening he would come to eat at her home. She could not tell him not to come, but, while he was in the house, she conducted herself in the most proper manner. Every day the rich man pestered her and sent her gifts, but she remained unimpressed.

One day the woman decided to end matters with her rich brother-in-law. She invited him to her house, but left before he came. He waited an hour, two, three—and then rose and left the house in anger. For days afterward he nursed the insult in his heart, and decided that he would revenge himself on this woman who had offended him.

One day, early in the morning, the rich man left his house and, on his way, met a poor man. Giving him money, he said, "In return for the money I want you to creep into the hall of such and such a house and remain there." Needless to say, this house was none other than the house of his sister-in-law.

Then the rich man went to one of the synagogues in the city and invited the men he found there to a *brit milah* which, he said, was taking place in that same building. The men opened the door and, there in the hall, saw a strange man. "What are you doing here?" they asked him. "Since the departure of this woman's husband I have always been here," the poor man answered. For this was what the rich man had ordered him to say, in return for the money he had given him.

The men believed the poor man, and so they beat the unfaithful woman and drove her out of the city.

All the woman's pleading was in vain. She started to explain to the men and her rich brother-in-law that she was not guilty of what they suspected, but they refused to listen. And so, she had no choice but to leave the place. When she was some hundreds of meters from the town, she fell, overcome with fatigue. And, as she lay on the ground, she groaned, but there was no one to help her.

Just at that time, a rabbi and his wife, a childless couple, were approaching the city. They heard the sound of moaning, and resolved that they must find the cause. And what did they see? A poor woman lying on the ground with bleeding wounds. They helped her up, bound her wounds, and decided to take her with them. In their hearts they thought: Perhaps we have done a good deed today and, in reward, will be granted a child.

And so it happened. After some time the couple had a child, and they asked the woman to be the child's nurse. The woman, of course, was very grateful to the couple, and she was, indeed, a faithful nurse.

Now, in the house of this rabbi there was a young student who fell in love with the beautiful woman. He asked her to marry him but she refused—for she was already married but did not wish to reveal her secret. The student decided to avenge himself on her. What did he do? In the middle of the night he arose and killed the infant in her care. Immediately afterwards, he ran away.

In the morning the parents were hysterical with grief and anger. The rabbi resolved that the ungrateful woman should not be punished. "It is the will of God," he said. "We must let her go, bearing the dead child."

The woman herself was now desperate. She had been driven from place to place by false accusations. Who knew better than she how false the accusations were?

Once again she went out into the desert, hungry and thirsty, carrying the dead child in her arms. Suddenly, she saw an old man, who told her that he was the Prophet Elijah and that she had nothing to fear. He gave her a potion which could revive the dead. And, lo and behold! Just as he said, the child came alive. Then he gave her another potion that cures all ills. He also gave her this advice: "Disguise yourself as a man, establish a big hospital, and in it cure all the sick who come to you. But, remember, do not cure those who have caused you this suffering."

The woman took the advice of the Prophet Elijah, donned men's clothes, and founded a hospital. The institution developed and expanded, for all sorts of maladies were cured there. The rabbi's son, who had been restored to life, thought that his disguised mother was his father and helped her in all her tasks. And the woman made provision that the young man study the Torah.

And all that Elijah prophesied came to pass. People came from all corners of the country to be cured. Among them was her wicked brother-in-law. There was also her husband who had fallen ill, after he had been told what his wife had done. There was the poor man who had stood in the hall of the woman's house and who had borne false witness against her; and there were the rabbi and his wife. Then too, there was the student who had wanted to marry her and whom she had refused.

The woman placed these patients in different wards, so that they could not see each other but could only hear. And there was one condition the woman laid down to those who came to be treated in her hospital: "Before receiving treatment, you must confess and reveal all your sins."

First among those who confessed was her rich brother-in-law, who told what he had done to his brother's wife. Then the Jew who had stood in the hall told his story. The husband heard these things and was very angry with those who had slandered his wife, but above all he was angry with himself for having believed the libels that had been told him. The couple who had driven out the woman after the death of their only child, and the student who had killed the child, all confessed their actions. The rabbi and his wife, when they heard the tale of the student, deeply regretted their hasty action against their nurse.

Only when they had confessed did the woman make herself known. She cured her husband who had returned to her, and to the old couple she returned their son, who had, in the meantime, grown up and was a promising scholar.

She did not cure the three others, and they remained sickly to the end of their days.

# Two Sisters

## INTRODUCTION

The following story is another about accused unfaithfulness, but in this tale the woman is guilty, and the message is quite different. It was told to me about ten years ago by my beautician in Jerusalem, Joe David, an observant Jew, as he remembers hearing it in Morocco. The story, based on and almost identical to the *midrash Bamidbar Rabbah* 9, 6, is often told by men. In such tellings, the story is a religious one and has a religious message: if a woman sins, she will be punished by God.

However, at a talk at the Jewish Storytelling Center (92nd Street YM and YWHA in New York City, December 1992), Professor Dov Noy related that during his vast experience, spanning over forty years of story collecting, he heard the story told by women to women. In such tellings, the story had two different endings:

1. The good sister, having passed the test, returns. The adulteress sister, seeing that she has gotten away with the crime, says, "Aha! I got away with it once. I'll do it again!" Professor Noy stated that the female audience, listening to the ending, clapped in approval. His explanation is that these women, from oriental Jewish ethnic groups where they were either secluded at home or lived within a female society, saw, in the ending, an outlet for their own secret wishes. These women, who had no possibility of interacting sexually with men other than their husbands, subconsciously desired such illicit relationships themselves.

2. The good sister, having passed the test, returns and says to the adulteress one, "You sinned once, and I agreed to save you. One sin does not make you a sinner forever. *But* I won't save you again. You must mend your ways." This constructive message is certainly one of female supporting female, sister supporting sister—and one which gives the woman the possibility of continuing her life as a Jewish woman, behaving in a righteous manner. This is an important message.

The adultery ordeal refers to Numbers 5:11-31, in which a woman suspected of unfaithfulness would be taken to the priest, there to receive the Lord's judgment by being force-fed a bitter "cocktail" of water and dust. If her stomach burst, she was considered guilty of her sin. However, the water would have no ill effect upon the innocent, who would be released to return to her home and, as is understood, to conceive new life.

# 69

# *Two Sisters*

nce there were two sisters who looked exactly alike. But they did not act alike: one was righteous; the other was an adulteress.

Now the husband of the evil sister suspected his wife's sin, and he decided to take her to the rabbi to drink the bitter water. If she were unfaithful, God would punish her. If she were innocent, she would remain unharmed.

The wife was distraught, for she knew that she could not pass the test. What could she do? She ran to her sister and begged, "My husband is going to take me to drink the poisoned water. Surely I will not survive. But you, my sister, are innocent, and you will pass the test. You are my dear sister, my flesh and blood. Please, please go in my place."

The good sister loved her sister, so she agreed to go. She was taken to the rabbi, and when she drank the poisoned drink, she remained well, for she was innocent. And she was released.

The evil sister waited for her sister's return, and when she saw her sister enter the house, she was so happy that she ran to her and threw her arms around her sister's neck, and kissed her. At that very moment, she smelled the bitter water in her sister's mouth, and at once fell to the floor, dead.

# The Hacham's Wife Who Was
# Turned to a Snake

## INTRODUCTION

This story, told by a Jewess from Morocco, is a love story: love between a husband and wife, and love of parents for a child. Although the father dotes on the child and adores her, it is the mother, seemingly dead but actually transformed into a snake, who rescues her. This is a women's message. The psychoanalytic school of folklore would give this element an erotic explanation, saying that the mother, in snake form (a male symbol), is actually finding a male for her daughter.

In addition to their love and devotion, the husband and wife are extremely pious and, because of this, are reunited at the end of the tale. This certainly is a strong Jewish message.

The wife's reluctance to gossip about others is a principle important to Jewish women; the Book of Proverbs (31:26) tells us, "She opened her mouth with wisdom, and the law of kindness is on her tongue."

In this tale, replete with supernatural elements, we see extremes of good and evil, in men and women alike. Regardless of sex, the evil are punished and the good are rewarded. As the Bible tells us, "The way of the wicked is an abomination to the Lord; But He loveth him that followeth after righteousness" (Proverbs 15:9). And what could be a greater reward than for one's daughter to marry King Solomon himself?

The story deals with woman-woman conflict between the stepmother and stepdaughter; this conflict is made even sharper because it was the girl who convinced her father to remarry.

# 70

# *The* Hacham's *Wife Who Was Turned to a Snake*

nce there was a pious *hacham* who had only one daughter whom he loved as he loved his own eye. So great was his love for her that if she did not accompany him at the table, he would refuse to eat.

Now, the family had a neighbor, a woman with an evil tongue. She would come and gossip, "This one's daughter went with this man. That one's wife went with that man." She had an evil word to say about everyone.

But the *hacham*'s wife would answer, "*Has veshalom. Has veshalom*—God forbid!" when she heard that kind of talk. She did not want to hear bad words about the daughters of Israel. And so she always answered, *"Has veshalom"* when she heard about *lashon hara.*

But one day the water carrier came to visit the *hacham* and, at that very same moment, the neighbor arrived to spread her gossip. And, because she was distracted, the *hacham*'s wife did not answer, *"Has veshalom,"* as usual. At that very moment she turned into a snake, and slithered into the logs of the house.

When the *hacham* returned, there was no wife. She had disappeared. He mourned for her and missed her deeply. And so, many years passed.

Now the *hacham* had a neighbor lady, who, from the very day that his wife disappeared, would come to visit the daughter. She cared for her, combed her, cleaned her. And one day she said, "You know, a rabbi shouldn't be without a wife. Convince your father to marry me. Pretend to be sad and he will not refuse you."

So the girl feigned illness. "Do not refuse me, Father," she cried. "Marry our neighbor. You know how she loves me and, besides, a rabbi shouldn't be without a wife."

"Ah," sighed the rabbi, "it will be difficult to take a wife after your pious mother, but I will do as you say."

And so the two were married, after which the new wife took good care of the daughter. But, as the months passed, her attitude changed, and she only wanted to be rid of the girl and to have the *hacham* to herself.

Now, the *hacham* had a certain student, a *talmid hacham*, whom he respected greatly. And so the woman called this young man to her and said, "If I find grace in your eyes, do me this favor. I will do anything you ask, if you take my daughter and leave her in the forest, there to be eaten by animals."

"But how can I do that?" protested the young man. "It would be a sin before God."

"Only *you* can do this task, for you are the only one who will not be suspected," argued the woman. And then, when the student smelled the money the woman promised him, he agreed.

The next day the wife approached the daughter. "My dear, you should go out for a breath of fresh air. The sunlight will do you good. Pretend to be sad, and your father will not refuse to let you go."

And so the girl said to the *hacham*, "Father, I want to see the sunlight and to walk in the fresh air. Do not refuse me." At this point the wife even suggested that the young student accompany the daughter, and she prepared food and drink for them to take along the way.

So it was that the young man took the girl to the forest. And there, in a place where there was grass and water, they stopped to eat. But, so much wine did the student give the girl that soon she was drunk, and the young man tied her to a tree and left.

Upon returning home, he told her father that an animal had eaten her, but that he, himself, had been able to escape. The *hacham* cried and mourned for the loss of his daughter.

Meanwhile, as the daughter stood tied to the tree, a snake glided toward her and bit away the ropes. Then the snake gave her signs as if it wanted her to follow. And the two went together, the girl walking, the snake slithering, until, at last, they arrived in Jerusalem at the court of King Solomon.

Now, King Solomon knew the language of all animals and was imbued with a holy spirit, so that he knew all. He knew who the snake was, and who the daughter was, as well. And, in the snake's own tongue, he asked the snake for her daughter in marriage—for the girl was truly a beauty. Upon the girl he bestowed endless gifts. And so it was that King Solomon took the girl as his hundredth wife.

Then King Solomon asked Heaven to permit the snake to return as the *hacham*'s wife. And so it was done! The king asked the husband to come to Jerusalem, for he knew that the husband's heart was pious and true. And so it was that the *hacham* and his wife were reunited.

As for the wicked wife and the student who was tempted by her, to them King Solomon sent a devil to destroy them.

And the daughter, the *hacham*, and his pious wife were thankful for the rest of their days to King Solomon for his wondrous deeds.

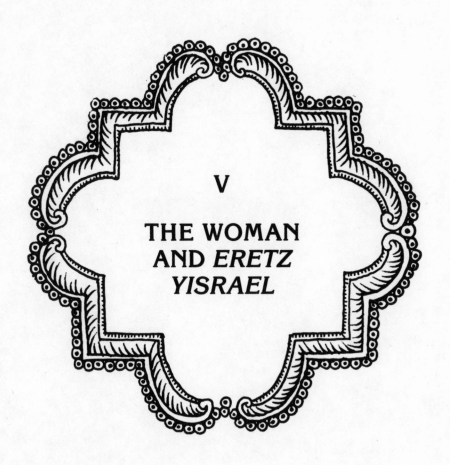

V

# THE WOMAN
# AND *ERETZ*
# *YISRAEL*

# The Woman and *Eretz Yisrael*

"If I forget thee, oh Jerusalem, let my right hand forget her cunning" (Psalm 137:5). The very syllables of the names *Jerusalem* and *Eretz Yisrael* have, for thousands of years, been a kind of prayer, a song, on the lips of Jews throughout the world. The very mention of these two places has created longing and yearning in the hearts of our people.

Just as Jews have written poetry and song about *Eretz Yisrael*, so too have they created legends about this holy place. These may be about Jerusalem, the Holy Temple, or the Wailing Wall, or about other sites in Israel, or they may be about coming to *Eretz Yisrael*, or other events that happened there.

These first two stories show the connection between Jewish women and *Eretz Yisrael* (that is, Jewish space).

# The Lawsuit of the Old Woman against the Wind

## INTRODUCTION

This story was narrated by an elderly Jewish woman from Larissa, Greece.

The story was very popular in literary chapbooks, and was adopted by some of the finest Hebrew and Yiddish authors, including Y. L. Peretz, Sh. F. Anski, and Haim N. Bialik. It combines the clever judge motif with a religious tale about the vindication of God's justice.

In almost all oral parables and literary adaptations, the woman is a widow. This stresses her unfortunate family status, in addition to her old age and poverty. The fact that she is an elderly and needy widow makes her piety, generosity, and strength of character even sharper, showing that she is truly worthy of God's intervention and reward.

The Holy Temple in Jerusalem is considered by Jews to be *the* sacred place, the remainder of the world being profane. In this story a woman's virtues have a direct influence on the building of the Holy Temple, the most sacred Jewish space of all. The very strong Jewish women's message is: A woman's piety can affect the holiest of Jewish places.

In a very similar tale, "The Widow and King Solomon," IFA 6732, told by a Jewess from Morocco, the widow sues the wind at King Solomon's court, but uses the captain's gifts to build a large house and make a wedding for her daughter. King Solomon, whom the woman forgets to invite to the wedding, sends his giant eagle to kidnap the young couple and separate them from each other. The daughter is shut in a tower, as Solomon did to his own daughter (see *Midrash Tanhuma*). The couple is eventually reunited — and all ends well, with King Solomon giving his blessing.

It is possible that, for the female teller of the second tale, the daughter's wedding is so important that she substituted it for the connection with the Holy Temple. Or, perhaps, the connection with King Solomon, who built and reigned at the Holy Temple, is a kind of connection with the Holy Temple itself.

# 71

# *The Lawsuit of the Old Woman against the Wind*

ears ago, in the days of King Solomon in Jeru-salem, there lived an old woman who followed the ways of God, and who practiced justice all her life. Now, this old woman was very poor and had to work hard to find enough money to feed herself and her young grandson.

One year there was a drought in the land, and in Jerusalem the shortage of food was even worse than elsewhere. Many were hungry for bread, and nothing was left for the old woman, not even a single loaf to revive her soul and that of her grandson.

But, try as she might, the old woman could not find work, and, in order not to die, she wandered the streets, begging for charity. Many people passed and looked aside, as if not to see her. But one day, as the sun was going down and evening was approaching, as people were hurrying home, one of the pass-ersby stopped, and, taking pity on the old woman, spoke these words, "Old woman, I have no charity to give you, but I can give you advice that may help. Each day sacks of wheat are carried to the Holy Temple. Follow the footsteps of the wheat carriers, and collect the grains which fall from their sacks. Grind them and bake bread, and, in this way, you will remain alive."

The old woman readily took the advice, and the very next day followed the steps of the wheat carriers. Bending down to the ground, she picked up grain after grain, collecting them in her robe.

But, in the evening, she found that her amount of wheat was so small that it would be useless to take it to the mill. And so she decided to pound the grain at home and bake what she could. And with dry tree branches that she collected from the field, she lit a fire, and, thus, baked three small loaves.

But even before the loaves had a chance to cool off, a poor man appeared at the door. "Old woman," he cried, "I am starving. Please give me a crust of bread, lest I die before your eyes."

Upon hearing these words, the poor old woman thought in her heart, "I have three loaves, and this poor man has nothing. Shall I let him starve? No, God would never accept it." And so she took one of the loaves and gave it to the stranger. The poor man blessed the old woman and turned away with his portion of bread.

And just at that very instant, her grandson approached. "Grandmother, help me. I am so hungry," he cried.

So, with joy and a full heart, the woman gave her grandson the second loaf of bread. Then, taking the third loaf in her hands, she walked to the water to eat it. Then she opened her mouth to utter a prayer of thanks to God: *Hamotzi lehem min haaretz*—but before she could even utter the words, behold! a strong wind arose, a wind which quickly turned to a storm.

The wind lashed fiercely, cutting everything in its way. Why, it even lifted the pan of bread, and took it away, far, far away— until it disappeared from the old woman's sight.

At first the woman was frightened, astonished, but then she became angry. "I gave a portion of my own bread for *tzedakah*," she thought. "Why then did the wind take my own share and leave me with an empty stomach? I shall go to King Solomon and ask him to call the wind to a trial of justice."

Without hesitation she approached the gates of the palace, and soon appeared before the king. There she told her story, pleading, "Please, oh king, call the wind to judgment. Punish him for the evil he did to me."

And while she was speaking, the king's messengers arrived, announcing that outside the palace was the captain of a foreign ship, surrounded by his sailors. They had come to Jerusalem to see the king and present him with a most distinguished gift. Indeed, they vowed that they would do a good deed for the God of Israel in His Temple in Jerusalem.

What an unexpected visitor! Who could it be?

The king asked the old woman to wait while he accepted the captain of the ship. And, in the presence of the old woman and the king, the captain spoke: "We were sailing on the open sea, our ship loaded with expensive cargo, when a storm arose, the likes of which we had never seen before. A hole was soon cut in the side of the ship, and the sea water began to pour in, so that we all knew that the ship would sink. What could we do? I, the captain, and all of my sailors, each in his own tongue, prayed to his own god. But the storm grew stronger. There was no help in sight."

At this the captain paused before the king. Then he continued: "It was then that we remembered the God of Israel, who, we had heard, has the power to perform miracles, and we prayed to Him and vowed that if He would save our lives, we would dedicate all of our cargo to His Holy Temple in Jerusalem.

"Then," said the captain, "while in the midst of prayer, we saw something carried by the wind, something which came very near to our ship, and which stuck into the hole and sealed it. We knew at once that we were saved. And so, as soon as the wind calmed and the waves rested, we rushed to see what it was that had sealed the hole. And there, there we found a loaf of bread stuck in the hole of the ship. The God of Israel had heard our prayers! We were saved from death!"

All this time King Solomon and the old woman had been listening patiently. And now the captain was ending his story: "So now we have come to fulfill our vow. All of the cargo aboard our ship we give as a gift to the God of Israel."

Then King Solomon turned to the woman. "Can you recognize this loaf of bread?"

"Yes," she answered, "it is mine," for the loaf had been undamaged by the sea waters, and had remained as dry as when she had baked it.

"You have heard with your own ears," said the king, "that there is no blaming the wind, for the wind was in a hurry to save these men's lives."

And then the king turned to the captain. "Know you that the loaf of bread belongs to this old woman. Therefore, I have decided to divide the cargo you have brought. Half will be given to the Holy Temple, and half will go to this old woman because of whose good deed your crew was saved."

And the judgment of King Solomon was willingly accepted by all those who were present.

The old woman lived happily ever afterward in richness and joy, doing good deeds for the poor and for all those in need.

May it be good for them and for us as well!

## The Amulet of Rabbi Shalom Sharabi

### INTRODUCTION

For as long as I can remember I have worn around my neck a gold charm, given to me by my mother, may her memory be blessed. The charm says *mazal*, which, in Hebrew, means "constellation" or "star" (indicating luck), and I do believe that the charm brings me luck. I also believe that when I wear it, my mother's spirit and protection are with me. That is why I never take it off.

The amulet in this story is also an amulet given by a mother to a child. But this charm is a very special one because it was written by a very holy man. Just as my mother's amulet brings luck to me, the amulet in this story brings luck to its wearer.

This story was told by Badur Seri, born in Yemen in 1888 but who came to Jerusalem at the age of three. She told the story to her daughter, Rachel Seri, in the 1960s. Rachel then related this tale and over fifty others from Yemen, mostly from her own family, to the IFA. (In addition, the archive now has over 400 stories collected by Rachel Seri from various ethnic groups in Israel.)

This is a tale of the greatness of Rabbi Shalom Sharabi of eighteenth-century Yemen, one of the most venerated of Yemenite sages, about whom many stories are told and about whom the IFA has collected over sixty tales. Most were told by the younger Yemenite generation, born in Israel, who heard them from their families.

Rabbi Shalom Sharabi, who came to Israel in 1739, was a great kabbalist and, because of this knowledge, was able to perform many miracles. The Jews of Yemen, who were treated as second-class citizens, and who, by law, were limited in dress, in occupation, and other aspects of daily life, created a great number of miracle stories; what they could not overcome by power they overcame via story. The miracles of Rabbi Shalom Sharabi, hero of many of these tales, were not doubted by the people; God helps those who believe.

The amulet, or *kamea* in Hebrew, of Shalom Sharabi was, therefore, believed to have magic virtues that could heal and save. As can be seen in the story, it was a treasured inheritance of the family, passed from woman to woman. Belief in holy amulets was common in Yemenite folk medicine. These were made of leather, and contained holy passages from the Bible and the names of angels.

Here, in this woman's version, the mother in the story becomes the heroine, for it is her faith that eventually saves her son. The educational women's message is: It is important to listen to one's parents. The stronger women's message is: Via a woman's death, she gives her son life.

The story also bridges the gap between folk belief and reality. The fact that the amulet kept the son safe during the War of Independence in Israel brings the story into a realistic framework, and ties it to the Holy Land. As the amulet was victorious over the enemies of Israel, the story shows the superiority of Judaism over the religions of her enemies.

# 72

# *The Amulet of Rabbi Shalom Sharabi*

 here once was a Yemenite woman in Jaffa, who received, as an inheritance from her mother, a holy amulet, a charm, which had been passed down to her mother by her grandmother, and to her grandmother by her mother before her. The charm was regarded in the family as a sacred and precious treasure, which had the power of saving its wearer from trouble or disaster. And why? Because it was prepared by the hand of none other than Rabbi Shalom Sharabi, may he rest in peace.

Now, this woman had a son, an only son, who wore the charm night and day from the time he was born. And the fact that this charm was close to her son made the mother happy, for she was certain that her boy would be protected from any danger.

But when the boy grew up, he resisted wearing the charm any longer. "How can a charm protect me?" he scoffed. "I don't believe in charms!" And despite his mother's efforts to plead with him and change his thinking, the boy was steadfast. "I don't believe in the charm, and I don't want to wear it," he insisted.

And so it was that the boy took that charm, which he had worn since the time of his birth, and removed it from his body. At this the mother became ill, convinced that her son would soon fall into danger, and, after much grieving, she died. Then the son began to feel remorse for not heeding the words of his mother. He suffered from guilt, and could find no rest. So, at last he decided that since he had not fulfilled his mother's wish during her lifetime, he would do so after her death. And so, once again, he put on the holy charm, and wore it always close to his heart.

Many years passed. During the War of Independence the young man went into battle, still wearing the charm of Rabbi Shalom Sharabi, according to the request of his mother. And, during the heat of battle, a bullet hit the young man, but as it came close to his body, it penetrated the charm. Thus the young man was saved from death and left the battle unharmed, indeed like one who has been reborn. And all this was due to the amulet of Rabbi Shalom Sharabi, may he rest in peace.

## Brotherly Love

### INTRODUCTION

This tale, told in 1991 to Sarah Davidovitz by Claudine Wasserman-Chatav, a Tunisian woman living in Netanya, Israel, is one of the most recent additions to the IFA collection. The legend is an old one, possibly rooted in *The Thousand and One Nights*, which has been retold and studied for hundreds of years.

The tale is one of a larger group of tales told about the Holy Temple and the Western Wall, from which, according to *Midrash*, the Divine Presence never budges. This particular story is an etiological one, that is, it explains why the Holy Temple was built where it is.

Yet, even though the story is very old, the storyteller breathes new life into it by injecting her excitement about brotherly love. She does this by adding her own comments to the text of the story. The concept of love between two brothers is so important to her that she has used it for the title of the story. This is her educational Jewish women's message.

In addition, the storyteller includes the number three several times in the story, showing that she is a natural storyteller. The number three is repeatedly found in folktales: There are three siblings; the hero repeats his action three times; etc. This adds more interest to the story and allows for many possibilities.

# 73

# *Brotherly Love*

t happened that there were two brothers. One had a wife and children; the other had no children—he was single, not married. They both worked at the same task, plowing the field. And, when they plowed the field, they divided

the bundles of wheat equally. One night, when they went to sleep, the first young man sat and thought, "I divided the wheat equally. But I have children who will worry about me, who will care for me. My brother has no one to care for him. He needs more than I. I will take part of my pile and put it on his." And so he did. (This is very exciting.)

The younger brother said, "I divided the wheat equally. But I have no family. My brother has children. He must educate them, raise them, marry them off. I will give him some of my wheat."

And so he took part of his wheat and put it on his brother's pile.

The two awoke in the morning and saw that the piles had not decreased. It was a mystery. How could this happen? And so, each brother refilled the other's stack of wheat, once, twice, three times, each time thinking, "My brother needs the wheat more than I." After three days and three nights each one said, "I must see who is doing this thing."

So they started to walk, one from this side of the wheat stack, and the other from the other side. And they met in the middle. They hugged and hugged. It was something, that scene, the love of brothers. And in that place the Holy Temple was built.

# *My Mother's Wedding Ring—A Story of* Aliyah

## INTRODUCTION

The State of Israel is, by its very nature, a place of ingathering. After the establishment of the State in 1948, immigrants began to arrive from post-war Europe, from North Africa, the Gulf States, Yemen. Later waves included large numbers from Romania, Russia, Ethiopia. And the people continue to come.

With each immigration came stories of *aliyah*, which in Hebrew literally means "going up" to *Eretz Yisrael*. These were tales of longing for a homeland, of traveling for days, sometimes years, individually or in small groups, of danger along the way, of walking for thousands of miles, or riding in a strange bird called an airplane. Thousands of such tales exist.

One, told to me by a friend in Haifa, is about his grandmother, who left Romania for Israel shortly after World War II, dressed in the finest array (fancy hat, dress, high-heeled shoes) in order to properly greet her new home. In such array she was prepared to *walk* to the Land of Israel. Unfortunately, circumstances delayed her arrival for four years, during which she *walked* through Hungary, Austria, Italy—until a ship finally brought her "home."

The following story was told to me in Haifa in the early '80s by a student of mine, then in her twenties, a member of a kibbutz in northern Israel. The story is based on the fact that there was a collection of jewelry and valuables, called for on a voluntary basis, by the government of Israel after the Sinai War in the 1950s, when the State was in need of money to cover its war debt. Jewelry was kept in the Central Bank until changed for currency. In many cases people who regretted, either for sentimental or other reasons, having donated their jewelry, could reclaim it.

# 74

# *My Mother's Wedding Ring— A Story of* Aliyah

 hortly after my parents were married, they decided to leave Russia and come to *Eretz Yisrael*, to live in a Jewish country. Before my parents could leave, the police demanded that they surrender all their gold. My mother gave up her earrings, but when it came time to hand over her wedding ring, she was very determined to keep it. So she thought of a plan. Taking a sharp knife, she cut her finger until it was swollen—and the ring would not come off. The Russian

official waved her on, and so she continued to *Eretz Yisrael* with her ring intact.

Some years later, when the government of Israel was badly in need of funds—for the soldiers, for the war—people were asked to donate jewelry: earrings, rings, whatever they could. My mother willingly gave up her wedding ring. As she told me, "For Russia I wouldn't give up my ring, but for a Jewish state, I gave it gladly."

VI

A CLOSING
TALE

## The Three-Eyed Daughter

### INTRODUCTION

This universal tale type, found in Grimm and known all over the European world, is a story of mother–daughter conflict. In this version, told by Miriam Shwili from Yemen, we see that "Three Eyes" accepts the decree of God for having been created different from everyone else. This Jewish concept is different from the attitude of the daughter in universal versions. An additional IFA version of this tale type was told by a Jewish woman from Afghanistan.

In our Yemenite tale little is told of the girl's character or virtues. Also, nothing is told of what happens to her afterwards. Personally, I wanted her to marry a prince and live happily ever after, as befits the persecuted heroine in fairy tales. Or, at the very least, I expected the wonderful tree to appear at her window, thereafter supplying her with food forever. The story deals, not with a just and happy outcome for the mistreated daughter (as in the fairy tales of Europe) but, rather, with the just and harsh punishment of the wicked mother. See what happens to an unappreciative, evil mother! This could be its message.

But, perhaps, the greatest message of the story (and what a wonderful note for ending this collection!) is:

May we all, mothers and fathers alike, treasure the imperfections in our children and cherish them as blessings from God!

# 75

# *The Three-Eyed Daughter*

nce there was a woman who had three daughters. Two were born with two eyes, like most other people, and their mother loved them very much. But the third was born with three eyes— and her mother didn't love her.

"Three eyes" was made to do all the work. Every morning

265

she had to take the goats a long way off to graze, and, in the evening, when she returned, hungry, she was given only scraps of food, the leftovers to eat.

One day, as she sat in the grass near her flock, hungry as always, she began to weep. And suddenly, an angel appeared: "Young girl, why are you crying?"

"Oh, it is because my mother does not love me the way God made me, thus, with three eyes, and she gives me only scraps of food to eat, and I am hungry indeed."

"Do not cry," replied the angel. "Tomorrow in this very place a young kid will appear and dance before you. Say to it: 'My kid, my kid, bring me food' and it will dig its horns into the earth and bring forth wonderful food. Eat and drink, and whatever remains you are to bury in the ground."

"Oh, thank you, thank you," cried the young girl in disbelief.

The next day, as the girl sat near her flock, a young kid did indeed appear and dance before her. "My kid, my kid, bring me food," she cried. And the kid dug its horns into the ground and brought forth delicious foods. The girl ate all that she could—and, as she had been instructed, buried the rest in the earth. The kid disappeared.

In the evening, when she returned, she did not even touch the food her mother gave her. "What is it? Why aren't you eating?" asked the mother.

But the girl replied, "Oh, I am just not hungry." In this way several days passed, but the mother and sisters continued to notice that the girl did not eat, and they grew suspicious.

"Someone must be feeding her," said the mother to her first daughter. "Tomorrow morning you shall follow her and see what is taking place."

So the daughter did as she was told and followed her sister to the grazing pasture. And that day, when the magic kid appeared and brought forth the wonderful food, she saw all that was happening. At once she ran home to report her findings to her mother.

"Ah, so that is the secret!" cried the mother. "I'll put a stop to that!" And the very next morning she took a sharp knife and went to the pasture, caught the kid, and slaughtered it. Its skin, horns, and bones she then threw behind the house. As for the meat, why, she and her daughters had a fine feast— and, of course, shared it not with their third sister. "Now she will surely die," thought the mother.

The next morning the girl went to the pasture and waited for her kid. The day passed, and the kid did not come. What was she to do? That evening she ate the scraps that her mother left her and, once again, she began to weep.

After several days the same angel appeared. "And why are you crying this time? You have all the food you need."

"Oh, no," cried the girl, "I am still hungry. My mother slaughtered my magic kid; only its skin, its horns, and its bones are left near the house."

"Good," answered the angel. "Fetch them. Bring them here."

So the girl brought forth what the angel requested. Then he dug a hole and buried the kid's remains inside. At once a tree grew in its place. "Tomorrow sweet fruit will grow from the tree," the angel told her. "Eat of it and you will be satisfied."

The next day, as the angel prophesied, magnificent fruit began to grow from the tree; soon it was covered with species from all the world. That day the girl ate her fill.

When she returned that evening, she once again did not eat the scraps her mother left her. The woman knew at once that someone was feeding the girl, so she turned to her second daughter and said, "Tomorrow you must follow your sister and see what is happening." So the daughter did what she was told, and when she saw that special tree, covered with fine fruits from all the world, she ran back to tell her mother.

The next morning the mother herself took a large axe, went to the pasture, and chopped down the tree—all its branches, all its leaves, down to the very roots. And the mother approached the roots to uproot them as well—when out slithered a giant snake.

Startled, the woman ran in the opposite direction, but behold! There in front of her was the sea.

She couldn't run forward: there was the water. She couldn't run backward: there was the snake.

She cried for help! But the people said, "How can we help you? The sea is on this side; the snake, on the other."

And so the woman remained in that place until she died of hunger and thirst.

# Comparative Sources—
## Explanation

The purpose of these comparative sources is to refer the researcher to published sources and retellings of these tales. The sources listed here are in addition to those given in the introduction to each story.

This list refers only to those tales found at the IFA. Tales that were told to me personally or obtained elsewhere are not listed here.

The following scheme has been used:

The IFA number refers to the tale's identification number in the Israel Folktale Archives.

AT refers to the Aarne-Thompson classification system, originally done by Aarne Thompson, to classify types or plots of universal tales. The AT system is used as the basis of the IFA Type Index. An asterisk *preceding* a number indicates that this is an additional number, not included in the AT index, but used in the IFA. This occurs when a tale is close to a universal type but has so many unique Jewish elements that it is granted its own number. This is called an oicotype.

Jewish tales (particularly legends) that are not close to AT (universal) types have *not* been classified by the IFA. Nor, as of this date, have stories with IFA numbers above 10,000 been classified.

Motif refers to the Thompson Motif classification system, which was expanded to include Jewish tales in the Neuman (Noy) Motif system. A narrative motif, according to Stith Thompson, author of this classification system, is "a part into which the tale can be analyzed" (*Funk and Wagnalls Standard Dictionary of Folklore,* p. 753). These motifs contain elements of magic or personality that are other than commonplace, in order that the folk remember them and include them in the tradition. A story may contain one motif or a combination of many.

Both the AT type index and the motif index are internationally accepted. Therefore, by using these indexes, a researcher can trace parallel tales from many cultures.

These sources are also meant to serve as a key to published IFA and other contemporary versions in which a telling by the *native* teller may be found.

"See" refers to an IFA publication in which the version I have retold here may be found. "See also" refers to background versions and/or IFA or other contemporary publications in which other versions or variants (similar tales) may be found. Publications are listed by name of the author or editor and, thus, may be identified in the bibliography.

The following abbreviations are used in the listing:

BJ = *Der Born Judas*
IFA = Israel Folktale Archives
JAT = *Jewish Animal Tales*
Marcus, *Fount* = *From the Fountainhead*
MMI = *Mimekor Yisrael*
Noy, *Folktales* = *Folktales of Israel*
RBJ = Revised *Born Judas*
TEM = *A Tale for Each Month*

Emphasized in this listing of sources are the publications of early collectors and retellers, such as Farhi, Cahan, Bin Gorion, Gaster, Ginzberg, and Bialik, whose invaluable pioneering works set the framework for our folktale studies today. More contemporary retellings, such as those by Patai, Rush, Sadeh, Schram, Schwartz, and Weinreich, may also be traced via the bibliography.

This listing shows comparative sources or works of Jewish nature. For comparative sources in world literature, see Gaster, *Exempla,* Schwarzbaum, *Studies, World,* and Noy, *Folktales,* headnotes to stories.

# Comparative Sources

1. Why Man Has an Adam's Apple
   IFA 9584
   Contains motifs:
      A 1319.1 "Origin of Adam's apple"
      A 1275 "Creation of man's mate"
      A 610 "Creation of the universe by creator"
   See *TEM*, 1973 #10
   For sources about the behavior of Adam, see Ginzberg, vol. 1, pp. 67, 74, 118; 3, p. 85; 5, p. 87, 133–134.
   For sources of Lilith's attacking both men and women, see Ginzberg, vol. 5, pp. 88, 148; 6, p. 338.
   For thought-provoking articles on the development of the Lilith legend, see Cantor, Lilith, and Schwartz, "Mermaid."

2. The Midwife's Reward
   IFA 279
   AT 476* "In the Frog's House"
   Contains motifs:
      C 242 "Tabu: eating food of witch (demon)"
      F 333 "Fairy grateful to human midwife"
   See Noy, *Folktales* #12
   See also Rand-Rush (English translation)
   For additional versions and background, see:
      Ben Yehezkel, vol. 4, pp. 33–37 "Circumciser as hero"
      Bin Gorion, *BJ*, vol. 6, pp. 63–67
      Grunwald, "Spaniolic" (Sephardic Jewish)
   For additional information about magic objects described in folktales, see Noy, "Archiving."

4. There Is No Escape from Fate
   IFA 5185
   AT 930 "Tales of Fate: The Predestined Wife"
   Contains motif T 22.2 "Predestined wife"
   See also Jason, *Types*, p. 188, and the IFA publications:
      Attias #9
      Noy, *Tunisia* #54, 66 and #6 note
      Noy, *Shwili* #99
      *TEM*, 1970 #2

Noy, *Iraq* #5, 80
Noy, *Folktales* #49
*TEM*, 1963 #4 = Marcus, *Fount* #12
For background versions, see:
Bin Gorion, *BJ* vol. 1, pp. 219, 221–224, 375, 887
_____ *MMI* (Hebrew) #82
Bialik, *And It Came to Pass*, p. 221
Abrahams, pp. 172–183
Ginzberg, vol. 4, pp. 175–176; 6, p. 303
Gaster, *Exempla* #336
Ben Yehezkel, rev. ed., vol. 5, pp. 47–66
For a Sephardic Jewish version, see Palacin, #111.
See also the excellent chapter in Shenhar, *Jewish and Israeli Folklore*.
See also notes in Schwarzbaum, *Studies, World*, pp. 273–275.

5.  The Match Made in Heaven
    IFA 3789
    AT 930*K
    Contains motif T 22.2 "Predestined wife"
    See also:
    Jason, *Types* 930*K
    Gaster, *Maaseh* #336
    Noy, *Tunisia* #54
    _____ , *Iraq* #70

6.  Sarah and Shlomo
    IFA 8596
    AT 930*E
    Contains motif T 22.2 "Predestined wife"
    See also:
    the variant in Bin Gorion, *MMI* vol. 3 #7
    and the IFA versions:
    Noy, *Morocco* #43
    _____ , *Shwili* #99
    Baharav, *Mi-Dor le-Dor* #4
    *TEM*, 1978 #2
    note to *TEM*, 1963 #4

7.  The Girl Swallowed Up by a Stone
    IFA 5418
    AT 706 "The Maiden Without Hands"
    See: Noy, *Libya* #61

8. King Solomon and Queen Kashira
   IFA 1071
   AT 888 "The Faithful Wife Rescues Her Enslaved Husband"
   For a rich tracing and bibliography of AT 1510 ("The Matron
       of Ephesus"), which is the first part of the story, see Bin
       Gorion, *MMI* (1990 ed.) #205 notes.
   See Noy, *Morocco* #44
   See also:
       Gaster, *Maaseh* #107
       _____ , *Exempla* #442
       Bin Gorion, *MMI* vol. 3., pp. 240, 315
   See also the IFA publications:
       Noy, *Tunisia* #68
       _____ , *Libya* #8
       Alexander, Noy #54
       *TEM*, 1964 #9 (Poland)
   See the interesting comments in:
       Schwarzbaum, "Female Fickleness"
       Shenhar, "On the Popularity"

9. The Ten Serpents
   IFA 386
   AT 425*Q "The Search for the Lost Husband: Marvelous
       Being Woos Princess"
   See Noy, *Folktales* #58
   See also Cahan, 1938 #20 (East Europe)
   For Sephardic Jewish versions, see:
       Grunwald #3, 6, 9, 46
       Meyuhas #5
   For other IFA versions on "the search for the lost husband,"
       see:
       *TEM*, 1963 #10
       Noy, *Tunisia* #71 note 13
       _____ , *Libya* #64
       *TEM*, 1968–1969 #10
       Avitsuk #28 (Iraqi Kurdistan)

10. The Ugly Daughter
    IFA 10258
    AT 510 "Cinderella"
    Contains motifs:
        N 711.6 "Prince sees heroine at ball and is enamored"
        H 36.1 "Slipper test"

See *TEM*, 1974–1975 #9
See also:
 Haviv, *Taba'at* #1 (Bukhara)
 Noy, *Shwili* #24
 Alexander, Noy #9 (Palestine Sephardi)
 Shenhar, *Shlomi* #3
For an interesting account of a present-day Cinderella story
 in Israel, see Bilu and Hasan-Rokem.

11. Seven Bags of Gold
 IFA 4871
 AT 676 "Open Sesame"
 AT 403 "The Black and White Bride"
 AT 450 "Little Brother and Little Sister"
 AT 76 "The Wolf and the Crane"
 Although this tale is typed in the IFA as AT 676 "Open
  Sesame," it is not true to this type since the secret
  password is missing.
 See Fus #7
 See also:
  Noy, *Tunisia* #7
  _____ , *Shwili* #35
  _____ , *Folktales* #23
  Baharav, *Ashqelon* #36
 For other IFA versions of AT 403, see:
  Noy, *Libya* #2, 67
  _____ , *Shwili* #24
 For other IFA versions of AT 450, see:
  Noy, *Libya* #67
  _____ , *Shwili* #20
  Marcus, *Fount* #11

12. The Garbage Girl Who Married the King
 IFA 7070
 AT 873 "The King Discovers His Unknown Son"
 Contains motifs:
  T 645 "King in disguise leaves a token with girl to give to
   their son if one is born"
  L 162 "King marries boy's mother"
 See *TEM*, 1966 #10
 See also:
  Bin Gorion, *BJ*, vol. 1, 200
  Noy, *Shwili* #76

13. The Baker's Daughter and the King's Son
    IFA 6839
    AT 879 "The Basil Maiden"
    Contains motifs:
    H 705.3 "Prince ridicules girl with rhyme but girl scorns
    him in turn—question and counter question"
    K 525.1 "Prince takes wife but first night seeks to avenge
    himself by cutting off head. She saves herself by
    putting in her place a puppet of sugar."
    See Noy, *Tunisia* #8
    See also Noy, *Shwili* #79

14. The Mountain of *Sheidim*
    IFA 1346
    AT 470* "The Hero Visits the Land of the Immortals"
    Contains motifs:
    F 302 "Fairy mistress"
    F 303 "Wedding of the mortal and fairy"
    F 302.3.4.1 "Fairy's kiss fatal"
    Q 247 "Punishment for desertion of fairy mistress"
    See Noy, *Shwili* #42 (Yemenite version in German transla-
    tion)
    This story has a long history. The story of the Jerusalemite
    first appeared in print bound together with "Divrei Ha-
    yamim Shel Moshe Rabbenu" (Chronicles of Moses) in
    Constantinople in 1517. It was later translated into Latin
    by J.C. Wagenseil in 1697, and appeared in Yiddish in
    Germany in 1711. An earlier fifteenth-century manu-
    script (Vatican Hebrew Codex 100) helped construct
    another version of the tale, and a seventeenth-century
    literary treatment was given in Jerusalem in 1889 by Ibn
    Sussan.
    Later versions include:
    Bin Gorion, *MMI* (Hebrew) #622; *MMI* (1990) #200, 201;
    *MMI* vol. 3 #10, 11
    _____ , *BJ*, vol. 1, pp. 224–243, 376, 378
    _____ , *RBJ* 1 #153
    For rich information about this tale, see also Aloni, Dan,
    Kagan, and Shenhar in the bibliography.
    For "The Weasel and the Well," see:
    Gaster, *Exempla* #89
    _____ , *Maaseh* #100

Maitlis (Yiddish) #21
Farhi, vol. 1, pp. 53–55
Bin Gorion, *MMI* (Hebrew) #295
_____ , *BJ*, vol. 1., pp. 124–128, 368
Eisenstein, pp. 161–162

15.  The Giving of Charity Is Repaid
IFA 2307
AT 706 "The Maiden Without Hands"
Contains motifs:
Q 451.1 "Hands cut off as punishment"
E 782.1 "Hands restored"
See Noy, *Tunisia* #52
See also:
Noy, *Morocco* #24 = Marcus, *Fount* #1
_____ , *Shwili* #38, 39, 22, note to #39
Avitsuk #33
For AT 706*D "The Slandered Maiden: The Wicked Father
Miraculously Punished"; "Punishment Fits the Crime"
See also:
Noy, *Shwili* #39
Baharav, *Ashqelon* #60
See also the excellent chapter in Shenhar, *Jewish and
Israeli Folklore.*

16.  Great Are the Deeds of God
IFA 4724
See *TEM*, 1962 #11

17.  The Deceived Girl and the Stone of Suffering
IFA 155
Contains motifs:
K 2251.1 "Treacherous slave girl"
H 13.2.2 "Recognition by overheard conversation with
stone"
See Noy, *Folktales* #48
See also:
Haviv, *Tangiers* #7
_____ , *Taba'at* #4
Note to Yehoshua #12

18.  The Enchanted Princess Who Became a Bouquet
IFA 3984
AT 407 "The Girl as Flower"

Contains motif D 212 "Maiden transformed into flower"
See also the note to Avitsuk #32

19.  The Pomegranate Girl
     IFA 6373
     AT 709 "Snow White"
     Contains motifs:
         S 31 "Cruel stepmother"
         L 55 "Stepdaughter heroine"
         F 451.5.1.2 "Dwarfs adopt girl as sister"
         F 852.1 "Glass coffin"
         N 711 "King (prince) accidentally finds maiden in woods
             and marries her"
         K 512.2 "Compassionate executioner; substituted heart"
     See also:
         Noy, *Libya* #2
         _____ , *Shwili* #20, 17

20.  The Girl with the Cow's Face, Redeemed by Elijah the Prophet
     IFA 5800
     AT 873*A "The Girl with the Animal Face" (a Jewish oi-
         cotype of AT 873) "The King Discovers His Unknown
         Son"
     See also:
         Jason, *Types*, p. 171
         Bin Gorion, *MMI* (Hebrew) #618
         _____ , *BJ*, vol. 6, pp. 200–216, 349–353, 375–385
         _____ , *RBJ*, vol. 1, #152
         Farhi, vol. 2, pp. 152–160
         and IFA versions:
             *TEM*, 1962 #2
             Baharav, *Ashqelon* #52
             Noy, *Iraq* #62
             _____ , *Morocco* #26
             Marcus, *Fount* #3
             as well as Alexander, Noy #7
     See also the excellent chapter in Shenhar, *Jewish and Israeli
         Folklore.*
     For information on deformities in Jewish sources, see Hol-
         den.

21.  He Who Has Found a Wife Has Found Good
     IFA 11459 (Persia) and 3063 (Egypt)
     AT 875 "The Clever Peasant Girl"

Contains a combination of motifs:

> H 586 "Riddling remarks of traveling companion inter-
> preted by girl at end of journey"
> H 586.1 "Man helps traveler and makes riddling remarks"
> J 1111.4 "Clever peasant daughter"
> H 561.1 "Clever peasant girl asked riddles by king"
> H 1152.1 "Task: selling a sheep and bringing it back along
> with the money"
> H 601 "Wise carving of the fowl. Clever person divides it
> symbolically"
> L 162 "Lowly heroine marries king"
> J 1191.1 "Reductio ad absurdum: the decision about the
> colt"
> J 1545.4 "The exiled wife's dearest possession"

See also:

> *Pesikta Rabbah*, 31
> Gaster, *Exempla* #196
> Bin Gorion, *MMI* (Hebrew) #743
> _____ , *BJ*, vol. 4, pp. 108–114, 280

and IFA versions:

> Baharav, *Ashqelon* #1 (Libya)
> *TEM*, 1962 #7 (Egypt)
> *TEM*, 1961 #4
> Noy, *Shwili* #77, 78, 79 (Yemen)
> _____ , *Iraq* #101
> *TEM*, 1971 #11 (Yemen)
> *TEM*, 1968–1969 #3 (Bukhara)
> Haimovits #8 (Yemen)

as well as:

> Kort #13 (Afghanistan)
> Alexander, Noy #98 (Palestine, Sephardi)

See also the excellent article, Noy, "Riddles at the Wedding
Feast."

See also the notes in Schwarzbaum, *Studies, World*, pp.
394–395, and for midrashic versions and influences of
the motif, "The exiled wife's dearest possesssion," see
p. 47 in the same volume.

24. The Hungry Bride
    IFA 5699
    AT 903C* "Mother-in-law and Daughter-in-law: The bad
    mother-in-law who lets her daughter-in-law be hungry is
    punished"

See *TEM*, 1963 #8

25. The Lost Princess and the Lost Prince
    IFA 2043
    AT 506 "The Rescued Princess"
    AT 304 "The Hunter"
    Contains motifs:
       R 61 "Person sold into slavery"
       H 117 "Identification by cut garment"
    See Noy, *Tunisia* #11

26. Lanjeh
    IFA 9021
    AT 444* "Enchanted Prince Disenchanted"
    See the notes on Solomon's daughter being locked in a
       tower, story #4.

27. Honor Your Mother
    IFA 6823
    AT 244C* "Raven Drowns His Young Who Promise to Aid
       Him When He Becomes Old"
    Contains motif J 267.1 "He saves one who admits he will not
       help, because he will have to carry his own young."
    See Gutter #1
    See also Noy, *JAT* #51
    For the treatment of mother by the rabbis, see Gaster,
       *Exempla* #189, 190, 191.

28. The Bird and Her Three Goslings
    IFA 7015
    AT 244C* "Raven Drowns His Young Who Promise to Aid
       Him When He Becomes Old"
    Contains motif J 267.1 "He saves one who admits he will not
       help, because he will have to carry his own young"
    See the notes to story #27.

30. The Mother
    IFA 7853
    AT 899 "Alcestis"
    See the notes to story #37.

31. The Experiment
    IFA 7405
    AT 982 "Supposed Chest of Gold Induces Children to Care
       for Aged Father"

See also:
Noy, *Tunisia* #61
_____ , *Libya* #60
Yehoshua #10 = *TEM*, 1966 #5
Baharav, *Mi-Dor le-Dor* #62 (Iraq)
Yeshiva #4 (Romania)

32. The Grandfather Who Was Thrown Out of the *Sukkah*
IFA 3257
AT 980A "The Half Carpet"
Contains motif J 121 "A man gives his old father half a carpet
to keep him warm. The child keeps the other half and
tells his father that he is keeping it for him when he
grows old."
See also:
Gaster, *Maaseh* #437
and the IFA versions:
Haviv, *Tangiers* #6, for the version told by Aliza Anidjar
Yehoshua #13
Marcus, *Fount* #28
Gutter #10 (Poland)

33. Charity Will Save From Death—1
IFA 876
AT 934*F
See also Jason, *Types*, pp. 58–59, 190
For talmudic and midrashic sources, see:
*Rosh Hashanah* 16b
*Baba Batra* 10a
*Midrash Ecclesiastes Rabbah* VII 14
*Seder Eliahu Rabbah*
For stories about charity saving from death, see also:
Yeshiva #1
Bin Gorion, *MMI* (Hebrew) #150
Gaster, *Exempla* #314, 394, and p. 204 for additional
sources
Gaster, *Maaseh* #83
Goldin, pp. 30–31 (sources)
For stories of giving charity saving one from a sinking ship,
see:
Goldin, pp. 30–31
Gaster, *Exempla*, #99, 298

Ha-Kohen, *Me'il Zedakah* 188, 189, 430.

For a story on giving of charity saving one from the King of Demons, see the Jerusalem Talmud *Peah* VIII 9.

For stories on the benevolence to a blind man rewarded by the Angel of Death with prolongation of life, see:

Jellinek, vol. 6, pp. 134–135

Gaster, *Exempla* #387.

For a story on how giving charity to an orphan saves from death, see Eisenstein, p. 39.

For a story on the giving of charity to a widow saving one from death, see:

Gaster, *Exempla* #100

Talmud, *Baba Batra* 11a

For IFA versions about charity saving from death, see also:

Noy, *Morocco* #16

Yeshivah #1 (Romania)

Marcus, *Fount* #35 (Persian Kurdistan)

*TEM*, 1965 #3 (Persian Kurdistan)

For further sources, see Schwarzbaum, *Studies, World*, pp. 278–280.

For versions about Rabbi Meir saving an uncharitable man from death, see:

Bin Gorion, *MMI* (1990) #165

Farhi, vol. 1, pp. 62–64

Ha-Kohen #441

and the suggestions in Schwarzbaum, *Studies, World*, p. 280.

34. Charity Will Save from Death—2

IFA 5113

AT 934*F

For this particular story, see also Gaster, *Exempla* #318.

For a talmudic version told in English (as well as other stories about charity saving from death), see Patai.

For additional sources, see Schwarzbaum, *Studies, World*, p. 280.

35. The Fate of a Son

IFA 8148

AT 934*G

For other sources about the bride saving the bridegroom from death, see also:

Jason, *Types*, pp. 59, 190

Bin Gorion, *MMI*, vol. 3, pp. 123–127

Noy, *Morocco* #63

For the story of Matanya, see:

Bin Gorion, *MMI* (Hebrew) #620; *MMI*, vol. 3 #8; *MMI* (1990) #199

_____ , *BJ*, vol. 1, pp. 153–155, 371–372

Gaster, *Exempla* #139

_____ , *Maaseh* #195

Jellinek, vol. 5, p. 52

Cronbach, pp. 503–567

For a rich article on this topic, see Schwarzbaum, "Hero Predestined."

36. By Right of His Wife's Charity

IFA 6505

See Stahl #20

37. A Mother's Love—2

IFA 7280

A variant of AT 899 "Wife Sacrifices Self For Husband When His Parents Refuse (Motif T 211.1)"

Can also be found under oicotype 934*G "Charity Saves from Death" in which the bride saves her husband from death.

See the excellent article by Schwarzbaum, "The Hero Predestined to Die on His Wedding Day."

See also:

Farhi, vol. 1 29a

Gaster, *Exempla* #139

Bin Gorion, *BJ*, vol. 1, pp. 149, 153–154, 156

and the more contemporary version in Cohen, *From the Mouths* #31

38. The Miracle of Elijah the Prophet

IFA 14579

AT *776 "Divine Rewards"

See also:

Farhi, vol. 3, pp. 354–355

Bin Gorion, *MMI*, vol. 2 #18; *MMI* (1990) #66

Gaster, *Maaseh* #35

_____ , *Exempla* #163, 409

Maitlis (Yiddish) #6

Stahl #4 and Rush, Marcus (English translation)

For more information on Elijah the Prophet in folktales, see
Noy, "Elijah," Schram, *Elijah*, and Weinreich, "Genres,
Elijah."

39. The *Shabbat* Candles
    IFA 2821
    See Weinstein #16

40. By Right of Observing the Sabbath
    IFA 6945
    AT *776 "Divine Rewards"
    See Haviv, *Tangiers* #5

41. The Rabbi Who Would Not Mourn on *Shabbat*
    IFA 3942
    AT *776 "Divine Rewards"
    See:
        Noy, *Morocco* #19
        Rush, Marcus (English translation) or Marcus, *Chag* #81
    See the *midrash* to Proverbs 31
    See also Gaster, *Exempla* #147

42. The Gifts of Elijah the Prophet—A Woman of Valor
    IFA 2112
    AT 750 "The Wishes"
    See also:
        Gaster, *Exempla* #355
        _____ , *Maaseh* #157
        Eisenstein, p. 342
        and the IFA version in Haviv, *Tangiers* #1

44. The Observance of the Sabbath
    IFA 7846
    See:
        Kort #116
        Rush, Marcus (English) or Marcus, *Chag* #71

45. A Disloyal Woman Honors the Sabbath
    IFA 6696

46. The Young Girl from Poland and the Baron de Rothschild
    IFA 2791
    See Weinstein #5

47. The Taste of the Sabbath Meal
    IFA 6494

See Stahl #25
See also:
   Gaster, *Maaseh* #5
   Rush, Marcus (English) or Marcus, *Chag* #87

48. The Cossacks
    IFA 1935
    For a beautiful literary account of the daughters of Matta-
       thias, see Bin Gorion, *MMI*, vol. 1 #128 or *MMI* (1990)
       #50. Although the tale is not found in the Book of
       Maccabees, its sources are old and date as far back as
       the second century. See "Midrash for Hanukkah" in
       Jellinek, vol. 6, pp. 2–3 and also Jellinek, vol. 1, p. 133.
       See also Eisenstein, vol. 1, pp. 189–190, 192; Bin
       Gorion, *MMI* (Hebrew) #118; Bin Gorion, *BJ*, vol. 1, pp.
       56–59, 324–325, 363, 385; *RBJ*, vol. 1, #46.
    The legend contains the motifs:
    T 161 "Jus primae noctis"
    J 87 "Men shamed for their cowardice by a woman
       standing naked before them"
    For sources about the legend, see Schwarzbaum, *Studies,
       World*, pp. 51–52 and Bin Gorion, *MMI* (1990), notes to
       #50.
    For the story of Judith, see:
    Bin Gorion, *MMI* (Hebrew) #116a, 116b, 116c; *MMI*, vol. 1
       #124, 125, 126; *MMI* (1990) #49
    _____ , *BJ*, vol. 1, pp. 148–155, 323, 362, 368
    _____ , *RBJ*, vol. 1 #45; vol. 2 #207–208
    Farhi, vol. 1, pp. 27–29
    Eisenstein, vol. 1, p. 204
    Gaster, *Exempla* #251
    Jellinek, vol. 1, pp. 130–131
    For a rich tracing of Judith in apocryphal, medieval, and
       midrashic texts, see Bin Gorion, *MMI* (1990) #49 notes.

49. The Brides
    IFA 14867

51. A Hannukah Guest
    IFA 3484
    AT 750*J
    See also:
       *TEM*, 1967 #8 (Lebanon)

Avitsuk #12 (Romania)

Noy, *Tunisia* #9

52. The Sabbath of Divorces

IFA 7299

See:

Noy, *Libya* #68 and

Rush, Marcus (English translation) or Marcus, *Chag* #89

53. Two Washerwomen on Pesah Eve

IFA 6840

AT 750*J

See:

Noy, *Tunisia* #9

Rush, Marcus (English translation) or Marcus, *Chag* #49

See also:

Avitsuk #12 (Romania)

*TEM*, 1967 #8 (Lebanon)

55. Love Like Salt

IFA 5691

AT 923 "Love Like Salt" (Motif H 592.1)

See also AT 510V1 "Value of Salt"

The ending comes from IFA 5956.

See also:

Cahan (Yiddish) (1931) #13

Gaster, *Exempla* #148

_____ , *Maaseh* #68

For an excellent analysis of this motif, see Dundes.

The IFA lists all subtypes of 923 under the main 923 heading;

for subtypes, see also:

Noy, *Tunisia* #32, 39

_____ , *Shwili* #21, 44

_____ , *Libya* #12 = *TEM*, 1961–62

_____ , *Folktales* #57

56. The Woman Will Humiliate and the Woman Will Raise

IFA 444

AT 923B "The Princess Who Was Responsible for Her Own
Fortune"

See references to story #55.

57. The Daughter Awaits the Gift of God

IFA 2875

AT 923B "The Princess Who Was Responsible for Her Own Fortune"
Contains motifs:
  M 21, N 145, L 419.2
See references to story #55.

59. The Clever Daughter of the *Poritz*
IFA 630
AT 983 "The Dishes of the Same Flavor"
Contains motif J 81 "Man thus shown that one woman is like another and dissuaded from his amorous purpose"
See Fus #1
For more background information on this tale type, see Schwarzbaum, *Studies, World*, p. 123.

63. The King's Daughter and Her Seven Brothers
IFA 12389
AT 451 "The Maiden Who Seeks Her Brothers"
Contains motifs:
  S 11 "Cruel father"
  P 253.0.5 "One sister plus six (seven, eleven, twelve) brothers"
  T 595 "Sign hung out informing brothers whether mother has borne boy or girl"
  N 344.1 "Wrong sign put out leads to boys' leaving home"
  S 272.1 "Flight of brothers from home to avoid being sacrificed"
  P 253.2 "Sister faithful to transformed brothers"
  H 1385.8 "Quest for lost brothers"

64. Money Comes and Money Goes but a Profession Lasts Forever
IFA 5610
AT 888A* "The Basket Maker"
See Haimovits #1 = Noy, *Tunisia* #44
See also:
  *TEM*, 1968–1969 (Syria)
  Alexander, Noy #9 (Palestine Sephardi)
  Marcus, *Fount* #13 (Persian Kurdistan)
  Noy, *Iraq* #45
  Yehoshua #3 (Afghanistan)
See also the article Noy, "Profession."

65. The Clever Wife
IFA 506

AT 899*H "The Lonely Wife"
Contains motifs:
  F 1041.1.4 "Death from longing"
  D 1624 "Image bleeding"
See Noy, *Folktales* #47 = Noy, *Iraq* #61
See also:
  Yehoshua #12, for the male version from Afghanistan
  Avitsuk #5 (Romania)

66. A Woman of Valor—Crown of Her Husband
    IFA 11272
    AT 545B "Puss in Boots"
    AT 859*E "Poor Suitor Pretends to Wealth"
    See also:
      Noy, *Tunisia* #16, 58
      _____ , *Shwili* #73

67. The Son Who Wanted to be a Merchant
    IFA 301
    AT 890 "A Pound of Flesh"
    Contains motifs:
      K 1837 "Disguises of woman in man's clothes"
      K 1825.2 "Woman masks as lawyer (judge) and frees her
          husband"
      J 1161.2 "Pound of Flesh. Literal pleading frees man from
          pound of flesh contract"
    For another story with the "pound of flesh" motif, see Noy,
        *Morocco* #7.
    See also:
      *TEM*, 1972 #4 (Syria)
      Marcus, *Fount* #14 (Persian Kurdistan)
      Noy, *Iraq* #24

68. The Faithful Woman
    IFA 2505
    AT 712 "Crescentia: The Slandered and Banished Wife is
        Reinstated Through Her Miraculous Healing Powers"
    See Noy, *Morocco* #70
    See also:
      Jason, *Types*, p. 160
      Gaster, *Exempla* #313
      _____ , *Maaseh* #204
      Maitlis (Yiddish) #74
      Lévi (French) p. 234

  Eisenstein, vol. 2 #2 pp. 343–344
  Bin Gorion, *MMI* (Hebrew) #625 a, b
  Ben-Yehezkel #135
  and the IFA publications:
   Noy, *Iraq* #6 notes
   _____ , *Shwili* #40
   _____ , *Libya* #3
   Marcus, *Fount* #4 notes
 For references to numerous non-Jewish Crescentia legends,
  see Gaster, *Exempla*, pp. 237–238.

70. The *Hacham's* Wife Who Was Turned into a Snake
  IFA 9542
  AT 830C "If God Wills "
  AT 450 "Little Brother and Little Sister"
  AT 510 "Cinderella"
  Contains motif N 385.1 "Person has successive misfortunes
   because he forgets to say, 'If God wills.' "

71. The Lawsuit of the Old Woman against the Wind
  IFA 10101
  AT 759C "The Widow's Meal"
  AT 920 "Clever Acts and Words"
  Contains motif J 355.1 Neuman
  See Attias #15 = Alexander, Noy #55
  See also:
   Bin Gorion, *MMI* (1990) #24; *MMI* (Hebrew) #64
   _____ , *BJ*, vol. 3, pp. 67–70, 266–267, 301, 318
   Gaster, *Exempla* #436, 444
   Ginzberg, vol. 6, p. 285
   Bialik, *And It Came to Pass*, p. 148
   Meyuhas, pp. 111–118
   and the IFA publication *TEM*, 1963 #5 note
 For the *midrash* about the presence of the *Shechinah* at the
  Western Wall, see *Midrash Tanhuma* in Buber, vol. II, p.
  6. Also see Vilnay.
 For another story about a woman's contribution to the
  Western Wall being more precious than that of the king,
  see Schwarzbaum, *Studies, World*, p. 124.

72. The Amulet of Rabbi Shalom Sharabi
  IFA 6031
  See Seri #8 = Stahl #28

For background information on amulets, see Trachtenberg
and see Budge.

For another source on amulets against misfortunes of war,
see Schwarzbaum, *Studies, World*, p. 431.

For further information about R. Shalom Sharabi and the
Jews of Yemen, see Brauer.

73. Brotherly Love
IFA 17545
For a Sephardic Jewish version, see Palacin.
For sources about the placing of the Temple, see Schwarz-
baum, *Studies, World*, p. 111.

75. The Three-Eyed Daughter
IFA 1553
AT 511 "One Eye, Two Eyes, Three Eyes"
Contains motifs:
.F 512.2.1.1 "Three-eyed person"
S 12 "Girl abused by mother"
N 825.3 "Wise old woman provides magic table"
D 830.1 "Sisters spy"
See Noy, *Shwili* #25

# Glossary

All words that are not otherwise identified are in Hebrew. In a few instances, I have indicated Ashkenazic (A) or Sephardic (S) pronunciation. Many of the Hebrew words are used in Yiddish as well.

**Afikoman** (Greek)   A special piece of *matzah* reserved as dessert during the Passover seder meal.

**Aggadah**   The nonlegalistic material in the Talmud, primarily of a legendary character.

**Aleichem Shalom**   A reply to *Shalom Aleichem,* "Peace unto you!"

**Aliyah**   Literally, "going up" to *Eretz Yisrael;* used as a synonym for immigration to *Eretz Yisrael.*

**Amol is geven** (Yiddish)   "Once upon a time."

**Bar mitzvah**   Literally, "son of the commandment"; a ceremony marking the rite of passage, the coming-of-age of 13-year-old Jewish boys.

**Beit din**   A rabbinic court which decides issues related to religious law.

**Beta Israel**   The Ethiopian Jewish community, literally, "House of Israel."

**Bo'i, bo'i, hamalkah**   "Come, come, (Sabbath) Queen."

**Brit milah**   Literally, "covenant"; a circumcision ceremony which takes place on the eighth day after a boy's birth.

**Couscous** (Arabic)   A semolina product; cooked widely in Mediterranean countries.

**Dayan**   Judge.

**Diaspora**   The Jewish community outside of *Eretz Yisrael.*

**Dod**   Uncle.

**Dodah**   Aunt.

**Eishet hayil**   A woman of valor; from the biblical verse Proverbs 31:10.

**El rahum vehanun**   "The Lord is compassionate and merciful." Part of the liturgy during the High Holy Days and on other holidays as well.

**Eretz Yisrael**   "The Land of Israel"; the sacred place to which Jews in the Diaspora have longed to return.

**Ganovim** (Yiddish) or *Ganevim* (Hebrew)   Thieves.

**Gefilte fish** (Yiddish)   A boiled ground fish dish eaten on Sabbath and festivals in East European homes.

**Get**   A Jewish divorce.

**Hacham**   Literally, "a wise man"; in Moslem lands, a term used by Jews for a wise or learned person.

**Halachah**   Jewish law.

**Halachic**   The body of religious law.

**Hallah** (plural, *Hallot*)   A white bread baked especially for the Sabbath.

**Hametz**   A leavened product (such as bread or a wheat by-product) that is forbidden to be eaten during the days of Passover.

**Hamotzi lehem min haaretz**   A prayer said before eating bread, "Bless the bread of the earth."

**Hanukkah**   An eight-day festival, beginning on the 25th of the month of Kislev, in remembrance of the victory of the Maccabees against the Syrians in 165 B.C.E.

**Hanukkiah** (plural, *Hanukkiot)*   An oil lamp or candelabra used on Hanukkah, with places for eight plus one or two extra candles, the latter which serve to light the others.

**Haroses** (A) or *Haroset* (S)   A mixture of nuts and apples, sometimes dates, and wine eaten at the Passover *seder,* which symbolizes the mortar used by the Israelites while they were enslaved in Egypt.

**Hasidic**   Referring to the practices of *hasidim.*

**Hasidim**   Followers of Hasidism.

**Hasidism**   A Jewish sect founded in eighteenth-century Poland by Israel ben Eliezer, known as the Baal Shem Tov, "master of the good name."

**Has veshalom**   A phrase akin to "heaven forbid."

**Hatzeir**   Courtyard. In hasidic lore, Jews gathered at the courtyard of the rebbe, or leader, to hear sermons, stories.

**Havdalah**   Ceremony held at the conclusion of the Sabbath to separate the holy Sabbath from the other days of the week.

**Hazan**   A cantor, a person who assists the rabbi by singing the liturgy.

**Hazanut**   The practice of singing the liturgy.

**Hupah**   A Jewish wedding canopy.

**Hutzpah**   Gall; nerve; cheek.

**Ich bin a Yood** (Yiddish) (Hungarian-German Dialect)   "I am a Jew."

**Ich k'nee nisht** (Yiddish)   "I don't kneel."

**In a guter sho** (Yiddish)   Literally, "in good hour"; "may it go well!"

**Kabbalist**   One devoted to the study of mystical Jewish texts, the *Kabbalah.*

**Kabbalat Shabbat**   Literally, receiving the Sabbath.

**Kadi**   A religious judge in Moslem lands.

**Kahal**   A black eye color made of burnt date pits and pomegranate peel; widely known in the Arab world.

**Kamea**   An amulet.

**Kapparah**   Indicating an evil or sin for which there is a sacrificial substitute; refers to the practice of *kapparot* on the eve of Yom Kippur, in which every male in the family is to take a rooster (every female, a hen) and swing it around the head several times, reciting, "May this be my substitute." This is based on the putting of one's sins upon the head of the goat, as described in Leviticus 16.

**Ketubah**   A written wedding contract.

**Kiddush**   Sanctification; a blessing said before the drinking of wine on Sabbath and at holiday meals.

**Kiddush Hashem**   Sanctification of God's name.

**Kohanim**   Priests of the Holy Temple.

**Kosher**   A term used in conjunction with dietary laws, as prescribed in the Torah; in a broader sense, religious items and sacred objects made according to religious specifications.

**Kislev**   The month in the Hebrew calendar in which Hanukkah is celebrated.

**Kriyah**   Literally, "tearing"; symbolic tearing of clothing by mourners.

**Kugel**   (Yiddish)   Pudding in Eastern Europe, often made with noodles.

**Lager**   (German)   Warehouse, barracks.

**Lamed vovnick**   Literally, "one of the thirty-six"; according to Jewish tradition, there are thirty-six just men in every generation, because of whose righteousness the world continues to exist.

**Lashon hara**   "Evil tongue."

**Lev**   Heart.

**Levivah**   (plural, *Levivot*)   Pancake.

**Lira**   A currency denomination.

**Maariv**   Daily evening prayer service.

**Mahsan**   An enclosed storage area.

**Matzah**   Unleavened bread, eaten during the week of Pesah in remembrance of the "bread of affliction" eaten by the Israelites during their hasty flight from Egypt.

**Marranos**   Jews, who, after the Spanish Inquisition, converted to Christianity while secretly retaining their Judaism.

**Mazel tov**   (Yiddish) or *Mazal tov* (Hebrew)   "Good luck!" or "Good fortune!" The literal translation is "Good Star" or "Good Constellation," referring to the Middle Ages when having a good astrological constellation meant having good luck.

**Mehutanim** (Yiddish, and also accepted in Hebrew)   Parents of a child's spouse.

**Midrash** (plural, *Midrashim*)   A method of interpreting Scripture to bring out lessons through story and homily. A *midrash* often explains a biblical story via the points of view of other characters in the biblical text.

**Midrashic**   Referring to *midrash*.

**Minhah**   Daily afternoon prayer service.

**Mishnah**   The earliest portion of the Talmud, believed to contain the Oral Law, transmitted from the giving of the Torah at Mount Sinai.

**Mitzvah** (plural, *Mitzvot*)   Commandment or good deed; one of 613 divine commandments listed in the Torah.

**Mohel**   One who performs circumcision.

**Moshav**   A type of agricultural settlement in Israel.

**Motzei Shabbat**   The conclusion of the Sabbath.

**Nahat** (A) or *nahas* (S)   A pleasurable fulfillment.

**Ner**   A candle.

**Nisan**   A month of the Jewish year in which the festival of Pesah occurs.

**Parnasah**   Livelihood.

**Pesah**   The holiday of Passover, a festival beginning on the fourteenth day of the Hebrew month of *Nisan,* commemorating the Exodus from Egypt and the liberation from bondage.

**Pita** (plural, *Pitot*)   A pocket bread, generally eaten in Mediterranean countries.

**Poritz** (Yiddish)   The landowner in Eastern Europe.

**Purim**   A holiday falling in the Hebrew month of *Adar,* celebrating the victory of the Jews over Ahasuerus, King of Persia, and his advisor, Haman; the story is told in the biblical Book of Esther.

**Rebbe** (Yiddish)   Rabbi; a term used for hasidic masters and leaders.

**Rimon**   Pomegranate.

**Rosh Hashanah**   Literally, "head of the year"; the holiday which begins the yearly calendar, on the first day of the Hebrew month of *Tishrei.*

**Ruggelach** (Yiddish)   Small rolled cakes of dough, chocolate, nuts.

**Sabbath**   The day of rest, falling on the seventh day of the week; a covenant between God and the Children of Israel, as prescribed in Exodus 31:16, 17.

**Saberr** (Arabic)   A black cream, used on the face against the Evil Eye; known amongst the Jews of Yemen.

**Samneh** (Arabic)   Hot butter, on the verge of boiling; known amongst the Jews of Yemen.

**Sandek**   Godfather.

**Sanhedrin**   The higher court of law which administered justice according to Mosaic law in Palestine during the latter period of the Second Temple.

**Seder**   "Order"; the meal eaten on Passover, which follows a pre-scribed order.

**Sefer Torah**   The Torah scroll.

**Shabbos** (A) or *Shabbat* (S)   Sabbath.

**Shabbat Hanukkah**   The Sabbath that falls during the week of Hanukkah.

**Shabbos Bereishis** (A)   The first portion of the Torah read after the holiday of *Simhat Torah,* when the weekly Torah reading begins anew.

**Shalom**   "Hello," "Good-bye," or "Peace"; a customary form of Jewish greeting.

**Shalom Aleichem**   "Peace be unto you."

**Shechinah**   The Divine presence, usually identified as a feminine aspect of the Divine, as the Sabbath Queen or Bride of God.

**Sheid** (plural, *Sheidim* [m], *Sheidot* [f])   Demon.

**Shivah**   Literally, "seven"; seven-day period of mourning for the dead.

**Shohet**   Ritual slaughterer of animals.

**Shtetl** (Yiddish)   Small town or village in Eastern Europe.

**Subah** (Arabic)   An illness, sometimes fatal, known amongst the Jews of Yemen.

**Sukkah**   A booth in which the family dwells during the festival of Sukkot.

**Sukkot**   "Booths"; the harvest festival that begins on the fifteenth day of the month of Tishrei in remembrance of the children of Israel living in booths after their exodus from Egypt.

**Tallis** (A) or *Tallit* (S)   A four-cornered prayer shawl with fringes at the corners, traditionally worn by men during prayer. Women are not obligated to wear a *tallit,* nor are they prohibited from doing so.

**Talmid hacham** (Yiddish) or *Talmud hacham* (Hebrew)   One learned in the Talmud and Jewish studies.

**Talmud**   The most sacred Jewish text after the Bible, consisting of both legal (halachic) and legendary (aggadic) material.

**Tam**   Taste.

**Tikkun hazot**   Literally, "Restoration at midnight"; a time of all-night learning just before Shavuot, when, mystics believe, the heavens open and a person can be at one with God.

**Torah**   The Five Books of Moses; in a broader sense it refers to the entire Bible and oral law.

**Tzimmes** (Yiddish)   Literally, "a stew"; indicates a tumult, fuss.

**Tzitzes** (A) or *Tzitzit* (S)   A tying of knots attached to a four-cornered garment, such as the *tallit*. Wearing of the *tzitzit* is commanded in Numbers 15:37–41.

**Tzedakah**   Justice, charity.

**Tzedakah tatzil mimavet**   "Charity will save from death"; a biblical phrase (Proverbs 10:2).

**Uvrachah**   "And blessing"; traditionally, given as an answer to "*Shalom*."

**Wadi**   A valley or ravine through which a stream flows during the rainy season.

**Yeshivah**   Traditional Jewish school, devoted primarily to the study of talmudic and rabbinic literature.

**Yiddish**   A Jewish language spoken in Eastern Europe; of German origin; written in Hebrew letters and influenced by the Hebrew language.

**Yiddishe Mamme** (Yiddish)   Literally, "a Jewish mother"; connotes an overprotective and self-sacrificing mother.

**Yom Kippur**   The Day of Atonement, occurring on the tenth of *Tishrei;* the holiest day of the Jewish year, to be spent in prayer and fasting with the hope of being inscribed for a year of life.

# Bibliography

Aarne, A., and Thompson, S. *The Types of the Folktale: A Classification and Bibliography.* 2nd rev. ed. Helsinki: Academia Scientarium Fennica, 1964.

Abrahams, I. *The Book of Delight.* Philadelphia, 1912.

Alexander, T., and Noy, D. *The Treasure of Father* (Hebrew). Jerusalem: Misgav Yerushalayim, 1989.

Aloni, N. "Bibliography of Maaseh Yerushalmi." In *Studies in Folklore and Ethnology,* vol. 1. Jerusalem: The Palestine Institute of Folklore and Ethnology, 1946: 85–100.

Attias, M. *The Golden Feather: Twenty Folktales Narrated by Greek Jews* (Hebrew). IFA #35. Ed. D. Noy. Haifa: Haifa Municipality Ethnological Museum and Folklore Archives, 1976.

Avitsuk, J. *The Tree that Absorbed Tears* (Hebrew). IFA #7. Ed. D. Noy. Haifa: Haifa Municipality Ethnological Museum and Folklore Archives, 1965.

*The Babylonian Talmud* (English). Trans. L. Epstein. London: Soncino Press, 1935–48.

Baharav, Z. *Mi-Dor le-Dor: One Generation to Another. Seventy-one Folktales Collected in Israel* (Hebrew). Ed. D. Noy. Tel Aviv: Tarbut Vechinuch, 1967.

————. *Sixty Folktales Collected from Narrators in Ashqelon* (Hebrew). IFA #5. Ed. D. Noy. Haifa: Haifa Municipality Ethnological Museum and Folklore Archives, 1964.

Ben-Yehezkel, M. *Sefer ha-Ma'asiyot* (Hebrew). 3 vols. Tel Aviv: Dvir, 1925–29; expanded 6 vols. Tel Aviv: Dvir, 1957.

Bialik, H. N., trans. *And It Came to Pass.* New York: Hebrew Publishing Co., 1938.

Bialik, H. N., and Ravnitsky, J. H. *Sefer Ha'agada.* Tel Aviv: Dvir, 1935. 1988.

Bilu, Y., and Hasan-Rokem, G. "Cinderella and the Saint: The Life Story of a Jewish Moroccan Female Healer in Israel." *Psychoanalytic Study of Society* 14 (1989): 227–260.

Bin Gorion, M. J., ed. *Der Born Judas: Legenden, Märchen und Erzählungen.* 6 vols. Trans. R. Bin Gorion. Leipzig: Insel, 1916–23. 2nd edition: vols. 1 and 2, 1918; vol. 3, 1919; vol. 4, 1924. 3rd edition: first 3 vols., 1924. Rev. ed. 1966–73.

————. ed. *Mimekor Yisrael: Classical Jewish Folktales* (Hebrew). Ed. E. Bin Gorion. Tel Aviv: Dvir, 1966. English edition. 3 vols. Trans.

I. M. Lask. "Introduction," D. Ben-Amos. Bloomington, IN: Indiana University Press, 1976. Abridged and annotated edition, "Introduction" and "Headnotes," D. Ben-Amos, Bloomington, IN: Indiana University Press, 1990.

Boccaccio, G. *The Decameron*. Trans. M. Musa. New York: Norton, 1983.

Brauer, E. *Die Ethnologie der jemenitischen Juden* (German). Heidelberg, 1934.

Buber, S., ed. *Midrash Tanhuma* (Hebrew). Vilna: 1885, 1913; reprinted 1946, 1964. Trans. J. J. Townsend. (English). Hoboken, NJ: KTAV Publishing House, 1989.

Budge, W. E. A. *Amulets and Superstitions*. New York: Dover, 1978.

Cahan, J. L., ed. *Yiddishe Folklor* (Yiddish). Vilna: YIVO Institute for Jewish Research, 1938.

———. ed. *Yiddishe Folkmaises* (Yiddish). New York, Vilna: Yiddishe Folklor Biblyotek, 1931.

Cantor, A. "The Lilith Question." In *On Being a Jewish Feminist, a Reader*, ed. S. Heschel, pp. 40–49. New York: Schocken, 1983.

Caspi, M. *Daughters of Yemen*. Berkeley, CA: University of California Press, 1985.

Cheichel, E., ed. *A Tale for Each Month, 1967* (Hebrew). IFA #22. Haifa: Haifa Municipality Ethnological Museum and Folklore Archives, 1968.

———, ed. *A Tale for Each Month, 1968–1969* (Hebrew). IFA #26. Haifa: Haifa Municipality Ethnological Museum and Folklore Archives, 1970.

———, ed. *A Tale for Each Month, 1972* (Hebrew). IFA #30. Haifa: Haifa Municipality Ethnological Museum and Folklore Archives, 1973.

Cohen, M. *From the Mouths of the Folk* (Hebrew). Tel Aviv: The Society for Research, "Yeda Am," 1974.

Cronbach, A. *Hebrew Union College Annual*. 1936: 503–567.

Dan, J. "Five Versions of the Story of the Jerusalemite" (Hebrew). *Proceedings of the American Academy For Jewish Research, (PAAJR)* 35 (1967): 99–111.

———. *The Hebrew Story in the Middle Ages* (Hebrew). Jerusalem: Keter, 1974: 95–99.

———. "The Story of the Dibbuk and the Demon Wife" (Hebrew). *Hasifrut* 18–19 (1974):74–84.

———. "The Version of the Story of the Jerusalemite." *Tales of Sendebar* (Hebrew). *Hasifrut* 4(1973):355–361.

Dundes, A. "To Love My Father All: A Psychoanalytic Study of the

Folktale Source of King Lear." In *Cinderella, a Casebook*, ed. A. Dundes, pp. 229–244. Madison, WI: University of Wisconsin Press, 1988.

Eisenstein, J. D., ed. *Otzar Midrashim: A Library of Two Hundred Minor Midrashim* (Hebrew). 2 vols. New York, 1915. Reprint ed., New York: Grossman's, 1956.

Farhi, Y. S. *Ose Pele* (Hebrew). 4 vols. Livorno, 1845, 1869, 1870. Leghorn, 1902. Jerusalem: Bakal, 1959.

Frazer, J. *Folklore in the Old Testament*. New York: Avenel Books, 1988.

Friedman, H., and Simon, M., trans. and ed. *Midrash Rabbah*. London: Soncino Press, 1951.

Friedman, M., ed. *Seder Eliahu Rabba*. Jerusalem, 1960.

Fus, D. *Seven Bags of Gold* (Hebrew). IFA #25. ed. O. Schnitzler. Haifa: Haifa Municipality Ethnological Museum and Folklore Archives, 1969.

Gaster, M. *The Exempla of the Rabbis*. Leipzig: The Asia Publishing Co., 1924. Reprint ed., New York: KTAV, 1968.

_____, trans. *The Maaseh Book: The Book of Jewish Tales and Legends*. 2 vols. Philadelphia: Jewish Publication Society, 1934.

Gaster, T. H. *Festivals of the Jewish Year: A Modern Interpretation and Guide*. New York: W. Morrow, 1952, 1972.

Ginzberg, L. *The Legends of the Jews*. 7 vols. Trans. H. Szold, vols. 1, 2, and 4. Trans. P. Radin, vol. 3. Philadelphia: The Jewish Publication Society of America, 1909–38.

Goldin, J., trans. *The Fathers According to Rabbi Nathan* (Hebrew). New York: Schocken, 1974.

Goldstein, D. *Jewish Folklore and Legend*. London: Hamlyn, 1980.

Grunwald, M. "Spaniolic Tales and their Motifs" (Hebrew). *Edoth 2* (1947):3, 4, 225–244.

Gutter, M. *Honour Your Mother: Twelve Folktales from Buczacy* (Hebrew). IFA #23. Ed. A. Shenhar. Haifa: Haifa Municipality Ethnological Museum and Folklore Archives, 1969.

Habermann, A. M. "Alphabet of Ben Sira, Third Version," *Tarbiz* 27 (1958):190–202.

Haimovits, Z. M. *Faithful Guardians* (Hebrew). IFA #34. Ed. D. Noy. Haifa: Haifa Municipality Ethnological Museum and Folklore Archives, 1976.

Ha-Kohen, E. *Me'il Zedakah*. Smyrna, 1731. Lemberg, 1859.

Haviv, Y. *Never Despair: Seven Folktales Related by Aliza Anidjar from Tangiers* (Hebrew). IFA #13. Ed. E. Cheichel. Haifa: Haifa Municipality Ethnological Museum and Folklore Archives, 1966.

_____. *Taba'at Hakesem B'Golani* (Hebrew). Ed. E. Hechal. Tel Aviv: Hakibbutz Ham'uchad, 1990.

Henry, O. *The Complete Works of O. Henry*. Garden City, NY: Doubleday, 1953.

Holden, L. *Forms of Deformity or Motif-Index of Abnormalities, Deformities, and Disabilities of the Human Form in Traditional Jewish Narrative*. Sheffield: Sheffield Academic Press, 1991.

Ibn Sussan, A. H. *Ma'aseh Zaddikim*. Jerusalem, 1889.

Jason, H. "Types of Jewish-Oriental Oral Tales," *Fabula* VII (1965): 115–224.

_____. *Types of Oral Tales in Israel*. Part 2. Jerusalem: Israel Ethnographic Society, 1975.

Jellinek, A., ed. *Beit Hamidrash* (Hebrew). 6 vols. Leipzig and Vienna, 1853–1877. 2nd ed. Jerusalem: Bamberger and Wahrmann, 1938.

Kagan, Z. "Marriages of Humans and Demons in Fable and Folktale." *Fourth World Congress of Jewish Studies Papers*, 2 vols. (Hebrew), World Union of Jewish Studies, (1968)2:344–351.

_____, ed. *A Tale for Each Month, 1963* (Hebrew). IFA #6. Haifa: Haifa Municipality Ethnological Museum and Folklore Archives, 1964.

_____, ed. *A Tale for Each Month, 1964* (Hebrew). IFA #9. Haifa: Haifa Municipality Ethnological Museum and Folklore Archives, 1965.

Kitov, E. *The Jewish Year and Its Days of Significance*. New York: Feldheim, 1970.

Kort, Z. *Folktales of the Jews of Afghanistan* (Hebrew). Ed. H. Schwarzbaum. Jerusalem: Dvir, 1983.

Legman, G. *The Horn Book: Studies in Exotic Folklore and Bibliography*. New Hyde Park, NY: University Books, 1964.

Lévi, I. "Un recueil de contes juifs médites" (French). *Revue des Etudes Juives* 77(1977):234–249.

Maitlis, J., ed. *The Book of Stories, Basel, 1602, and Studies on the Jewish Literature* (Yiddish). Musterverk fun der Yiddisher Literatur, #38. Buenos Aires: Ateneo en el Instituto Cientifico Judio, 1969.

Marcus, E. *Chag La'am* (*A Holiday for the People*) (Hebrew). Jerusalem: Keter, 1990.

_____. *Min ha-Mabua (From the Fountainhead): Forty-Four Folktales Collected by the "Mabuim" School-Pupils* (Hebrew). IFA #12. Ed. D. Noy. Haifa: Haifa Municipality Ethnological Museum and Folklore Archives, 1966.

_____. "The Confrontation Between Jews and Non-Jews in Folktales of Jews from Islamic Countries." Ph.D. diss., The Hebrew University of Jerusalem, 1977.

Meyuhas, J. *Oriental Folktales* (Hebrew). Tel Aviv, 1938.

Mizrachi, H. *With Elders in Wisdom* (Hebrew). IFA #16. Ed. D. Noy. Haifa: Haifa Municipality Ethnological Museum and Folklore Archives, 1967.

Nadich, J. *Jewish Legends of the Second Commonwealth.* Philadelphia: Jewish Publication Society, 1983.

Neuman (Noy), D. *Motif-Index of Talmudic-Midrashic Literature.* Doctoral dissertation. Bloomington, IN: Indiana University Press, 1954.

Niedermüller, P. "From the Stories of Life to the Life History: Historic Context, Sociological Processes, and the Biographical Method." *Proceedings of the Third American-Hungarian Folklore Conference,* ed. T. and P. N. Hofer. Budapest, August 1987.

Noy, D. "Archiving and Presenting Folk Literature in an Ethnological Museum." *Journal of American Folklore* 25 (1962):23–28.

_____. "Elijah the Prophet at the Seder Night" (Hebrew). *Machanayim* 43 (March 1960).

_____, ed. *Folktales of Israel.* Trans. G. Baharav. Chicago: The University of Chicago Press, 1963.

_____, trans. and ed. *Jefet Shwili Erzählt* (Yemenite folktales in German translation). Fabula Supplement Series A, vol. 4. Berlin: Walter de Gruyter, 1963.

_____. *The Jewish Animal Tale of Oral Tradition* (Hebrew). IFA #29. Haifa: Haifa Municipality Ethnological Museum and Folklore Archives, 1976.

_____, ed. *Jewish Folktales from Libya* (Hebrew). Jerusalem: Bi-Tefutsot ha Golah, 1967.

_____, ed. *Jewish Iraqi Folktales* (Hebrew). Tel Aviv: Am Oved, 1965.

_____, ed. *Moroccan Jewish Folktales.* New York: Herzl Press, 1966.

_____. "A Profession Saves from Death." In *Sefer Ze'evi,* ed. Y. Zigelman (Hebrew). "Beitenu" Literature and Folklore Club at the Cultural and Education Department of the Haifa Labour Council, 1966.

_____. "Riddles at the Wedding Feast" (Hebrew). *Machanayim* #83 (1963):64–71.

_____, ed. *71 Jewish Folktales from Tunisia* (Hebrew). Jerusalem: Bi-Tefutsot ha-Golah, 1966.

_____, ed. *A Tale for Each Month, 1961* (Hebrew). IFA #1. Haifa:

Haifa Municipality Ethnological Museum and Folklore Archives, 1962.

————, ed. *A Tale for Each Month, 1962* (Hebrew). IFA #3. Haifa: Haifa Municipality Ethnological Museum and Folklore Archives, 1963.

————, ed. *A Tale for Each Month, 1965* (Hebrew). IFA #11. Haifa: Haifa Municipality Ethnological Museum and Folklore Archives, 1966.

————, ed. *A Tale for Each Month, 1966* (Hebrew). IFA #18. Haifa: Haifa Municipality Ethnological Museum and Folklore Archives, 1967.

————, ed. *A Tale for Each Month, 1970* (Hebrew). IFA #27. Haifa: Haifa Municipality Ethnological Museum and Folklore Archives, 1971.

————, ed. *A Tale for Each Month, 1971* (Hebrew). IFA #28. Haifa: Haifa Municipality Ethnological Museum and Folklore Archives, 1972.

————, ed. *A Tale for Each Month, 1974–1975* (Hebrew). IFA #36. Haifa: Haifa Municipality Ethnological Museum and Folklore Archives, 1978.

————, ed. *A Tale for Each Month, 1978* (Hebrew). IFA #40. Haifa: University of Haifa Folktale Archives, 1979.

Palacin, A. *Cuentos Populares de los Judios del Norte de Marruecas* (Spanish). 2 vols. Tetuan, 1952.

Patai, R. *Gates to the Old City*. New York: Avon, 1980.

————. *Historical Traditions of Mortuary Customs of the Jews of Meshed*, pp. 49–51. Jerusalem: Community of Meshed in Jerusalem, 1945.

Payne, J. *The Book of the Thousand and One Nights*. London, 1906.

Pipe, S. Z. *Twelve Folktales from Sanok* (Hebrew). IFA #15. Ed. D. Noy. Haifa: Haifa Municipality Ethnological Museum and Folklore Archives, 1967.

Rand, B., and Rush, B. *Around the World with Jewish Folktales: The Jews of Kurdistan*. Toledo, OH: Board of Jewish Education and the American Association for Jewish Education, 1978–79.

Rush, B., and Marcus, E. *Seventy and One Tales for the Jewish Year: Folktales for the Festivals*. New York: American Zionist Youth Foundation, 1980.

Sabar, Y., ed. and trans. *The Folk Literature of the Kurdistani Jews: An Anthology*. Yale Judaica Series, vol. 23. New Haven, CT: Yale University Press, 1982.

Sadeh, P. *Jewish Folktales*. Trans. H. Halkin. New York: Doubleday, 1989.

Schram, P. *Jewish Stories One Generation Tells Another.* Northvale, NJ: Jason Aronson, 1987.

_____. *Tales of Elijah the Prophet.* Northvale, NJ: Jason Aronson, 1991.

Schwartz, H. *Elijah's Violin and Other Jewish Fairy Tales.* New York: Harper and Row, 1983.

_____. *Lilith's Cave: Jewish Tales of the Supernatural.* San Francisco: Harper and Row, 1988.

_____. "Mermaid and Siren: The Polar Roles of Lilith and Eve in Jewish Lore." *The Sagarin Review, The Saint Louis Literary Journal* 2 (1992): 105–116.

_____. *Miriam's Tambourine: Jewish Folktales from Around the World.* New York: Seth Press, 1988.

Schwarzbaum, H. "Female Fickleness in Jewish Folklore." In *Jewish Folklore Between East and West.* Ed. E. Yassif. Beersheva: Ben-Gurion University of the Negev Press, 1989.

_____. "The Hero Predestined to Die on His Wedding Day (AT 934B)." In "Studies in Marriage Customs," *Folklore Research Center Studies* 4:223–252. Jerusalem: The Magnes Press, 1974.

_____. *Studies in Jewish and World Folklore.* Berlin: Walter de Gruyter, 1968.

Seri, R. *The Holy Amulet* (Hebrew). IFA #21. Ed. A. Shenhar. Haifa: Haifa Municipality Ethnological Museum and Folklore Archives, 1968.

Shenhar, A. "Concerning the Nature of the Motif 'Death by a Kiss' " (Hebrew). *Fabula* 19(1978):62–73.

_____. *Jewish and Israeli Folklore.* New Delhi: South Asian Publishers, 1987.

_____. "On the Popularity of the Legend of Beruriah, Wife of Rabbi Meir" (Hebrew). In *Folklore Research Center Studies,* Jerusalem: The Magnes Press, 1972.

_____, ed. "The Story of the Jerusalemite" (Hebrew). In *The Folktales of Israeli Ethnic Groups,* pp. 83–97. Tel Aviv: Tcherikover, 1982.

_____, ed. *A Tale for Each Month, 1973* (Hebrew). IFA #32. Haifa: Haifa Municipality Ethnological Museum and Folklore Archives, 1974.

Shenhar, A., and Bar-Yitzhak, H. *Tales of Shlomi* (Hebrew). Haifa: University of Haifa, 1982.

Shinan, A. *The World of the Aggadah.* Trans. J. Glucker. Tel Aviv: MOD Books, 1990.

Stahl, A. *Stories of Faith and Morals* (Hebrew). IFA #17. Haifa: Haifa Municipality Ethnological Museum and Folklore Archives, 1976.

Steinschneider, M., ed. *Alphabet of Ben Sira* (Hebrew). Berlin: 1858.

Stern, D., and Mirsky, M. J. *Rabbinic Fantasies*. Philadelphia: Jewish Publication Society, 1990.

*Talmud Yerushalmi* (English). Trans. J. Neusner. Chicago: University of Chicago Press, 1982–91.

Thompson, S. *Motif-Index of Folk Literature. A Classification of Narrative Elements in Folktales, Ballads, Myths, Fables, Mediaeval Romances, Exempla, Fabliaux, Jest-Books and Local Legends.* New Enlarged and Revised Edition. 6 vols. Bloomington: Indiana University Press, 1955–1958. Rev. ed. 6 vols. Bloomington, IN, and London: Indiana University Press, 1966.

Trachtenberg, J. *Jewish Magic and Superstition: A Study in Folk Religion*. New York: Behrman's Jewish Book House, 1939. New York: Atheneum, 1974.

Vilnay, Z. *Aggadot Eretz Yisrael* (Hebrew). Jerusalem, 1959.

Weinreich, B. S. "Genres and Types of Yiddish Folktales about the Prophet Elijah." In *The Field of Yiddish Studies in Language, Folklore and Literature*, ed. U. Weinreich, pp. 202–231. The Hague: Mouton, 1965.

———. *Yiddish Folktales*. New York: Pantheon Books and YIVO Institute for Jewish Research, 1988.

Weinstein, E. *Grandma Esther Relates . . .* (Hebrew). IFA #4. Ed. Z. Kagan. Haifa: Haifa Municipality Ethnological Museum and Folklore Archives, 1964.

Yehoshua, B. *The Father's Will* (Hebrew). IFA #24. Ed. Z. Kagan. Haifa: Haifa Municipality Ethnological Museum and Folklore Archives, 1969.

Yeshivah, M. *Seven Folktales, 1963* (Hebrew). IFA #2. Ed. D. Noy. Haifa: Haifa Municipality Ethnological Museum and Folklore Archives, 1963.

## GENERAL REFERENCES

*Encyclopaedia Judaica*. Jerusalem: Keter, 1976.

*Funk and Wagnalls Standard Dictionary of Folklore, Mythology, and Legend*. Ed. M. Leach. 1950.

## REFERENCES TO THE BIBLE AND APOCRYPHA

*The Apocrypha and Pseudepigrapha of the Old Testament in English With Introductions and Critical and Explanatory Notes to the Several Books*, vol. 1. Ed. R. H. Charles. Oxford: Clarendon Press, 1963.

*The Exhaustive Concordance of The Bible With Comparative Concor-*
*dance.* Ed. J. Strong. Nashville, TN: Abingdon, 1894. Thirty-sixth
printing, 1977.

*The First Book of the Maccabees.* Commentator H. A. Fischel. New
York: Schocken, 1948.

*The First Book of the Maccabees.* Trans. S. Tedesche. New York:
Harper and Bros., 1950.

*The Hebrew Bible With English Translation* (Hebrew/English). Ed. M.
Friedlander. Jerusalem: Jerusalem Bible Publishing Co., Ha-
madpis Liphshitz Press, n.d.

*The Holy Scriptures According to the Masoretic Text.* Philadelphia:
The Jewish Publication Society, 1952.

*The Holy Scriptures: Tora* (Hebrew/English). Jerusalem: Koren Publishers, 1989.

*The New Bible Dictionary.* Ed. J. M. Douglas. Grand Rapids, MI: Wm.
B. Eerdmans, 1965.

Bibliography

# Index of Tales by Country

The country refers to the native country of the storyteller, as far as can be determined. The number refers to the story number in this collection.

## About the Author

For over twenty-five years, Barbara Rush has been known throughout the United States and Israel as a professional storyteller and collector of tales. A retired librarian, she received a master of library science degree from Queens College and is currently a teacher of library science at the Library School of the Hebrew University of Jerusalem. She also holds a master of arts degree in Jewish studies and is the author or co-author of seven books, including *The Diamond Tree: Jewish Tales from Around the World*, which won the 1991 Sydney Taylor Book Award as the best Judaica children's book, and *The Sabbath Lion: A Jewish Folktale from Algeria*.